D0948454

BREAKING BARRIERS

BREAKING BARRIERS

A History of Integration in Professional Basketball

Douglas Stark

ROWMAN & LITTLEFIELD
Lanham • Boulder • New York • London

Published by Rowman & Littlefield
An imprint of The Rowman & Littlefield Publishing Group, Inc.
4501 Forbes Boulevard, Suite 200, Lanham, Maryland 20706
www.rowman.com

6 Tinworth Street, London SE11 5AL

British Library Cataloguing in Publication Information Available

Library of Congress Cataloging-in-Publication Data

Name: Stark, Douglas (Douglas Andrew), 1972–, author.
Title: Breaking barriers : a history of integration in professional basketball / Douglas Stark.
Description: Lanham : Rowman & Littlefield, [2019] | Includes bibliographical references and index.
Identifiers: LCCN 2018029419 (print) | LCCN 2018042853 (ebook) | ISBN 9781442277540 (electronic) | ISBN 9781442277533 (cloth : alk. paper)
Subjects: LCSH: Basketball—United States—History. | African American basketball players. | Racism in sports—United States—History. | National Basketball Association—History.
Classification: LCC GV885.5 (ebook) | LCC GV885.5 .S73 2019 (print) | DDC 796.323/64—dc23
LC record available at https://lccn.loc.gov/2018029419

∞ ™ The paper used in this publication meets the minimum requirements of American National Standard for Information Sciences Permanence of Paper for Printed Library Materials, ANSI/NISO Z39.48-1992.

Printed in the United States of America

For Benjamin Hunter

Basketball is in your future.

CONTENTS

Acknowledgments ix

Prologue xi

1 Early Black Professional Basketball 1

2 The World Professional Basketball Tournament 35

3 The National Basketball League 95

4 Early Black NBA Pioneers 135

5 The Rise of African American Stars in the NBA 169

6 The Shadow of Michael Jordan 203

Notes 229

Bibliography 245

Index 249

About the Author 259

ACKNOWLEDGMENTS

Each book project is a labor of love, and this certainly was. As always, it is a wonderful journey but one that requires the assistance of many individuals. This was no different, and without their help this book would not have been possible. To everyone involved, I thank you from the bottom of my heart.

As always, Matt Zeysing, historian at the Naismith Memorial Basketball Hall of Fame, proved especially helpful in allowing me to view the clipping, nomination, and photo files of many individuals. Bill Himmelman recently completed his online encyclopedia of early basketball players. The site www.probasketballencyclopedia.com is an indispensable resource for player stats and leagues from the game's formative years. It is a valuable resource, as is he. Robin Deutsch was a sounding board for how to frame the modern story in a way that was compelling. To all, my deepest thanks.

Photographs for this book were generously provided by Bill Himmelman, Steve Lipofsky, and Monica Smith, as well as the Associated Press, Cleveland State University, Duquesne University, Naismith Memorial Basketball Hall of Fame, North Carolina Central University, Saint Francis College (Pennsylvania), Schomburg Center for Research in Black Culture, Syracuse *Post-Standard*, UCLA, and University of Massachusetts Lowell.

Christen Karniski, my editor at Rowman & Littlefield, was enthusiastic about this project from the beginning and carefully guided it to its finished product. She was also very patient as due dates came and went and understanding throughout the entire process. Many thanks, Christen, for your support.

As always, family plays an important role—Mom, Dad, Jim, Sunday, Bennett, Nick, Rachel, and Alexis—thank you all.

My wife, Melanie, was a constant source of good cheer, even as we juggled parenthood for the first time and a new house. Fitting in this book was, at times, a challenge but ultimately worth it. Thanks again for your undivided love.

While I was writing this book, Benjamin Hunter entered our life. What a joy having a baby in the house. Each day is a blessing. As he grew, he learned a few of the key moves of basketball—dribbling and the pick and roll—the wonders of being a baby. Eventually, he will have an inside-outside game. Hopefully, one day he will develop an appreciation for the wonderful game of basketball. This book is for you, my buddy boy, with all my love.

PROLOGUE

My first full-time job in the sports museum industry came in January 1998. The Naismith Memorial Basketball Hall of Fame hired me to be its librarian and archivist. Growing up in Holyoke, Massachusetts, right up the road on Route 91, working at the Basketball Hall of Fame was a dream job. I learned the game at the Holyoke YMCA, where, incidentally, the game of volleyball was invented in 1895 by William Morgan, a student of James Naismith, basketball's inventor. As a child, I played basketball all day in the backyard of my parents' house and read all I could about the game. Mostly, it was about the Boston Celtics. The *Boston Globe* was my newspaper, and Bob Ryan, Jackie MacMullen, Peter May, and Dan Shaughnessy were all must reading—more so than Hemingway, Salinger, and Faulkner.

As the librarian and archivist, I spent my first several months organizing collections, answering reference requests (usually settling bar bets on a Monday morning), and generally being excited about any task that came my way (that last part would change as I got older and wiser). Nine months later, I was experiencing my first enshrinement weekend, in which a new class of Hall of Famers was being inducted. The class of 1998 was headlined by Larry Bird, the one player I followed more closely than any other (another reason that this was my dream job!). Also in that class was Marques Haynes, the world's greatest dribbler and the first player with the famed Harlem Globetrotters to be inducted.

The night before the ceremony, a welcome dinner was held, headlined by a few awards. Wilt Chamberlain returned to support Marques Haynes, a teammate on the Globetrotters. As everyone was filing into the room, an elderly gentleman sat in a chair, wearing his Hall of Fame jacket, impeccably dressed, and receiving many handshakes. He was still as trim as in his playing days. I kept watching as returning Hall of Famers, board members, and supporters all made sure to stop by and say hello. Finally, I asked a colleague, "Who is that person?" "Oh, that's Pop Gates." Pop Gates?

A few years later, we opened a new exhibit, *Freedom to Play*, about African American basketball pioneers. To assist us with that exhibit, we assembled a small advisory group that included John McLendon, a pioneer African American coach who learned the game from Naismith. John spent some time at the Hall of Fame with the staff, telling stories and making sure we understood that what Clarence "Big House" Gaines accomplished with Winston Salem State University was far more important than Texas Western University defeating the University of Kentucky to win the 1966 NCAA championship. On the exhibit's opening night, Earl Lloyd, the first African American to play in a National Basketball Association (NBA) game on October 31, 1950, participated in a panel discussion. I remember calling Earl "Moonfixer." He laughed and said he had not been called that since college. A few months later, Bill Jones, who played a season with the Toledo Jim White Chevrolets in the 1942–43 National Basketball League (NBL), visited and shared his thoughts about the NBL and his playing days.

In a short period of time, I had met Pop Gates, John McLendon, Earl Lloyd, Marques Haynes, and Bill Jones. All five of these individuals played instrumental roles in integrating basketball. All five were some of the nicest people I had ever met, an accomplishment that far transcends their playing and coaching accomplishments. Why were they not in the basketball books I was reading? Why were these names not as well known as Jackie Robinson? Who else out there had I not heard about?

Despite my interest, time passed. I changed jobs a few times. I moved. I married. I became a father. I approached middle age. But in that time my deep interest in the history of basketball never wavered. If anything, it only grew stronger.

I started writing books several years ago. My first was *The SPHAS: The Life and Times of Basketball's Greatest Jewish Team*. The SPHAS were the South Philadelphia Hebrew Association, founded in 1918 and still playing in 1959 as a touring team with the Harlem Globetrotters. Their heyday was the 1930s and early 1940s, during the Great Depression, the rise of anti-Semitism, and the coming of World War II. They persevered and laid the foundation for the game we know today.

In writing that book, I devoted some space to World War II and how the game was fundamentally changed for the better. That led to my second book, *Wartime Basketball: The Emergence of a National Sport during World War II*. This book charted the war years, the professional leagues, and the importance of the World Professional Basketball Tournament, the original March Madness, and the tournament that helped save the professional game during the war. One chapter discussed the color line falling and noted how professional basketball integrated in 1942, five years before Jackie Robinson and baseball. It did so with less fanfare and conflict. It was a tremendous feat that largely has gone unrecognized nearly seventy years later.

Writers tend to find their next subjects where they least expect. For me, it was the integration of professional basketball, which comes full circle to my first job at the Basketball Hall of Fame. In writing this book, I wanted to explore who these fellows were and the contributions they made. This book is meant to be a one-volume overview of the integration of professional basketball from Bucky Lew to the present. As I researched this book, I realized that bits and pieces of this story had appeared in different formats, but the entire story had never been told in one volume. This book attempts to present a clearer narrative of the game's integration. By no means is it the most complete or in-depth analysis of the black basketball experience. It is not a social or cultural history. Rather, it is meant to put in one place these fellows—Pop Gates, John McLendon, Bill Jones, Marques Haynes, Earl Lloyd— whom I met many years ago.

The other thing I learned in writing this is that these books form a loose trilogy about the early history of the game. That was not my intent. I was just following my interest wherever it took me. The game prior to 1950 and the emergence of the NBA always fascinated me the most. I tend to spend more time living in the past than I do in the present: How did the game develop and why? What were the early players and leagues really like? How did the game's ethnic roots affect how the game developed? How did the urbanization of the country impact the game's growth? How did World War II change the game?

So my books explore the game's early roots in the Northeast, early professional leagues and their struggles, Jewish players, black players, barnstorming, and independent ball. They focus on players and leagues and a time period often absent in the discussion of modern basketball. The goal is to showcase the game's roots so that those who made the game of basketball what it is today are not forgotten. I do not know the best way to read these three books; I will leave that to the reader. I will say that finding lost stories and telling them is very rewarding.

In some small part, I hope this book presents a clearer narrative of the integration of the game and contributes to this oft-neglected aspect of basketball history.

I

EARLY BLACK PROFESSIONAL BASKETBALL

November 6, 1902

Harry "Bucky" Lew joined his teammates for a game of basketball. His team was Lowell's Pawtucketville Athletic Club. Their opponent was a team from Marlborough, Massachusetts. Both teams played in the New England Basketball League, one of the early professional basketball leagues founded a decade after the game of basketball was invented by James Naismith at the International YMCA Training School in Springfield, Massachusetts, in December 1891. The new century was not two years old, and basketball was gaining a foothold in the United States, however small at the time. Lew made his way to Marlborough for the game. His teammates, players named Alby Allard, Skip Field, Oscar McFarland, and Jim Harrington, were ready to welcome Lew as part of the squad. The team was prepared to play, having practiced and played some warm-up contests against local squads over the past several weeks.

The city of Marlborough was excited to start this new basketball season. A crowd of five hundred people filed in to see the first game; the city's mayor, Walter B. Morse, put the ball in play. He briefly addressed the spectators and said he would give one dollar to the first person who scored a basket. The game was played in three periods, the norm for that time. Marlborough held a slim 7–6 lead after the first intermission. The teams were tied at fourteen after the second stanza.

In the final frame, Marlborough's Healey scored four quick baskets to give the hometown team the win, 28–19.

The *Lowell Courier-Citizen* covered the game, as it would the team all season, and noted in its story the following day, "The features were the playing of [Jim] Healey and W. [Bill] Sheridan for the Marlboro [*sic*] team and of McFarland and Lew for the P.A.C."[1] In many respects, it was an ordinary game, except that Lew was the first black to play in a professional basketball game. It was a singular moment, one that went unmentioned in the local newspapers of the day and that largely has been forgotten more than a century later. His achievement on that night, November 6, 1902, paved the way for all of the great African American players to have played professional basketball.

Lew would never forget that first game, when he entered the court for the first time, and his experiences. In 1958, Lew sat for an interview with sportswriter Gerry Finn of Springfield, Massachusetts, who chronicled Lew's place in basketball history. Lew's story about breaking the color barrier is best told by Lew himself:

> I can almost see the faces of those Marlboro [*sic*] players when I got into that game. Our Lowell team had been getting players from New York, New Jersey, Pennsylvania, and some of the local papers put the pressure on by demanding that they give this little Negro from around the corner a chance to play.
>
> Well, at first the team just ignored the publicity. But a series of injuries forced the manager to take me on for the Marlboro [*sic*] game. I made the sixth player that night, and he said all I had to do was sit on the bench for my five bucks pay. There was no such thing as fouling out in those days so he figured he'd be safe all around.
>
> It just so happens that one of the Lowell players got himself injured and had to leave the game. At first this manager refused to put me in. He let them play us five on four, but the fans got real mad and almost started a riot, screaming to let me play.
>
> That did it. I went in there and you know . . . all those things you read about Jackie Robinson the abuse, the name-calling, extra effort to put him down . . . they're all true. I got the same treatment and even worse. Basketball was a rough game then. I took the bumps, the elbows in the gut, knees here and everything else that went with it. But I gave it right back. It was rough but worth it. Once they knew I could take it, I had it made. Some of those same old boys who gave

Bucky Lew became the first black to play professionally when he suited up for Lowell on November 6, 1902. *University of Massachusetts Lowell.*

the hardest licks turned out to be among my best friends in the years that followed.[2]

Lew's pioneering spirit was forged in a household that could be said to be "the first" of many moments in American history. Bucky Lew was born on January 4, 1884, to William and Isabell Lew. His family's lineage and their remarkable story began in the decades prior to the American Revolution. In the 1740s, his great-great-great-grandfather and great-great-great-grandmother, Primus and Margaret Lew, were married. Both were former slaves in Groton, Massachusetts. Primus distinguished himself by fighting with the Americans in the French and Indian War.

By the time of the American Revolution, Lew's great-great-grandfather Barzillia Lew fought in the Battle of Bunker Hill in 1775. Barzillia was a free man, and he later freed his wife, Dinah, for $400. Barzillia's remarkable life has been memorialized in an oil painting of him that hangs in the U.S. Department of State in Washington, D.C. In addition, Duke Ellington composed a song titled "Barzillia Lew." Barzillia's daughter, Lucy Dalton, and her husband, Thomas Dalton, were extremely active in an antislavery movement in Boston; Thomas served as president of an all-black antislavery society that predated the noted white abolitionist William Lloyd Garrison.

In the 1840s, Bucky Lew's grandfather and grandmother, Adrastus and Elizabeth Lew, purchased property near Riverside Street in Lowell. Over the ensuing two decades, this property became a well-known, documented stop on the Underground Railroad. The property was in a secluded forest area in Lowell, and the runaway slaves hid in a closet upstairs in the house. More than likely, these runaway slaves were en route to Canada. Laura Ashe, whose great-grandparents were Adrastus and Elizabeth, recalled decades later the remarkable role they played in this period of American history. "My [great-]grandparents would put a pallet down there and the slave would sleep there during the day and come down to the kitchen at night." After eating and telling stories, Ashe's great-grandfather would gather the slaves and hide them in a horse-drawn carriage under piles of hay.[3]

Afterward they would be on their way, as Ashe recalled: "They would take them to the Pelham, N.H., line. They were met by someone else to take them to Canada. If no one else was there to take them, then my [great-]grandfather or Elizabeth Lew would." Nearing the end of her life, Elizabeth recalled their participation in the Underground Railroad. "My husband and I helped many of the escaping slaves to get safely to Canada, giving them rest for the night, food and clothing and money to help them on their way. Those were terrible times."[4]

In the 1880s, Lew's parents opened a dry cleaning business in Lowell, and in 1891, the year basketball was invented, Lew's father, William, was a delegate representing Lowell at the 1891 Equal Rights Convention in Boston.

Bucky's siblings were equally impressive in their achievements. His sister Theresa graduated as the salutatorian from Lowell High School and later earned a law degree from the Portis Law School in Boston. His brother Girard was a cofounder of the first African American Museum, now known as the DuSable Museum. Among the artifacts in its collection is a powder horn Barzillia Lew used in the American Revolution.

With such an impressive family pedigree, it was only natural to assume that Lew would make his mark. Basketball would be that field. He quickly took an interest in a game that was invented when he was seven years old. There were no coaches or instructional manuals to guide him. He learned by watching others play and by experimenting. It was a crude form of the game, but soon Lew made his mark based on his quickness, speed, and agility. He caught the attention of the local basketball scene and as an eighteen-year-old was signed by the Lowell basketball team prior to the 1902–3 New England Basketball League season. It was quite an achievement for a local boy.

With that first game over, Lew played the rest of the season with Lowell and acquitted himself well. His exploits did not go unnoticed as evidenced by a December 2, 1902, article in the *Lowell Courier-Citizen*. It notes that "his playing has been of the phenomenal kind, and his success in caging the elusive sphere has been remarkable." One month later, Lew was again singled out for his exploits on the court, this time for his defensive performance. Playing in Manchester, Massachusetts, Lew was guarding Harry Hough from Trenton, New Jersey, an early pioneer of the game and one of its best players at that time: "he had the heralded champion player of the world on the weary list. Three baskets were all that Hough succeeded in landing." By the first week of January 1903, Lew was being recognized for his all-around efforts. Writing in the *Citizen* of Manchester, New Hampshire, the article notes that "Lew is now recognized as one of the very best floor workers in the business."[5]

After a season in Lowell, his contract was purchased by a rival team, Haverhill, in the New England Basketball League. Lew spent two years with Haverhill before moving on to Peabody in 1906. According to historian Bill Himmelman,

He enjoyed an outstanding sophomore year as a professional until late in the season when he was slowed by a dislocated shoulder. Lew dislocated his shoulder again in a collision early the following season, but still managed to play in more games than any other player on the team.[6]

He was a consistent contributor on his team, even if he did not score many points. In those early years, the game was not the high-scoring affair that it is today. Scores were low, and players passed the ball around to their teammates looking for the best shot. Possession and taking care of the ball were strategically important.

Lew was not known as a big scorer. He once tallied fourteen points in a game in 1902, but that was an anomaly. Instead, he was better known for his defensive prowess. Himmelman notes, "He was probably one of the best defenders of his time on the planet." He continues, "His real talent was as a defensive guard during a period when guards were responsible for guarding forwards, unlike today when forwards cover forwards and guards cover guards. He had a real talent for shutting down high-scoring forwards." His scoring average of about three points per game would be equal to a pro player today scoring an average of eleven points per game.[7]

During his two seasons with Haverhill, Lew developed into a defensive player and set shooter. As Himmelman states,

> Generally the teams would groom people to be defensive specialists, and that's what Bucky Lew was. They weren't asked to score; they were just asked to shut down opposing forwards. And he was one of the best at that time. He was one of the best ten defensive players of that first era, but not one of the best overall players.[8]

Lew recalled in 1958,

> The finest players in the country were in that league just before it disbanded and I always wound up playing our opponent's best shooter. I like to throw from outside but wasn't much around the basket. Of course we had no backboards in those days and everything had to go in clean. Naturally, there was no rebounding and after a shot there was a brawl to get the ball. There were no out-of-bounds markers. We had a fence around the court with nets hanging from the ceilings. The ball was always in play and you were guarded from the

moment you touched it. Hardly had time to breathe, let alone think about what you were going to do with the ball.[9]

In fact, his defense was so good that in some cases it was regarded as *the* reason, not race or prejudice, some teams refused to play against Lew. In an early season game in November 1904, the sportswriter for the *Lowell Courier-Citizen* suggested,

> Many are of the belief that the star basketball shooter of the Natick team had other reasons for not wanting to play Lew than the mere fact that he was colored. It has been noted in the past that [Harry] Hough has found that the goals from the floor do not come with the usual frequency when he is pitted against the Lowell boy.[10]

According to Himmelman,

> Haverhill finished in first place during the first-half of the split season ahead of the highly favored Natick club that featured Harry Hough and Joe Fogarty. While Lew was generally well-received by fans and players alike, he did face some episodes of discrimination. After some rough matchups early in the 1904–05 season, some Natick players protested Lew's presence in the league. President Fred Cunningham quickly fined the Natick team $50 and said there would be no color line in the New England Basketball League. The same two teams met in the playoffs, with Natick winning the championship without any further incidents. . . . Teams would go up and play there and nobody ever voiced an objection to playing against him as a black player until they played him and he would shut down their best player. Then all of a sudden, they would say we don't want to play against a Negro player. They just used that tactic to get him off the court for the next game. It was like using race as a scapegoat-type excuse.[11]

While playing for Haverhill, he scored 236 points in sixty-seven games during the 1903–4 season. The following year, he returned to Haverhill and scored 102 points in forty-seven games. He played for Peabody in 1906. According to Himmelman,

> In the end, Lew's professional career was cut short not by prejudice, but by harsh realities of early professional basketball. The NEBL, dependent on highly-paid [*sic*] stars from Philadelphia, Trenton,

Camden area, disappeared under a sea of red ink after the 1904–05 season. Major-league basketball in New England did not take hold again until after World War I.[12]

After the league disbanded in 1906, Lew organized his own team, the Lowell Five, and played for another twenty seasons up and down the East Coast. Lew's last game came in 1926 in St. Johnsbury, Vermont, at the age of forty-two.

During his years with the Lowell Five, one of Lew's teammates and later a good friend was Dan O'Connor. In an interview later in life, he recalled that "Bucky was considered the best dribbler in pro basketball, and it was almost impossible to take the ball away from him. He used two hands and kept spinning." Players in those years were also tough; it was part of basketball's creed then. Lew was no exception. "Bucky Lew had a severe toothache, and we had to stop in Haverhill to see a dentist in route to the game," O'Connor recalled. "After having the tooth pulled, we continued to Gloucester, where Bucky played the entire game with a blob of gauze in his mouth."[13]

During his career, he was regarded as an equal of contemporaries Ed Wachter, Florenz "Flo" Harvey, Paddy Grand, George Renkert, Jim Crowley, and Francis "Flo" Haggerty, all early stars of the game in New England, particularly Wachter, who is a member of the Naismith Memorial Basketball Hall of Fame. Lew made a contribution as the first black professional basketball player, but his achievement was not part of a larger movement. For historical perspective, it most closely resembles baseball player Moses Fleetwood Walker's contribution as the first black baseball player to play professionally in the 1880s. "The addition of both these players [Lew and Walker] to professional team rosters was singular, localized events. Neither started a movement in their time that allowed others of their race to gain playing spots," Himmelman noted in a *Boston Globe* article in 1997. "Robinson was good, and owners realized there was money to be made by recruiting the best players, regardless of race, so we begin to see other blacks in professional baseball as part of a continuous trend."[14]

In 1997, Lew's daughter, Phyllis, reflected both on her father's remarkable achievements and some of the adversity he faced.

My father talked often about playing basketball but I was too young to remember seeing him play. When people would talk about the discrimination that Jackie Robinson experienced in baseball, my father would chime in with his own experiences. When his team traveled to Fitchburg or Haverhill, he had to find different eating accommodations, for example.[15]

"Lew deserves credit for not only being the first African-American professional player, but for his passion for the sport and his efforts to help it grow in New England," Himmelman states. "There is a spot [in the Hall] for the breaking of the color line, and obviously Lew did it." Himmelman, however, correctly points out that the game has changed considerably, and it is easy to overlook a player who scored few points and was a defensive specialist. Lew averaged three to five points a game, which in those days was considered a lot because most teams did not score more than twenty points a game.[16]

Bucky Lew's role as the first black basketball player to play in a professional game in 1902 was singular in its impact. Although he had an opportunity to play on a white team, there did not yet exist all-black teams or leagues where black children could learn and play the game of basketball. That was about to change, and the man responsible was Edwin Bancroft Henderson. Known as the "father of black basketball," Henderson single-handedly was responsible for ushering in this next phase in the development of black basketball.

Born in 1883 in southwest Washington, D.C., Henderson grew up in a segregated community. His father was a day laborer. His mother was the daughter of a white Virginia landowner and his slave. She worked as a domestic, but it was she who taught her son to read. His love of learning and the importance of education placed on him by his parents would prove invaluable throughout his life. When he was twelve years old, he played on a local baseball team. As he recalled, "After each game, I would walk over to the *Washington Star* newspaper office and write up the story of the game."[17] His story and scores were published, and he later received a penny a word. He attended the segregated M Street High School (now Dunbar High School) and later matriculated at Miner Normal School, a two-year teachers' college, where he graduated in 1904 at the top of his class. He found a job as an elementary school teacher, but prior to starting his new position, he spent some time furthering his education.

In the summer of 1904, he made an important decision that would affect the rest of his life's work. He ventured to the Dudley Allen

Edwin B. Henderson was a pivotal figure in introducing basketball to the Washington, D.C., area. *Courtesy of the Moorland-Spingarn Research Center, Howard University Archives, Howard University, Washington, D.C.*

Sargent School of Physical Training at Harvard University, where he intended to study physical education. He would spend the summers of 1904, 1905, and 1907 at Harvard learning physical education, but it was that first summer that changed his life. There, he learned the game of basketball. It consumed his time when he was not in class or working odd jobs to earn his room and board. The game was merely thirteen years old, but its possibilities seemed endless to Henderson. It met all of his requirements—physical, mental, and emotional.

When his summer studies were complete, he returned to Washington, D.C., and embarked on his life's passion of physical education opportunities for black children. In this field, he would become a legend. As he stated about the importance of physical education,

> It has been my feeling that athletics has done more to bring Negroes
> into the mainstream of our American Society than possibly any other
> medium. They create tolerance from the prejudiced, and then fel-
> lowship. . . . To a large extent this carries over to the classrooms and
> unto other life situations.[18]

In reflecting on his accomplishments later in life, he said,

> But sports were my vehicle. I always claimed sports ranked with
> music and the theatre as a medium for recognition of the colored
> people as we termed ourselves in my day. . . . I think the most
> heartwarming thing about all this is the progress made by the black
> athlete. I have always believed that sports bring about an under-
> standing difficult to achieve in so many other fields.[19]

In the fall of 1904, he became the first certified African American male
physical educator in the country. A year later, in 1905, he organized the
Eastern Board of Officials (EBO) for African Americans. That same
year, he again developed another first for African Americans, this one
being the Public School Athletic League (PSAL). Using the PSAL, basketball became part of the physical education curriculum in the public
school system. "I had to ride a bicycle to get to all the schools, which
included two high schools and all of the widely scattered elementary
schools," recalled Henderson.[20] He was not finished. Instead, he was
just getting started.

   In 1906, he organized the first African American athletic conference,
the Inter-Scholastic Athletic Association (ISAA), and he instituted the
first black high school and college track meets in the United States. The
ISAA became the forerunner of the Central (originally Colored) Intercollegiate Athletic Association (CIAA), Southwestern Athletic Conference (SWAC), Mid-Eastern Athletic Conference (MEAC), and the
Southern Intercollegiate Athletic Association (SIAC). "When I came
back to Washington to teach, I began to instruct the boys in basketball
and later organized some city basketball teams and this led to the Inter-
Scholastic Athletic Association. This was the first league ever formed
for Negroes. It included two teams in Washington, one in Baltimore
and some of the schools."[21]

   While working as a physical education instructor, he found time to
earn a medical degree from Howard University (1905–1907). Educa-

tion was also a lifelong passion, and he would go on to earn a doctor of chiropractic degree, a bachelor of arts, and a master of arts over the ensuing decades. From 1926 until he retired in 1954, he was the director of health and physical education for the black schools in Washington, D.C. Desegregating sporting events at Uline Arena was a ten-year battle that he fought and won. In 1937, he founded the Washington Pigskin Club. During his career, he taught and wrote books and articles, including coediting the Spalding official athletic handbook, *The Official Handbook of the Interscholastic Athletic Association of the Middle Athletic States*, and writing *The Negro in Sport* in 1939. *The Negro in Sport* was the first book to chronicle and discuss the black experience in sports.

A pioneer and activist, Henderson was a prolific contributor to issues of civil rights. Among his accomplishments, he assisted in the organization of the Fairfax County (Virginia) branch of the NAACP. Upon retiring in 1954, he was recognized for his life's work by receiving the National Honor Fellowship from the American Association for Health, Physical Education and Recreation. He was the first black to receive this award. The Black Athletes Hall of Fame inducted him in 1974.

Despite all of the accomplishments, and there were many, Henderson was most passionate about the sport of basketball. As he reflected,

> There was this still-young sport called basketball. I played it at Harvard and when I got back to Washington I organized the 12th Street YMCA team. We played the best teams available in Washington, Baltimore, Philadelphia and New York and claimed the national championship in 1909 and 1910.[22]

When he returned to Washington, D.C., he realized there were no avenues for black children to play basketball. To address this, he became the first to introduce and promote basketball to African Americans in Washington, D.C. To him, basketball could be used as a tool for African Americans to combat images of inferiority. It was a way for African Americans to gain respect and equality. Part of introducing basketball included forming his team, the 12th Street YMCA team. The 12th Street Y was the nation's first black YMCA. For several years, he played center and also coached the team. At the time, he was considered one of the best centers in black basketball.

In the early years of black basketball, a rivalry existed between Washington, D.C., and New York. The first great black basketball team was the Smart Set Athletic Club from Brooklyn, which claimed the Colored World Basketball Championship in 1908 and 1909. By 1910, Henderson's team was making a name for itself. A championship match with the Smart Set Athletic Club was on the horizon. On March 31, 1910, the two clubs met at Brooklyn's Fourteenth Regiment Armory, and Henderson's team won, 20–17. They were now undisputed champions. The team eventually became the first basketball varsity squad at Howard University, which would go on to claim the Colored Basketball Championship in 1910–11.

Over the first quarter of the twentieth century, many great black basketball teams emerged including the Monticello Athletic Association, Alpha Physical Culture Club, St. Christopher Club, Marathon Athletic Club, New York Incorporators, and the Leondi Big Five. The Smart Set Athletic Club, St. Christopher Club, and Marathon Athletic

Edwin Henderson founded the 12th Street Basketball Team, which was part of the nation's first black YMCA. *Courtesy of the Moorland-Spingarn Research Center, Howard University Archives, Howard University, Washington, D.C.*

Club formed the Olympian Athletic League (OAL). New members Alpha Physical Culture Club, St. Cyprian Athletic Club, and the Jersey City YMCA were added to the OAL. By the mid-1920s, the New York Renaissance were regarded as the premier black team. The Rens, as they were known, would emerge as one of the best basketball teams in the country and have a profound impact on the game's growth, eventual integration, and the emergence of a new, more exciting style of play. The Rens were the brainchild of Bob Douglas, a jovial person known as "Smiling Bob," but someone who possessed a strong competitive streak when it came to his team.

Born in 1882, in St. Kitts in the British West Indies, Douglas left his home country and ventured to the United States, where he settled in Harlem. He was active as a child in the community, playing with friends on the street and earning money with a series of jobs. Douglas recalled, "I was then working at 312 Manhattan Avenue near 114th Street as a doorboy for $22 a month. I roomed downstairs in the basement, where I paid the superintendent $3 a month for the room." He continued, "I saw my first basketball game on 52nd Street and Tenth Avenue in 1903. I was from St. Kitts . . . and soccer was the game played there. But when I saw that basketball game, I thought it was the most remarkable game ever. . . . That's when I started with basketball. You couldn't keep me off the court after that."[23]

Professional basketball at that time was still in its infancy, and not many teams or leagues were available to black players. This was the same time that Bucky Lew was playing for Lowell and Haverhill, and Edwin Henderson was spending his summers at Harvard University learning the game of basketball. As Douglas remembered,

> Around that time George Abbott, J. Foster Phillips, and I formed the Spartan Field Club, which took part in all types of games. We played soccer, cricket, basketball, and track. The basketball team was known as the Spartan Braves and we were very successful. . . . We played in an amateur league called the Metropolitan Basketball Association. It consisted of three teams in the New York area; they were the Alpha Big Five, the Puritans, and the St. Christophers. We played games as far away as Pittsburgh to meet the Leondi Big Five and Chicago to go against the Forty Club. We played our home games at Young's Casino at 131st Street and Park Avenue. Members of the Spartan Braves were Frank Forbes (who later played in the Negro National

Bob Douglas was the founder, owner, and manager of the New York Renaissance.
Courtesy of Bill Himmelman.

League and became a prominent boxing official with the New York
Athletic Commission), Leon Monde, George Capers, Hilton Slocum,
Richie Wallace, Hobey Johnson, Jimmy Ross, J. Foster Phillips,
Charles Robinson, and me. Despite being the coach and owner,
upon occasion I also took the floor.[24]

The Spartan Field Club was successful for many years and was one of
the dominant amateur black basketball teams in New York. Other clubs
that competed against Spartan included the Alpha Club, St. Christopher's, Salem Church, and St. Philip's Church. As Douglas recalled,
"Near the end of 1921, the Metropolitan Basketball Association, who

protected against professionalism in amateur basketball, directed us to release Frank Forbes and Leon Monde because they'd played sports for money during the summer months. We ignored the association and, by doing this, they accused the Spartans of threatening to wreck the organization."[25]

Douglas was at a crossroads with his Spartan club on whether he should turn professional, which, in the end, he did. According to Douglas,

> But you know, I loved the professional game so much and needed a real home court, so in October 1923 I approached William Roach, owner of the Renaissance Ballroom on 137th Street and Seventh Avenue. I asked him about having a basketball team playing there and he said, "Definitely not. You guys will play rough basketball and those rough crowds will break my place." But I guaranteed him we wouldn't do any damage to his ballroom. Since it was a new place, first opening in 1920, I told him the team would give the place publicity and I'd name the team the Renaissance, although I didn't like the name. I wanted to call the team the Spartans after my old club. I told Roach he'd make money with the percentage of the gate he'd receive. He finally said yes.[26]

The building, which in 1923, showed movies and contained a ballroom on the second floor where basketball games were held.

> So on November 30, 1923, the Renaissance Big Five played their first professional game at the ballroom against the Collegiate Big Five. We won 28–22. . . . On that first team we had Harold Slocum, who was the captain until 1932, the year he left the squad. We also had Frank Forbes, Harold Mayers, Zack Anderson, Hy Monte, and Leon Monde. . . . The following year Clarence "Fats" Jenkins, George Fiall, James "Pappy" Ricks, and "Clix" Garcia joined the team. Monde, Harold Jankins, Anderson, Forbes, and Wardell left. The substituting of Walter Saunders for Garcia in 1925 and the addition in 1926 of Eyre "Bruiser" Saitch were the only changes in the club until 1930, when Fiall was replaced by Bill Yancey, who also played shortstop with the New York Black Yankees of the Negro National League. In 1932, Johnny "Casey" Holt made the grade and replaced Harold Mayers. I'd say that the team I had from 1932–1935 was the greatest that ever played any kind of basketball. . . . That team had Charles "Tarzan" Cooper, Wee Willie Smith, Holt, Saitch,

Yancey, Ricks, and Jenkins. We won eighty-eight consecutive games. That team used to beat the hell out of the famous Celtics [white team]. . . . Pappy Ricks left the Rens after the 1935 season. John Isaacs replaced Jackie Bethards in 1936 and then Al Johnson replaced Yancey. . . . In 1939 we had William "Pop" Gates, who was a standout at Benjamin Franklin High School; Clarence "Puggy" Bell, a great player from the Harlem YMCA, and Zack Clayton, a beautiful defensive player from Central High School in Philadelphia. In addition to these three, Jenkins, Smith, Isaacs, and Saitch made up the team.[27]

The Renaissance Ballroom served not only as the team's home court, but also as an important part of the social scene for well-off African Americans. As Gates remembered,

It was rectangular, but more box-like. They set up a basketball post on each end of the floor. The floor was very slippery and they outlined the sidelines and foul lines. It wasn't a big floor. It was far from being a regular basketball floor. Other than high schools or armories, they had very few places to play at, except the Negro college. It was a well-decorated area—chandeliers, a bandstand. All the big [dance bands] played the Renaissance—Fatha Hines, Duke Ellington, Count Basie, Ella Fitzgerald, Chick Webb's band. They had the dancing prior to the game, at halftime, and after the game. . . . It was a very slippery floor. They had baskets that they put up before every ball game and markers they put down for the foul lines and so forth. The spectators were seated at tables in loges in the second tier and in boxes in the third tier. That was supposed to be an elite area. . . . The ballroom had a high ceiling, so you didn't have to worry about your shots. All you had to worry about was running into that hard wooden barrier around the floor because it had sharp edges. Sometimes when the game got rough, the guys would be flying over that barrier into people's laps.[28]

According to Zack Clayton, "It was a class thing—the pinnacle of black sport. People dressed like they were going to Heaven." As Bruiser Saitch recalled, "We had to have a dance afterwards or nobody would come to the damn thing . . . the Renaissance [Ballroom] was right across the street from The Red Rooster [nightclub] . . . if you didn't get there by seven o'clock, you didn't start until 10 o'clock."[29]

Fats Jenkins was a key member of the New York Renaissance during the 1920s and early 1930s. © *Morgan and Marvin Smith Photographs and Prints Division, Schomburg Center for Research in Black Culture.*

John J. O'Brien Jr. was the commissioner of the American Basketball League for several decades, and many of his league teams made the trip to Harlem to square off against the Rens. "The fans were the wealthiest black people in Harlem, dressed, believe it or not, in tuxedos. A good-

A native of Philadelphia, Zack Clayton was a key defensive player for the New York Renaissance during the 1930s. © *Morgan and Marvin Smith Photographs and Prints Division, Schomburg Center for Research in Black Culture.*

looking crowd—handsome women, good-looking guys—and they loved the basketball game, but they loved to get the game over for dancing afterwards."[30]

By the mid-1920s, the Rens were asserting themselves as a top team. They traveled around the country and played games wherever they could find a basket, a court, and a willing opponent. As Bruiser Saitch stated, "We played in some areas where they didn't have backboards; just a net attached to an iron pipe." Saitch continued, "In those days . . . we played by halves and then changed to fifteen-minute quarters . . . the referees only called flagrant fouls . . . with no jump ball, we just outran everybody." As they outran and outgunned teams, they were getting noticed more and more; before long, they sought to challenge the top professional team, the Original Celtics. The Original Celtics were basketball's top team with Dutch Denhert, Horse Haggerty, Johnny Beckman, Joe Lapchick, and Nat Holman, among others. The two teams first played each other in 1924–25, with the Original Celtics winning the first two contests. It took five tries, but the Rens finally defeated the Original Celtics in December 1925. This coincided at a time when the American Basketball League (1925–1931) was founded. The Original Celtics were asked to join the league but declined because black players and teams such as the Rens were not asked to become members.[31]

According to Arthur Ashe,

> This snub of blacks came in the same year the National Football League began to ease its black players from its member teams. But like the best white major-league baseball squads, the best white professional teams actually sought out confrontations against the premier black aggregations. These interracial games virtually guaranteed a jammed box office.[32]

Johnny Isaacs noted how important these games were to the Rens. "The Rens learned a lot from the Celtics. They played with their heads. And when we played other teams, we instituted a lot of their stuff—playing smart basketball, setting each other up." As Douglas recounted, "We always played in a war, but often it was a race war. When we played against most white teams, we were colored. Against the Celtics, we were men. Over those last years a real brotherhood was born out of competition and travel."[33]

During the 1920s, these Rens teams were quite popular with the residents of Harlem. Pop Gates, who would later star for them in the 1930s, remembered watching them play as a child. "Our basketball heroes were the New York Rens and I used to see them play. I'd sneak in or get 50 cents to watch them play." These players were his idols, ones he tried to emulate on the playground and who would have a big influence on his development as a player. As he proudly concluded, "It was the aspiration of every Negro basketball player in the country to play for the Renaissance."[34]

> Remember, this was the only well-known, premier black team in the country, so they would have the best ballplayers come in from all over. The fact that the Renaissance had played for so many years meant that Bob Douglas and Eric Illidge had created friendships in small towns and big cities everywhere. So if people thought they had a ballplayer who could play with the Renaissance, they would let Bob Douglas know about it and he would invite them to the training camp the following year.[35]

Each year, Douglas would hold tryouts, and players from all over would come for a chance to play for the New York Renaissance.

> You know, every October we'd try out dozens of young players who hoped to make the team. I'd pay the fare and all the living expenses while each youngster was making his bid. If they didn't make it, I would pay his fare to go home. . . . I paid all the living expenses of the members of the team while they were on the road. Guys like Fats Jenkins and Tarzan Cooper were getting $250 a month, plus expenses, plus $3 a day for meals—which was big money at that time. . . . In later years, the highest-paid player on the team was Pop Gates, who got $1,000 per month. Funny thing . . . when we broke up, he went with the Harlem Globetrotters and only got $600 a month.[36]

Playing on the Rens was an honor. Not many black professional teams were comparable with the Rens. In addition, scholarships to colleges were not being handed out as they are today. As Gates concluded, "We saw that most of the Negro ballplayers in the New York area were not offered scholarships to go to various colleges in this area. . . . Basketball offered no opportunity at that time, especially to black players. When you finished playing, you had to hurry and get yourself a job if you wanted to eat. You didn't get to go down to Florida and play golf."[37]

Unlike baseball, which had the Negro Leagues, no separate all-black leagues existed for all-black professional teams. Because the all-white leagues would not accept the Rens or any other black teams, the Rens were forced to barnstorm throughout the country. As Johnny Isaacs stated, "We'd leave [Harlem] right after New Year's and wouldn't come back until April. We were barnstorming."[38]

> Life was tough on the road as a barnstorming team, as Gates recounted, "We played every day in the week, sometimes twice on Saturdays and Sundays. We'd get in the bus and ride anywhere from 100 to 300 miles to get to the ball game. In certain areas, we had to ride another few hundred miles to find a place to sleep, due to the conditions in the country at that particular time.
>
> We barnstormed between New York and Chicago, and then we'd set up a base of operations in Chicago and cover the area within 300 or 400 miles, maybe further. We'd play in Kansas City, St. Louis, Milwaukee, into Minnesota. We played all the big arenas of the Middle West at that time. We had to play in small cities, too, because of the fact that you couldn't play in big cities all the time; to keep the money coming in, you had to play the small towns—wherever we could go to in time to make the ball game.
>
> We had no particular problems playing in the eastern part of the country, even though certain areas of the East were just as prejudiced at that time as the South. They wanted to see the Renaissance play because of the popularity of the team, and I guess you could say we were accepted because they wanted to see us.
>
> We found prejudice all over the South—and not just the South. Take Illinois, Indiana and Ohio—those states border on the South and there was prejudice there also as far as staying in hotels and eating is concerned.
>
> So we would do what we called eating out of a grocery store bag. You buy your stuff in a grocery store and make your own sandwiches. That was automatic when we left a big town to barnstorm through small towns. Even when I was with the Globetrotters in the middle of the 1950s we had to stay in private homes in Negro areas in the South and even in some places in the Middle West.[39]

During those years, Jim Crow existed in all facets of society. Finding a place to stay presented its own set of challenges. As Bruiser Saitch remembered,

[We] slept in jails because they wouldn't put us up in hotels . . . standard equipment for us was a flint [Flit] gun; we'd spray all the bedbugs before we went out to play and they'd be dead when we got back. . . . We sometimes had over a thousand damn dollars in our pockets and we couldn't get a good god-damn meal. Our per diem was $2.50 a day. "Fats" Jenkins was so tight that he'd save the tea balls and later ask for a cup of hot water. Man, he was tight.[40]

As Gates stated,

We had to eat in the bus because we weren't allowed to eat in the restaurants. We'd stop in grocery stores along the way to buy sandwiches and whatnot. We'd call it grocery bag lunches. Even changed uniforms in the bus because we weren't allowed in white dressing rooms. A lot of times we'd have to drive another 150 miles to find a place to sleep.[41]

Bill Yancey recalled decades later,

When I played with the Renaissance in basketball, sometimes we used to get treated something awful. We'd go in town and couldn't get any food, and then they'd expect us to make 'em look good! In baseball we didn't get bothered too much expect in the South. In the North, we never had problems, not that you'd notice. Because the white ballplayers thought it was an honor to play us. Oh, we used to have problems getting food in the North. The restaurants didn't want to serve us. That was general in the North, but we never had too far to ride. If we were going from New York to Philadelphia, how long is that going to take? And if you were going to Pittsburgh, you could stop in Harrisburg. There's always ways. Our biggest problem was when we were on the road all the time, like when I was playing basketball. I'll never forget the time we went into West Virginia for the first time and there was no hotel at all where we could go. It took us maybe a couple of hours to find lodging for eight or nine fellas— one stay here, two stay here, like that.[42]

The team barnstormed throughout the country in a bus bought and modified by Bob Douglas. Douglas recalled,

> The team would cover about thirty-eight thousand miles each season and they'd travel in the team bus. The club would appear at places like Iowa, Wyoming, New Orleans, and other faraway sections of the country. I'd never travel with the team; I would stay in New York and arrange the bookings and map out the itinerary. We had a club secretary, Eric Illidge; a trainer, Doc Bryant; and my assistant Frank Richards, who handled the publicity. He got out releases, posters, and whatnot.[43]

There existed a culture on the bus, a pecking order in terms of who sat where. Gates recalled,

> All the rookies on the Rens used to have to ride in the back of the bus. Tarzan Cooper used to give all the young guys a hard time—taking food and drinks from them. He felt he was a veteran and was entitled to do that. . . . It was a lot of fun, laughing and talking in the bus. Ride the bus from four to eight hours, and if you're not running your mouth, you're sleeping.[44]

Despite the camaraderie engendered on those long trips, the team faced racism as they traveled throughout the country. Gates remembered,

> We'd tour the South and play the Negro colleges, sometimes playing three teams in the same day. In Atlanta, we'd play Morehouse, Morris Brown, and Clark twenty-minute periods each. Many times when we played in the South, we'd have to fight our way in and out of the arenas. One time in Marion, Ohio, [Clarence] "Puggy" Bell went into the crowd scrambling for a ball and a woman kicked him from behind. One time in Cicero, Illinois, where we were playing, a fight broke out. The lights went out and when we came back on, twelve of us were in the middle of the floor with chairs in our hands. Then another time in Indianapolis, Indiana, some white guys kept yelling nigger-this and nigger-that. After we picked out who was yelling, I conveniently missed a Puggy Bell pass and the basketball knocked the guy right off his chair. We did that a lot of times.[45]

The team quickly realized that racism factored into where they played, who they played against, and who refereed the games. "You got ten points as fast as you could because you assumed those were the ten points you weren't going to get from officiating," remarked Isaacs.[46]

Isaacs's teammate, Puggy Bell, agreed with Isaacs's assessment:

> [The team] was so good we'd spot clubs ten points, with the racists officiating taken into account. At that time we had a policy not to beat a team by more than ten points. In other words, hold the score down so we could come back and play them again. Don't show the other team up so bad they wouldn't play us again. After all, we had to make money.[47]

Making money was an important aspect to their basketball barnstorming days. Eric Illidge, the team's manager was in charge of making sure that his team was paid at each venue. He would tell the team, "Never come out on the court unless I have the money. We would not let anyone deny us our right to make a living." Illidge would remember, "That was a whole lot of money to me at the time."[48]

As Johnny Isaacs recalled about one trip,

> We played one team in Bedford, Indiana. It was one of those rough games where bodies were bumping up against each other a lot. And one of their guys slammed against Puggy Bell, one of our teammates. It was an accident, but it made the fans angry. Several people, including a county police officer, jumped over the railing and began kicking Puggy in the shins. There was a lot of pushing and shoving going on. It was rough.
>
> I remember once we traveled to Bloomington, Indiana. Eric Illidge had a schedule on a little piece of paper that said "Bloomington." So he assumed it was Bloomington, Indiana. But unfortunately for us, it was Bloomington, Illinois. Well, we pulled into the gym in Indiana and got dressed to play. I went out early to check on the crowd, and there was nobody around. I saw this young boy, and I asked him when the game was supposed to start. He asked, "What game?" I knew there were a bunch of cars parked outside the arena. I assumed that they were there for the game. But the boy told me, "Oh, no. There is a magician here in town tonight."
>
> So I ran down and told the team that there was a mistake. That's when Illidge realized that we were supposed to be in Bloomington,

Illinois. Boy, were the guys angry! We had to jump into the bus quickly and drive 400 miles over to Illinois for the game. We stopped at a roadside phone and called the promoters in Illinois and told them we had an accident, and we were running late. We didn't even get into town until 11:00 that night. And would you believe it?! The people were all there still waiting for us. We were so tired and angry, but we still played a great game that night. . . . The worst part of all was that we had no place to stay in Illinois that night, so we had to drive all the way back to Indianapolis to stay. In all, we must have traveled nearly 1,000 miles that day.[49]

Isaacs remembered,

> We were always impressed by Indiana. We mostly played in high school gyms there. And those high school gyms were larger than most of the college gyms in New York City. Most folks back east couldn't believe it when we told them about the popularity of the game in Indiana.[50]

As the 1930s dawned, the Rens were quickly becoming one of the best teams in the nation. During the 1933 season, they won eighty-eight straight games. One of their best shooters was Bill Yancey. Before embarking on a Hall of Fame career as the UCLA coach, John Wooden was building an equally impressive Hall of Fame career as a player following graduation from Purdue University. While teaching and coaching, Wooden found time to play professionally for a few years in the early to mid-1930s and faced off against the Rens many times. He clearly remembered Yancey and his awesome shooting ability.

> Even with a ball that was none too round in those days, he would hit every shot from nine different positions. [He] was the greatest outside shooter I ever saw. I remember once before a game, he laid out nine spots on the floor, all from a distance of today's three-point line, and he'd shoot from each spot. He'd hit from all nine spots, then turn around and hit nine more coming back the other way, all without a miss. . . . Yancey used a two-handed set shot and got that shot away very quickly. I don't think there's anybody in the game today who could shoot any better or more accurately.
>
> I played many games against the New York Rens in the thirties and continue to feel that they were the finest exponents of team play

that I have ever seen. . . . To this day, I have never seen a team play better team basketball.[51]

That team set the tone and pace for style, creativity, and a sense of teamwork in which the ball moved effortlessly from one player to the next. According to Gates, "When we played, you had to check your man. Make him take two steps to get one. Nobody guards nobody now. . . . When we played you had to earn your grits." Saitch said, "We didn't even have a coach! We didn't have positions; we played the man." Douglas stated, "Years ago a man wouldn't dare try to take the ball up-court without passing to a fellow player. If a player had started that one-on-one stuff you see so much of today, I would have yanked him right away. We called it hogging the ball." Isaacs believes that the Rens and then the Washington Bears invented the pick-and-roll and motion offense, not Red Auerbach's Celtics. "Auerbach was in the Navy and he would go watch the Washington Bears play in Turner's Arena, a small fight club in Washington, DC."[52]

The Rens would play about 140 to 150 games a year and lose no more than 20. The Rens were a draw, and fans would come out just to see them play. Gates noted,

> Most games were sold out, because many of them were advertised weeks in advance. Bob Douglas and [manager] Eric Illidge were arranging games throughout Indiana and the Midwest through the Chambers of Commerce in each of the towns we played in. So each of them had a lot of time to advertise that the Rens were coming to town.[53]

Frank Baird, who played against the Rens, remembered the challenges the team faced when they arrived in town:

> When the Renaissance came in, they had to stay at the colored YMCA at Sennet and Michigan [Streets]. We'd go out with them and play around the state. There was no place they could get anything to eat, so they brown-bagged it. We'd get to the gym at 6 or 6:30 for an 8 o'clock game, and they'd be down in the locker room already dressed and having a sandwich or something. Maybe they'd save part of it to eat on the way back to Indianapolis. I thought that was one of the most unfair things. They were nice guys and they were tough. I'm sure over the years they beat us more than we beat them.[54]

Pat Malaska, an opposing player, recalled,

> They had some difficulty in getting places to stay because most folks didn't want to house blacks. But on the court they were pretty well respected, I'd say. They were a clean bunch. They weren't dirty ballplayers. People liked them. People liked seeing them play. I'd say, all in all, they were very well respected. [55]

The respect the team generated did not prevent them from experiencing difficulty finding a place to stay. Gerald Archibald, whose father played in the first game of basketball at the YMCA Training School by James Naismith, arranged games in Warren, Pennsylvania, and he recalled trying to find a hotel in town for the team.

> Normally the Rens never tried to stay here [Warren, PA]. They always stayed in Jamestown, N.Y., when they came in to play us. But for this one game they had come in from Indiana, and they said they hadn't had time to make a reservation so they asked me if I could find a place for them. I said, "I think I can," and I called the Sitler House and asked if they could handle a basketball team. I didn't say they were black. The hotel said yes, so I returned to the Rens' manager and said, "I got a place for you." So we drove to the Sitler House and the Rens' manager and a couple of the players went in with me. I'll never forget the look on the poor girl's face at the desk when we opened the door. She turned white as a sheet and she said, "Mr. Archibald, I just can't do it," and she burst out crying. Just like that, the Rens turned around and said, "Okay, Gerry, we'll find some place." And boy, did they ever put on a show that night! I beat 'em a couple of times, but not that night! [56]

Throughout all the successes and failures, trials and tribulations, the one person who stood tall was Bob Douglas. He was the Rens and a man who was respected by everyone, friend and opponent alike. Douglas demanded respect from his players, and as Gates recalled, "By showing respect, Bob Douglas said we'd earn respect. We were so widely known that everybody was watching us. So Bob didn't want anybody acting up or making the team look bad. He didn't want any blemishes on our reputation." [57]

Douglas lived and worked during a period when a person's word was his word, and a handshake was your word. Bill Yancey, one of his players, reflected on the influence Douglas had on the team:

> First if Bob gave you his word or a hand shake it was better to me than any contract I have ever signed and that has been quite a few, he made us go first class and he kept basketball alive for a number of years when it was really on the rocks. When we walked on the floor we had the best uniforms that money could buy and every man had to have his on right. I remember when maybe one man would wear his basketball shoes out a little quicker than another, Bob would get us all new shoes so we would be uniformed. [58]

In addition to the Original Celtics, the Rens also traveled and played against the Philadelphia SPHAS (South Philadelphia Hebrew Association), a team owned and managed by Eddie Gottlieb, who said,

> We never had a telegram or written letter or anything as far as a guarantee. Everything was done over the phone and never any problems. I have been associated with basketball for over fifty years and I have never found a better businessman than Bob. My various teams have locked horns with the Rens over seventy times and I can tell you we lost more than we won; but those good pay days sometimes take the hurt out of losing, and that's what we had when we played Bob's team. [59]

Later in life, Douglas was nominated for the Naismith Memorial Basketball Hall of Fame. Nat Holman, who played and coached against Douglas during the 1920s and 1930s and no less an authority on basketball, wrote a letter of support for Douglas's candidacy. In it, he summed up Douglas's influence on the game and what his contributions to the game meant:

> No man's life has been more dedicated to the game of basketball for more than half a century. . . . His contribution to basketball isn't measurable. The tendency is to look back at the record of achievement, but no applicant, I am sure, has made greater progress under greater odds. When one considers the exhausting, backbreaking pace his teams had to go through, having been the target for discrimination in the early days of the sport—his leadership, his integrity, his intelligence, qualified Bob Douglas for a place in the Hall of Fame.

His greatest reward is written in the heart of his players. His influence in the black community on both amateur and professional
players will remain long after he and the rest of us are forgotten and
he will not be forgotten for a long time. I have always appreciated
loyalty to one's friends but loyalty to the game, that it be played
properly, is one of the trademarks of this high-minded, decent and
enlightened citizen.[60]

Douglas eventually was enshrined into the Basketball Hall of Fame,
and as time passed he was able to reflect on the legacy the Rens left:

For all the years that the team was in existence we treated the fans to
some of the classiest basketball in the world. At the end of the 1939
season, we'd won 112 games and lost 7. In the years after that, we
never failed to win at least 100 games every season. In Chicago in
1939, we went through the toughest clubs in the country to win the
first world professional basketball championship tournament on
record. The victory in Chicago was one of the team's greatest
achievements. The Rens had brought full realization to the world
that they were the best.[61]

That was not lost on his players either, as Gates proudly stated long
after his playing days: "Playing for the Rens was the greatest thing in the
world for a player at that time—be he black or white. The Rens were
the premier ball club in the country. We played the best and beat the
best."[62]

The New York Renaissance was not the only black professional basketball team with national appeal and recognition. The other was the
Harlem Globetrotters, based in Chicago. Their origins are controversial
and still lack complete clarity nearly ninety years later. The team was
founded by Dick Hudson and comprised of players from Wendell Phillips High School but was billed as the Giles Post American Legion
basketball squad. The team was led by Dick Hudson, a twenty-eight-
year-old former professional football player. The players from Wendell
Phillips included Tommy Brookins, Randolph Ramsey, Toots Wright,
and Lester Johnson; also added to the squad was Joe Lillard. The Giles
Post American tour of Wisconsin began on December 21, 1926, and
continued into January 1927. The team traveled across the state and
played eighteen games from Sheboygan to Fond du Luc to La Crosse.

The purported first game of the Harlem Globetrotters on January 7, 1927, never occurred; the Globetrotters had yet to exist.

By the end of 1927, the Giles Post team began playing games in the Savoy Ballroom and was soon referred to as the Savoy Big Five. Inman Jackson and Runt Pullins eventually joined the team. After some internal disagreement with the team, Tommy Brookins left and developed his own team, the Tommy Brookins Globe Trotters, which started traveling the Midwest. A booking agent, Abe Saperstein, who was helping Dick Hudson and the Giles Post team, started booking games for Brookins. It also appears that Saperstein had created his own team, a

Abe Saperstein managed and coached the Harlem Globetrotters for many decades. *Courtesy of Bill Himmelman.*

Bernie Price played for the Harlem Globetrotters during the 1940s. *Courtesy of Bill Himmelman.*

second team called the Globe Trotters that was barnstorming the Midwest. Eventually, Tommy Brookins left the team, and some of his team members were absorbed into Saperstein's squad. This team eventually became the Globetrotters.

Like the Rens, the Globetrotters traveled throughout the country playing the best competition and facing discrimination. Oftentimes, the team slept in its car, an old Model T, because they could not find any other place to stay. Bernie Price recalled,

> We were treated poor practically everywhere. I remember one occasion in Omaha, Nebraska. After the game a boy came by and said, "I got a place for you." So we go by this big fine hotel. The kids on the desk must have been younger or new on the job because he gave us rooms, but about 4 o'clock in the morning we had to get up and get out. So we got in the bus and drove on down toward the town where we were playing next. We drove all night, just kept going. Saperstein would intercede for us, but hell, there wasn't anything he could do about it. But we were mostly young and we didn't pay much attention to it.[63]

Soon enough, they became a juggernaut, winning most every game they played. Many of the games were not very close. The fans became bored. If the games were not close, why would the team be asked back the following year to play again? Sensing this, Saperstein believed that his team would need to make it fun for the spectators and keep it close, yet not too close that winning was ever in jeopardy. They still won by a comfortable margin. The fans had a good time, and an invitation to return the following year was offered soon thereafter.

In the ensuing decades, the team added the Magic Circle as part of its routine set to the music of "Sweet Georgia Brown." With the music playing, the players would stand around in a circle and make trick passes behind their back, between their legs, down their arms, and over the shoulder. The crowds loved it, and soon they became the most popular basketball team in the country. By the 1940s and 1950s, the Globetrotters single-handedly were keeping the NBA afloat financially. They became known for their trick plays and fun ways on the court, which masked the fact that they were excellent players. As Pop Gates declared, "This is a fallacy that people have, that the Globetrotters were not good ballplayers. They were excellent ballplayers." Gates continued,

"They think that's all we were doing—clowning. Against the teams we played, you couldn't clown," said Bernie Price.[64]

Indeed, they were great players; in the 1930s, they and the Rens were the two best black basketball teams. They crisscrossed the country, playing games and winning over fans with their fine play. However, the call was growing for them and the Rens to play each other, to settle once and for all which was the best black basketball team. As the 1930s came to a close, that desire among the fans became a reality.

2

THE WORLD PROFESSIONAL
BASKETBALL TOURNAMENT

March 27, 1939

Finally. The game everyone had been hoping for was finally here. For much of the 1930s, basketball fans were anticipating a game between the Harlem Globetrotters and the New York Renaissance (Rens). On March 27, 1939, in Chicago, the two best black basketball teams finally met. It was the semifinals of the inaugural World Professional Basketball Tournament. In many ways, it was the signature game of the decade, one that would put to rest which black basketball team was the best. Much had been written about these two teams as both squads and fan bases could lay claim to their team being the best. For the Rens, the 1930s had been a dominant decade as the team crisscrossed the country and became a household name. They faced all comers while winning more than fifteen hundred games. Meanwhile, the Globetrotters were no slouch. They, too, traveled the country, winning games, and earning a reputation as a fun bunch of basketball players. They were opposites, but both had strong followings and both employed highly skilled basketball players—the best black basketball players.

Many attempts had been made to have the teams face each other and settle the dispute once and for all. It had not happened. Instead, it became a battle of words, trash-talking and one-upmanship that never resolved anything. In February 1939, Eric Illidge, the Rens manager, openly challenged the Globetrotters to a series, a winner-take-all match. To him, the Globetrotters were "clowns," not nearly as skilled or worthy of the attention bestowed on his Rens. The Globetrotters were entertainers, not basketball purists like the Rens, whose artful display of passing, teamwork, and timely scoring elevated basketball to an art form. Illidge issued this challenge:

> We will play the Harlem Globetrotters anytime, anywhere. They've been going around telling folks how good they are, and how they will beat us, but we issued them a public challenge and they're afraid to answer it. Listen, we'll pass the ball around those guys so fast they'll think they're on the Rhine.[1]

His claim was further endorsed by the *Pittsburgh Courier*'s Wendell Smith, who declared,

> The Renaissance are demanding the Globetrotters answer this time or keep their traps shut forevermore. . . . It is now the duty of Mr. Abe Saperstein, owner of the Harlemites, to offer some kind of answer. If all this talk about the Globetrotters being able to beat the Renaissance has been issued by "Ile Abe," and we have reason to believe that it has, for publicity purposes, we would suggest that he put a muffler on his ballyhoo. For the last time, Mr. Saperstein should answer this challenge or forevermore hold his peace.[2]

Saperstein continued to duck the challenge and keep his team on the road. At times, he offered to play the Rens; but for whatever reasons, he and Bob Douglas could not agree on the financial terms of such a match. It would not last; they were on a collision course to meet. The occasion was the inaugural World Professional Basketball Tournament.

The World Professional Basketball Tournament saved professional basketball during World War II. The tournament did more to help professional basketball and the game's integration than any other basketball event of this time. It was a key aspect that contributed to the game's survival and growth after World War II. John Schleppi, the author of *Chicago's Showcase of Basketball: The World Tournament of Professional Basketball and the College All-Star Game*, notes,

> During the Great Depression many organizations and events, as well as several college football bowls (the Sugar, Cotton, and Sun), the National Collegiate Athletic Association (NCAA) basketball tournament, the National Invitational Tournament (NIT), the National As-

sociation of Intercollegiate Basketball (present NAIA) tournament, and Amateur Softball Association tournament, were all promotions born out of financial necessity to put backsides in arena seats. The developing World Tournament of Professional Basketball was to become another of these events.[3]

That attention was needed, because, Schleppi stated,

> Professional basketball was in disarray in the late 1930s due to poor financial backing, quixotic leadership, and the effects of the Depression. Against this background entrepreneur Harry Hannin and Leo Fischer of the *Chicago Herald American* promoted the World Tournament of Professional Basketball, which began in March 1939. Attracting the best available teams, they included the leading black and integrated teams. This was the first time blacks competed with whites on an even footing for a professional team championship. Using major facilities, including the Amphitheatre and the Stadium, attention was drawn to the game during the war years.[4]

From 1939 to 1948, the World Professional Basketball Tournament played a significant role in promoting the game, establishing the professional game on a national level, drawing teams from across the country, and providing a forum for quality professional basketball during World War II. Held in Chicago, the country's second largest city and the midway point in the country, the tournament was operated by the *Chicago Herald American*.

Four individuals were most responsible for the successful promotion and operation of the tournament. Harry Wilson was the tournament secretary, and Harry Hannin served as director of arrangements. The publicity fell to Leo Fischer, who wrote articles about the team, published the annual program, and later served as commissioner of the National Basketball League (NBL). His affiliation with the NBL provided the tournament with a decidedly Midwestern flavor as many of the teams who competed over the years hailed from the Midwest or were affiliated at some point with the NBL. Many eastern-based teams chose not to participate. Finally, Edward Cochrane, sports editor of the newspaper, rounded out the group of four men in charge of operating the tournament. Due to the great support of the *Chicago Herald American*, the tournament always received extensive coverage in the newspaper and attracted record crowds. It was during those days in March from 1939 to 1948 that the Original March Madness was born.

The early years of the tournament, though, belonged to those players who, playing in unheated armories and driving seven players to a car, built professional basketball during the 1930s. Players such as Leroy "Cowboy" Edwards, Buddy Jeannette, Bobby McDermott, and George Mikan all won the tournament at some point. Jeannette (Detroit Eagles, 1941, and Fort Wayne Zollner Pistons, 1945) and Mikan (Chicago American Gears, 1946, and Minneapolis Lakers, 1948) each won two MVP awards as the tournament's best player. The Oshkosh All-Stars made five trips to the finals, winning once, and the Fort Wayne Zollner Pistons won the tournament three times, 1944 through 1946. Three teams—the Oshkosh All-Stars (1942), the Fort Wayne Zollner Pistons (1944 and 1945), and the Minneapolis Lakers (1948)— won the tournament in the same year they captured the NBL title. Seven teams that competed—Fort Wayne Zollner Pistons, Minneapolis Lakers, Sheboygan Red Skins, Anderson Duffey Packers, Tri-Cities Blackhawks, Syracuse Nationals, and Baltimore Bullets—later became NBA franchises. Cities such as Clarksburg, Toledo, and Kenosha also fielded teams at some point during the tournament's ten-year run.

The World Professional Basketball Tournament's most important and lasting legacy: the tournament served as the first venue for all-black and integrated teams to play for a professional championship. From its very first year in 1939 until it concluded ten years later, in 1948, the World Professional Basketball Tournament invited the best black teams to participate.

The New York Rens won the inaugural tournament in 1939. One of the Rens' best players, William "Pop" Gates, was the only player to compete in all ten years, although not all with the Rens. The following year, the Harlem Globetrotters won the title. Thus, in the first two years, the two best black teams each captured the title as basketball champions of the world. In 1943, the Washington Bears, whose roster greatly resembled the New York Rens of previous seasons, won the tournament, thus making it three all-black squads to win the tournament in the first five years.

As black teams won, recognition went to their players. A strong array of black players competed in the tournament, including Robert "Sonny" Wood, Nat "Sweetwater" Clifton, George Crowe, Pop Gates, Zack

Clayton, Bernie Price, William "Dolly" King, Johnny Isaacs, Clarence "Puggy" Bell, Louis "Babe" Pressley, and Wyatt "Sonny" Boswell, and all garnered recognition. Except for the 1946 and 1947 tournaments, at least one black player was named to the all-tournament first or second team every year. Other players such as Al Price, Tarzan "Chuck" Cooper, and Willie Smith all made contributions to integrating the game. In addition, Dolly King and Tarzan Cooper earned the unique distinction of coaching teams in the tournament, the first time a black player coached either integrated teams (Dolly King) or all-black teams (Tarzan Cooper). The World Professional Basketball Tournament was an important part of the game's history, particularly integration, and its significance is largely lost today.

The 1939 tournament was scheduled for March 26–28. From the beginning, it seemed as if the Rens and Globetrotters were on a collision course. The field, still being assembled up to the final days before the tournament, featured, in addition to the Rens and Globetrotters, the House of David, New York Yankees, Fort Wayne Harvesters, Oshkosh All-Stars, Sheboygan Red Skins, Illinois Grads, Clarksburg Oilers, Chicago Harmons, and New York Celtics. To lend some prestige to the tournament, football's George Halas was named commissioner, and City College of New York (CCNY) basketball coach Nat Holman was named the honorary referee. The prize was $1,000.

The Rens and Globetrotters were placed in the same bracket, meaning that they could only face each other in the semifinals but not in the finals. This was not lost on either Douglas or Saperstein. Why were the two black teams placed in the same bracket? Was it by chance, or was it racism? Did the organizers believe that having two black teams in the finals would undermine the tournament or be bad for business? Wendell Smith of the *Pittsburgh Courier* wondered the same thing. "If they hadn't paired [the Globetrotters] in the same brackets with the flawless Rens, we might have two sepia teams playing for the title. But, of course, they just couldn't let that happen, could they?" Douglas and Saperstein decided that they would play the matches as they came.[5]

Ben Green, author of *Spinning the Globe: The Rise, Fall, and Return to Greatness of the Harlem Globetrotters*, discusses the rivalry and how this was viewed quite differently by the black and white press on the eve of the tournament.

The rivalry between the Trotters and Rens might have been a hot story in the black press, but the white papers treated it like so many other issues in the African American community: they ignored it completely. Even when the *Chicago Tribune* got around to mentioning the pro tournament, the *Trib*'s sports editors couldn't bring themselves to face the race issue head-on. They reported that the "lone Chicago representative" in the tournament was the Chicago Harmons, completely ignoring the fact that the Globe Trotters were from Chicago, too. The Trotters has been in business for over a decade, yet through either ignorance or intent, the *Tribune* still couldn't accept them as a hometown team.[6]

The Rens arrived in Chicago a day before the tournament and headed to their usual place of residence when staying in the Windy City, the Hotel Grand on South Parkway. It was comfortable and felt like home to the team, who spent many weeks on the road in the Midwest and used Chicago as a base city. As John Isaacs recalled about the Hotel Grand, "We could look out our windows and see people riding horses up and down the media of South Parkway."[7] Well rested and with a first-round bye, the Rens opened the tournament facing the New York Yankees, who won their opening round match against the House of David from Benton Harbor, Michigan. On paper, the game appeared to be lopsided. Instead, the contest turned into a tougher affair for the Rens than they had expected or hoped. A close contest for much of the first half, the Rens finally pulled away for a 30–21 win with Tarzan Cooper scoring ten points. The game turned when Eric Illidge replaced Fats Jenkins and Eyre Saitch with his younger players, Johnny Isaacs and Puggy Bell. They injected new life into the team, which proved the difference.

Writing after the first day of games, the *Sheboygan Press* sang the praises of the Rens: "The Renaissance displayed the most class, and to most observers, they appear to be the team to beat, although anything can happen in a tournament of this kind."[8] The Rens could sit back and wait for their next opponent.

Meanwhile, the Globetrotters would need to win two games in one day to advance to the semifinals and a date with the Rens. The following day, in the afternoon match, they defeated the Fort Wayne Harvesters' team, 41–33, behind fifteen points from Ted Strong. The game was tied 7–7 before Larry Bleach broke the tie, and thereafter the Globetrotters had little trouble with the team from Fort Wayne. After gaining a comfortable margin, the Globetrotters focused on defense and held the Harvesters scoreless for nearly five minutes as they coasted to victory. After showering, grabbing a bite to eat, and getting some rest, the Globetrotters returned to play the final game of the evening's tripleheader, which did not tip off until after 10 p.m. Facing the other Chicago entry, the Chicago Harmons, the Globetrotters slogged through a tough affair to win, 31–25. It was a long day of basketball for the Globetrotters, but two hard-fought wins earned them a chance to play another day.

That set up the match the black press and fans had awaited for years: the Rens versus the Globetrotters. New York versus Chicago. The site was the 132nd Regiment Armory. Leo Fischer understood the importance of the game when he wrote in the *Chicago Herald American,*

> The second game on the program will bring together for the first time the two great Negro professional teams—the Rens of New York and the Harlem Globe Trotters, more or less a Chicago club. For years they have been dodging each other and tonight's meeting not only will decide which goes into tomorrow night's final at the Coliseum, but also will determine the Negro's world championship.[9]

Seven thousand fans passed through the turnstiles to witness this historic and long overdue match. The game, though, had an inauspicious beginning. The Rens quickly established themselves with an 8–1 margin that swelled to 11–2 before settling in at 15–10 at the half. The Rens were dominating inside and hitting their shots. They were bigger, stronger, and more athletic. The methodical, structured, and patient play of the Rens proved too much for the younger Globetrotters, who failed to dictate the pace of play to which they were most accustomed. They were frustrated when they could not find a good shot; their offense was predicated on quick scores and an up-and-down tempo. The threesome of Fat Jenkins, Willie Smith, and Tarzan Cooper proved too much on the inside. The Globetrotters had their shots, but were ice-cold from the field; they could not score for fifteen minutes.

As the *Chicago Defender* observed the next day, "At no time did the Globetrotters get a chance to put on an exhibition of ball handling or passing. They were guarded so close that most of their shots were from a distance." The second half played out much the same way until a late surge by the Globetrotters knotted the game at 23–23. A basket in the final fifteen seconds by Cooper help seal a 27–23 win. Exuberant at finally playing and defeating their nemesis, the Rens still needed to win one more game to become world champions. Isaacs remembered, "When the game was over, we all hung out together. No problem. But once we got out on the floor, it was who's going to come out. You beat us or we beat you."[10]

The following night, the Rens faced the Oshkosh All-Stars, who had already defeated them twice in three contests during the season. Only three thousand fans, fewer than half of the previous evening, ventured out to watch the championship match, to see "a rough and tumble affair with spectacular passwork and close guarding mixed in great profusion." The game was close early on before "the Rens proceeded to go to town in a big way. Isaacs, Cooper and Gates rung up five baskets in a row among them while Oshkosh was being blanked."[11] The Rens held a 24–11 halftime lead, too large for Oshkosh to mount a serious challenge. The Rens won, 34–25, to claim the first World Professional Basketball Tournament title. In the third-place game, the Globetrotters defeated Sheboygan, 36–34.

Pop Gates led the team with twelve points. Earning tournament MVP honors was Clarence "Puggy" Bell. A New Yorker, Bell was a basketball player from the beginning. A versatile player, he possessed both strength and a soft touch, able to be physical under the basket while displaying speed and quickness in the open court. Growing up, he was considered too small to play high school; instead, he played for the Harlem Midgets, Harlem YMCA Seniors, Passaic Crescents, and the Harlem Yankees. His ambition was always to play for his hometown team. As he said, "The idols of the basketball world whenever they have played, the Rens, to Harlem, their hometown, are veritable demigods on the court, and it is the dream of nine out of ten promising young basketball players in the community to get a chance to play with them."[12]

He joined his hometown Rens in 1938–39 and alternated between them and the Washington Bears until 1945–46. He was an integral member of the 1943 Bears team that won the World Professional Basketball Tournament. After the war, he played in the minor leagues for teams in Saratoga, Bridgeport, Troy, Bristol, Manchester, Wilkes-Barre, and Glens Falls. He ended his playing career in 1952–53 with Saratoga-

Manchester of the American Basketball League. He was the player-coach when the team won the championship. Thus, in a career that spanned parts of three decades, he began and ended his career on championship teams. In 1939, his career was just getting started, and his play helped the Rens make history.

After winning the World Championship, Bob Douglas stated,

> At the end of 1939, we'd won 112 games and lost 7. In Chicago in 1939, we went through the toughest clubs in the country to win the first world professional basketball tournament on record. The victory in Chicago was one of the team's greatest achievements. The Rens had brought full realization to the world that they were the best. [13]

After their historic win, the team celebrated at the Hotel Grand. Douglas gave them championship jackets that said "Colored World Champions." Isaacs did not like the wording and took a razor and cut away "Colored." Douglas was flabbergasted: "You're ruining the jacket!" Isaacs responded, "No, just making it better." Indeed, it was the full realization of Douglas's dreams. As Chester Washington Jr. perfectly summed up in the *Pittsburgh Courier*, "You just can't take it away from them. The Rens still reign supreme as the greatest pro basketball team in the country." [14]

The Globetrotters spent the next year licking their wounds. Payback was on their mind. Like the previous year, both the Rens and the Globetrotters were seeded in the same bracket; and if both won their opening-round games, they would face each other in the quarterfinals. The Rens, again coming off a strong basketball campaign, opened against the Canton Bulldogs. The Bulldogs kept the game close in the first ten minutes, but playing without any bench players due to illness, the Bulldogs did not have enough firepower to keep it close. The Rens led at the half, 30–15, before putting Canton away, 42–21, in the second half. Puggy Bell's thirteen points and John Isaacs's ten points paced the Rens. Meanwhile, the Globetrotters easily defeated the Kenosha Royals, 50–26, with Bernie Price (fourteen) and Babe Pressley (thirteen) leading the way. The Globetrotters were so strong defensively that they limited Kenosha to three points in the second half.

That set up the rematch for which everyone had been waiting. Scheduled for March 18, the Globetrotters–Rens matchup was the fourth and final quarterfinal game. The site was the Madison Street

Puggy Bell was a key contributor for the 1939 New York Renaissance that won the World Professional Basketball Tournament. © *Morgan and Marvin Smith Photographs and Prints Division, Schomburg Center for Research in Black Culture.*

Armory. Five thousand fans packed the arena with excitement. The game started after 10 p.m., but the wait was worth it. Unlike the previous year, when the Rens jumped to an early lead and controlled much of the game, this year the Globetrotters were ready from the outset.

The 1938–39 New York Renaissance team won the first World Professional Basketball Tournament in 1939. © *Morgan and Marvin Smith Photographs and Prints Division, Schomburg Center for Research in Black Culture.*

The first quarter was close and ended with a 12–11 lead for the Rens. The second quarter was similar, more defense and less scoring, as the Rens held a slim 18–16 margin. Both teams found their offense in the third quarter. The Rens held a 31–30 lead entering the final frame. Unlike the previous year, these teams were evenly matched.

At that point, both teams went ice-cold as if the basket had a barrier on top preventing each team from scoring. With a few minutes remaining, the Rens held a 36–34 lead. The Globetrotters scored, and then moments later Sonny Boswell was fouled; he hit a shot to make it 37–36 for the Globetrotters. It was his nineteenth and final point of the contest. The Rens had one last chance. With a change of possession, the Rens had the ball. It was in the hands of Puggy Bell. He raced down the floor hoping to score the winning basket before the clock expired. With their season on the line and remembering the bitter taste of defeat last year, the Globetrotters' Inman Jackson, the senior member of the squad, raced down the court. An elder statesman now, he was not the spry, quick player of thirteen years before. His presence startled Bell, who took a shot underneath the basket, a tough one to make. Jackson rebounded, sealing victory for the Globetrotters. The old guy has one more play left in him. Sonny Boswell proved the difference as he led all scorers with nineteen points.

The following day, the *Chicago Defender* sang Boswell's praises: "If the Rens could have tied Sonny Boswell's hands behind him, the 1939 world champs might have repeated." For the Globetrotters, it was sweet revenge. For the Rens, it was a bitter defeat. As Bob Douglas summed up, "I can't understand it. Everything my boys did was wrong in those last minutes of the game. I have never seen anything like it." For John Isaacs, the defeat was simply explained: "If Puggy had hit that shot, we would have won by one point. But Inman Jackson got the rebound, and the horn sounded."[15]

The Globetrotters still had two games to win before being declared champions. In the semifinals, they pulled away for a 34–25 win over the Syracuse Reds. That set them up in the finals.

Championship night arrived, and for the fans of Chicago's South Side, this was a momentous occasion. The all-black Harlem Globetrotters were playing for the world championship. There that night was a young man who would later go on to notoriety as a lawyer and civil rights activist. As recalled decades later by Timuel D. Black Jr., "I was right there at Chicago Stadium. The fact that they were going to be playing for the championship was momentous for the South Side, not just young people but for older people, too."[16] One of the key players for the hometown Globetrotters was Ted Strong.

A native of South Bend, Indiana, Strong joined the Globetrotters in 1935–36 and played with them until 1941–42 before joining the integrated Chicago Studebakers in 1942–43 for ten games. After serving in the military for three years, he rejoined the Globetrotters from 1945–46 to 1948–49 before retiring. When not playing basketball, he was a star baseball player in the Negro American League. Strong was a solid contributor, never a high scorer, but a key component in the Globetrotters' run to the championship. He was also a source of pride for the black Chicago community.

Black continued,

> I remember Ted Strong when he performed in Captain Walter Henri Dyett's "High Jinx" variety show. He sang the song, "Shoe Shine

Ted Strong starred for the Harlem Globetrotters during the 1940 World Professional Basketball tournament. *Courtesy of Bill Himmelman.*

Boy." Ted had a marvelous voice. He sung the song in the same spirit and elegance with his own voice as a Louis Armstrong singing that song. We were fascinated by this guy who was such a good athlete also being able to sing and perform. As he sang, he was performing like a shoeshine boy. As he was singing he was strokin' a shoe. Those of my generation cherish and remember Ted and his contemporaries of that period. They were not that much older but they were like big brothers. And Ted playing baseball . . . he could hit a ball . . . oh, man. If we were playing in Phillips play yard, he could hit the ball and break someone's window a block away . . . and he did! So those memories or experiences were inspirational to those of us who were less talented and somewhat younger. He was a hero to those of us who remember Ted Strong.[17]

The championship game featured the Globetrotters versus the Chicago Bruins, a battle of Chicago. If the Globetrotters finally were going to win the championship, it would take all they had. The Bruins would not go quietly. The first quarter was sluggish as the Globetrotters held a slim 7–6 lead. They started to exert themselves in the second quarter and pulled ahead, 20–13. Having a little breathing room may have led the Globetrotters to pull up on the gas pedal as the Bruins fought back to take a 21–20 lead. Gaining momentum, the Bruins continued to push the action, hoping to connect on a knockout punch. They led by eight points with five minutes remaining. At that point, the Globetrotters made their move. Chipping away, they tied the game at twenty-nine with a minute remaining. The Globetrotters had the ball, and Bernie Price dribbled into the frontcourt. Sensing an opening, he stopped and put up a shot that had all of the Globetrotters holding their breath. The ball went through the basket for a 31–29 lead. The Bruins had one last chance. Eddie Oram launched the ball from mid-court. The ball hit the rim, bounced high in the air, hit the rim again before rolling around and falling out. The Globetrotters and their faithful finally could exhale.

The Reverend Morris Gordon recalled,

> We were so proud of them. We used to sneak up to Ted's room and get his Globetrotter jacket and wear it around the neighborhood. Bernie Price was the nicest guy you would ever meet. I remember when he came out to the vacant lot where we were playing basketball and played with us in his street clothes. Man, did we get a kick out of that. Here he is a professional athlete coming out in his street clothes to play with us and show us some moves. [18]

"They were glad to talk to people they knew. They showed us that it was possible to overcome the impossible . . . racial barriers," Tim Black remembered. "I had fond memories of Ted Strong as a gentleman in terms of his social style. To us he was great because he was an example of what could be accomplished." [19] And what was accomplished was a world championship for the Harlem Globetrotters.

The 1941 tournament marked the first time in the tournament's brief history that an integrated team participated. Based in Toledo, Ohio, the Toledo White Huts were a semiprofessional team that toured Ohio and the Midwest. The White Huts joined a sixteen-team field and opened their first-round game against the Sheboygan Red Skins, a perennial NBL favorite. The lone black player was Bill Jones who, in December 1942, would help integrate the NBL with the Toledo Jim White Chevrolets. A native of Toledo, Jones played on all-black independent

and semiprofessional teams after graduating from the University of Toledo. He was a natural selection to join Toledo's entry in the field.

In this tournament, the White Huts opened strong against Sheboygan and held on for a 36–28 win. Jones did not score. Waiting for
Toledo in the second round were the Chicago Bruins, one of the two
hometown teams. Paced again by Chuck Chuckovits, the White Huts
surprised the Bruins with a 43–33 victory. Jones scored one point on a
free throw. Moving on to the semifinals, Toledo faced Oshkosh, another
perennial power in the NBL and the tournament. Still riding the hot
hand of Chuckovits, the White Huts stayed close until the end but
lacked enough scoring besides Chuckovits to pull out a victory. Jones
scored one bucket for two points. That semifinal loss put them into the
third-place game as their magical ride through the tournament was
coming to an end.

Also joining the White Huts in the field were the 1939 champion
New York Rens and 1940 winner, the Harlem Globetrotters. During
the tournament, the basketball community lost a valued member when
legendary Rens player Pappy Ricks died of cancer. Tributes poured out
of the black press. In its article on Ricks, the *Pittsburgh Courier* stated,

> Owner Bob Douglas, of the Renaissance, said in a recent interview
> that Pappy Ricks was the greatest player he had ever seen, white or
> colored, because in addition to his teamwork, he could put his shots
> in the basket from any angle and from all distances.[20]

Saddened by the loss of Ricks, the Rens were still focused on winning
the tournament for the second time in three years. Seeking to add some
scoring punch and another inside presence, Bob Douglas signed former
Long Island University star William "Dolly" King. Basketball historian
Peter C. Bjarkman once said, "If there is a lost name in the history of
basketball integration, it is most certainly the name of LIU's Dolly
King." A gifted athlete, King was a three-sport star at Alexander Hamil-
ton High School in New York in football, basketball, and baseball. After
graduating, King enrolled at Long Island University and played under
head coach Clair Bee. By the late 1930s, Bee had emerged as one of the
best college coaches in America. He was also one of the first college
coaches to address the issues of integration and civil rights. As Basketball Hall of Fame coach John McLendon, himself a pioneering coach

on the issues of integration and civil rights, once noted, "[Clair Bee was] the first college coach to schedule a game with an all-black college."[21]

Dolly King, it should be noted, was not Bee's first black varsity player. That distinction fell to Jimmy Gladden who played on the 1933–34 team. However, Gladden was a bench player who rarely saw meaningful action. It was King, though, who was Bee's first great black player, but not the only one. During the war years, Bee also reached out to King's brother Haldane, Eddie Younger, and Larry Doby and offered them all scholarships to play for him. Doby, who eventually broke base-ball's color barrier in the American League shortly after Jackie Robin-son, never did finish his freshman year as the war intervened. He later transferred to Virginia Union University, which had an ROTC program. On his way out of Brooklyn, Doby noted that "when [Bee] knew I might be drafted he gave me $10 for transportation home. He wished me luck, and said I could come back after the war was over to finish my educa-tion."[22] Although Doby did not return to LIU, he never forgot the gesture Bee made.

King was one of Bee's star players, which caused Bee to rethink his team's travel schedule and opponents. During the 1937–38 season, Bee faced several decisions regarding his team. Late in the season, the team was scheduled to visit Washington, D.C., to play George Washington University and Catholic University. However, it became apparent that the two schools did not want to play a team with a black player. Shortly before the trip, Clair Bee canceled the two games. The *Amsterdam News* noted this in an article that appeared several days later:

> Answering implications that he condoned the Jim Crow benching of Bill King when his Long Island University Blackbirds played teams of Dixie schools, Coach Clair Bee revealed this week that he had cancelled all games against those southern school fives who object to King playing.[23]

Shortly thereafter, LIU went on its final road trip of the season and headed to Huntington, West Virginia, for a rematch with Marshall Uni-versity. On this trip, they encountered Jim Crow face-to-face when they tried to register at the Governor Cabell Hotel. Informed that the hotel would not accept a black player staying and eating there, Bee said that if King could not stay there, then the whole team would find another place. Eventually, the matter was settled: the team stayed there, and

A star at Long Island University, Dolly King was a pivotal person in the integration of the game during the 1940s. *Courtesy of Bill Himmelman.*

LIU went on to win, 38–33. Later that season Bee scheduled his first games against all-black schools when LIU faced Virginia Union and Morgan State University.

Dolly King's play and ability to command attention and respect from his teammates earned him the honor of serving as captain of the team. In 1939, Long Island enjoyed an undefeated season, and the team was seeking a second undefeated season in 1941 when King left school to begin a professional career. He formed his own team, the Long Island Blackbirds, which also was known as the Dolly King All Stars. He quickly realized that operating his own squad was not so easy, particularly in the middle of the basketball season, so he joined the Harlem Yankees, which, at the time, was a feeder team for the Rens. He quickly established himself and was signed by the Rens in time to play in the 1941 Max Rosenblum Tournament in Cleveland. The Rosenblum Tournament was a smaller version of the World Professional Basketball Tournament and often played either before or after Chicago's main event.

In the semifinals against the Philadelphia SPHAs, he led all scorers with eighteen points. Despite the loss, the Rens defeated the Detroit Eagles in the third-place game. King tallied eleven points. His twenty-nine points in the two games in Cleveland boded well for the Rens as they ventured to Chicago. In 1946, after the war, King joined the Rochester Royals of the NBL, helping to integrate the league postwar. One of their game programs that season extolled the virtues of King and his contributions to the team: "As a scoring threat Dolly can hold his own with the top courtsters in the National circuit. His real value to the team, however, is his floor work. There he is beyond reproach."[24]

After one year with Rochester, King returned to the New York Rens for a season before joining the Dayton Rens as they made history in 1948–49 by becoming the first all-black team to play in a professional league. By then, King's days as a top-flight player were waning, although he continued playing professionally for another four years for teams in Mohawk, Scranton, and Saratoga, in what today would be considered minor leagues. He played three years with the Scranton Minors of the ABL in 1948–49, 1949–50, and 1950–51. For two years, his team made the finals, and he finally earned a championship in 1949–50. That team was integrated, and joining King were longtime friends and teammates Eddie Younger and Pop Gates.

Despite all he had accomplished, King still faced discrimination in the late 1940s as a member of the Scranton Minors. His coach was Red Sarachek, who recounted this story decades later:

> I remember going to a hotel in Scranton where the price was three dollars a night for a person and they wanted maybe fourteen from Dolly King. So I walked out of the hotel and I never came back, though they wanted us to come back. I would not even have had a victory banquet at that hotel. I felt it was unfair. On an individual basis we lived together. I do not think there was this business of blacks on one side of a bench and whites on another. I think they lived together, and we still live together, those who played with us.[25]

In addition to playing, he enjoyed coaching; and during the war years, he returned to his alma mater to serve as assistant coach to Red Wolfe, a former player with the Philadelphia SPHAS. Later in life, he served as athletic director and professor of student life at Manhattan Community College. While on a trip with the basketball team in 1969, he died of a heart attack at the age of fifty-one.

Prior to King joining the team, the Rens were again coming off a stellar season touring the country and sought to avenge their loss to the Globetrotters in the previous year's tournament. In their opening game, the Rens easily handled the Dayton Sucher Wonders, 43–20, behind balanced scoring as three players, Pop Gates, Puggy Bell, and Dolly King, each tallied eight points. Tarzan Cooper returned to the Rens solely for the tournament after playing much of the season with the Washington Bruins, another all-black touring team. The score was close in the first half until Cooper entered the game and ignited his team; it pulled out a 26–13 halftime margin. It was a lead they would not relinquish as they coasted in the second half. In the quarterfinals, the Rens faced the Kenosha Royals, who pulled the tournament's first big upset by defeating the Rochester Seagrams. Kenosha was no match for the Rens, who easily handled them, 43–15, behind fourteen points from Dolly King. That set up a semifinal match with the Detroit Eagles.

It proved to be the tournament's best game.

Detroit had quickly become the crowd favorite over the first few days of the tournament. Against both Indianapolis and the Harlem Globetrotters, they came from behind to earn two big wins. The trend reversed itself against the Rens as the Eagles set the pace and tone early. Rather than playing from behind, the Eagles took charge early in the contest. Throughout the first half, Ed Sadowski led a ferocious attack under the boards as Detroit commanded a comfortable 24–15 lead at intermission. The third quarter followed the same pattern, although the Rens started to chip at the lead bit by bit. Entering the final period, the Eagles still led, 34–31. The game was nip and tuck and with four minutes remaining, the Eagles held a 41–38 margin. Tight defense held for the next few minutes, and with forty seconds left the game entered a furious finish. Wilmet Sidat-Singh made a basket to cut the Detroit lead to 41–40. Then "came break No. 1. A blind Detroit pass from out-of-bounds went direct to 'Pop' Gates, alone under the hoop, and he caged it to put the Rens ahead, 42–41, with twenty-two seconds left." With seconds remaining, Detroit found a way to respond as "Jake Ahearn scooped the sphere from an opponent's grasp, fired a pass to [Buddy] Jeannette under the basket and the latter calmly tossed it through for the winning points." Despite a valiant effort, the Rens fell short even as Gates and Sidat-Singh each tallied eleven points. But the Rens were their own worst enemy as they missed nine of fifteen foul shots. If they had shot their normal percentage, they most likely would have advanced to the finals. Their chance at another title would have to wait another year. [26]

Sidat-Singh, a player on that 1941 Rens squad, was born William Webb. After his father died at a young age, his mother remarried an Indian medical student, Dr. Samuel Sidat-Singh, and he became Wilmeth Sadat-Singh. His adopted father relocated his family from Washington, D.C., to Harlem, and Wilmeth soon became involved with sports, particularly basketball. Growing up in the neighborhood, he played against Johnny Isaacs, a future teammate with the Rens and Washington Bears. "Sidat was something," Isaacs said. "So competitive, so disciplined that anything he put his mind to he would do it. A great first step, maybe as quick as (ex-Boys High and Duquesne star) Sihugo Green's." He and Isaacs "used to play football on sandlots, in playclothes—no pads, no Jordans, no nothing." Sidat-Singh led DeWitt Clinton High School to the city championship in 1935 and became one of the first African American all-Americans as voted by the city newspapers. He enrolled as a medical student at Syracuse University and played for the basketball team. The team went 40–13 during his first three years and was undefeated, 14–0, when he was a senior. As a basketball player, he was a stellar athlete as noted by the Reverend John Schroeder, a former college teammate of his: "I've often thought he introduced a lot of moves you didn't see in those days. He was a dandy ballhandler, really tricky." His style was more expressive than his time might indicate. He often threw the no-look pass and could be seen with his tongue hanging out of his mouth, a gesture later made famous by Michael Jordan in the 1990s. As his roommate on the road, Richard Jensen, noted, "He could fake you right out of your jock." [27]

His legend in college grew as he became a two-sport star. One day during an intramural football game, an assistant football coach, Roy Simmons, discovered him and suggested he try out for the football team. He played quarterback for the football team and soon became a

Wilmeth Sidat-Singh was a star at Syracuse University, but his career was cut short when he suffered a fatal accident training with the Tuskegee Airmen. © *Morgan and Marvin Smith Photographs and Prints Division, Schomburg Center for Research in Black Culture.*

star. He even earned the praise of noted sportswriter Grantland Rice: "A new forward-pass hero slipped in front of the great white spotlight of fame at Syracuse today. The phenomenon of the rifle shot event went on beyond Sid Luckman and Sammy Baugh. His name is Wilmeth Sidat-Singh." As the only black player, he faced discrimination and sat out road games against the University of Maryland and the Naval Academy, which refused to play integrated squads. Prior to those games, noted sportswriter Sam Lacy revealed in an article that he wasn't really "Hindu" as the white press had associated with him, but rather "Negro." Well, this ignited an uproar with Maryland and Navy and forced his coaches to sit him against those teams. As his aunt Adelaide Webb Henley, who was there that day against Maryland, remembered, "Wilmeth was just sitting there, with his head down, so embarrassed and humiliated." Despite the indignities that he faced, he never let those setbacks get to him, as Gates recalled: "He was a warm person, who had this ability to make anyone around him feel good. All those years, all the things he went through, and I don't think I ever saw him get really mad once." But, as Isaacs emphatically stated decades later, "He never presented himself as anything except a black man from Harlem."[28]

Despite those setbacks, Sidat-Singh became the first star African American athlete at Syracuse. After graduation, in 1938–39, he started to play professional basketball on independent teams including the All-Syracuse, Syracuse Reds, Rochester Seagrams, and then the New York Rens. With the outbreak of World War II, he returned to Washington, D.C., and became a police officer. He soon found out it was not for him. "I remember one time he told me he was at Griffith Stadium and a fight broke out," Isaacs said, "and he yelled, 'Somebody get the police,' until somebody yelled back, 'You are the police!'"[29]

Instead, he set his sights on something bigger. Sidat-Singh was accepted into the prestigious Tuskegee Airmen program. He continued to play basketball during the war with the Rens and Washington Bears while he was training. On May 9, 1943, he was performing a routine training mission when the engine failed. He jumped out but made the fatal mistake of not releasing his parachute before hitting the water. He drowned in Lake Huron at the age of twenty-five. His untimely passing occurred as his star as a basketball player was rising. His teammate Pop Gates wondered what might have been: "If Wilmeth had lived long enough, if he had played long enough, there is no telling how great he would have been."[30]

Despite its tough loss to Detroit, the Rens had a chance to claim third place. Standing in their way were the Toledo White Huts. Toledo started off strong and held a 17–10 lead before Dolly King started to make his move. Scoring inside and pounding the boards, King made his presence felt as he quickly turned the tide of the game, and the Rens took a 28–21 lead into halftime. The second half was more of the same as the Rens extended their margin. Despite the efforts of Chuck Chuckovits and Jimmy Johnson, Toledo had no other scorers and fell 57–42. A nice tournament run ended with fourth place. King paced the Rens with twenty-three points as they finished in third place. For his effort, King was named to the All-Tournament Team, the only black player to earn that honor. Bill Jones scored one basket for Toledo in the consolation round. This would prove to be Jones's only appearance in the World Professional Basketball Tournament. He scored five points for a 1.3 points per game average. He also dished out five assists. His contributions to integrating the game on a larger level would need to wait another year.

When the tournament began, the Harlem Globetrotters sought to become the tournament's first repeat winner. Since their victory the year before, the Globetrotters had played extremely well as "Sonny Boswell, Babe Pressley, Hillery Brown, Ted Strong and Inman Jackson—heroes of the all-star game, are going better than ever and it's going to take some tough competition to keep the Globe Trotters from repeating their triumph of last year in the world championship meet."[31]

In their opening round match, they easily defeated the Newark (New York) Elks. In the quarterfinals, the Globetrotters faced the Detroit Eagles. The Globetrotters opened strong with a quick 5–0 lead. They continued their strong play and led 17–11 at the half. The third quarter still belonged to the Globetrotters; they held steady with a 28–24 margin. Things looked positive for the team to move into the next round. Balanced scoring helped as Babe Pressley (ten points) and Hillery Brown (seven points) paced the team. In the last period, though, Detroit finally made a sustained run. Bob Calihan and Jimmy Brown were the difference makers; together they tallied a quick five points on a hook basket, free throw, and shot at mid-court that gave Detroit its first lead, 33–32, with five minutes remaining. Strong foul shooting also helped the Eagles' cause. The final five minutes proved to be a wild affair as the lead seesawed back and forth with Detroit holding on for a wild 37–36 win, sending the defending champions home early.

For the Globetrotters, it was a bitter disappointment. Sherman L. Jenkins, in his biography of Ted Strong Jr., posits this theory as to why the Globetrotters quickly lost their chance to defend their title:

> A combination of factors contributed to the Globetrotters' loss of the world champion title. First, a punishing traveling basketball schedule intended to generate revenue for owner Saperstein undoubtedly took a toll on the players. Second, the Globetrotters may have been overconfident; they were racking up wins against some of the nation's best professional and semiprofessional basketball teams. Why not relax and enjoy yourself a couple of days before you begin tournament play? You are at home, not on the road, and you will have a day or two to recover in order to compete. And maybe the Detroit Eagles were just a better basketball team in 1941. They defeated the 1939 world champions New York Rens in the semifinal round and then became the 1941 world champions by trouncing the Oshkosh All-Stars in the finals. [32]

Jenkins's theories all lend credence as to why the Globetrotters lost their title. First and foremost, Saperstein was a businessman; the more the team was on the road, the more money they made. In addition to their travels through the Midwest and many of the smaller towns in Middle America, Saperstein booked the team's first California trip to be followed by an extensive trip through the East. Both were important trips that allowed Saperstein to size up the potential on both coasts for future tours and exhibitions. After finishing up their California swing, the team headed to the opposite side of the country where they played in Ohio, Pennsylvania, Maryland, South Carolina, West Virginia, Virginia, Washington, D.C., New York State, and finally New York City. By the time they were finished, the team needed to head home to Chicago to defend its world championship. It was not only a lot of travel, but it was a lot of games against some of the better teams in a short amount of time. The team simply may have run out of gas.

The second theory Jenkins posited suggests that some players might have enjoyed themselves too much prior to the start of the tournament. The *Chicago Defender* certainly agreed with this assessment. The day following their defeat, the *Defender* noted that a handful of the players stayed too late at some of the more frequented nightclubs in Bronze-ville, "until the rays of the morning sun were breaking over Lake Michigan." The *Defender* pulled no punches in stating that the team "disappointed many of their followers by their poor performance."[33] The Eagles, however, were a good team coached by legendary player Dutch Dehnert. Balanced scoring from Ed Sadowski, Bob Calihan, Jake Ahearn, Jerry Bush, and future Hall of Famer Buddy Jeannette proved to be the right combination for Detroit. For the Globetrotters, their brief stay as world champions was now over as they returned to the road. Although they would play in most of the remaining World Professional Basketball Tournaments, the Globetrotters would never find the magic to claim another title as world champions.

By 1942, the war was in full bloom, and many of the best players were serving in the military and playing on service teams. The year also marked the first time that military teams played in the tournament. One of the teams was the Aberdeen (Maryland) Army Ordnance Training Center. Another team was the Long Island Grumman Flyers, one of two integrated teams in the field. Grumman Aircraft made airplanes for the World War II military effort. The players worked in the Grumman factory and were deferred from military service. As the *Chicago Defender* wrote,

> The easterners had three Negro players on their squad and all three got into the game. Talk about a real All-American democratic outfit—this was one. There were Tarzan Cooper and Pop Gates, two ex-New York Ren players, and Dolly King, who gained fame at Long Island University and later played one year with the Rens.[34]

The Grumman Flyers were a very good team and consisted of former New York Renaissance players such as Dolly King, Pop Gates, and Tarzan Cooper, along with former Long Island University players such as Ossie Schectman, Irv Torgoff, Butch Schwartz, and Si Lobello. Torgoff and Gates served as cocaptains. They were a well-balanced squad that amassed a 20–2 record playing a variety of teams including the Brooklyn Celtics, Brooklyn Jewels, Stan Lomax All-Stars, Paterson Pros, Colored Chain Gang, Detroit Clowns, and Fordham Giants.

They opened the tournament against the Indianapolis Kautskys and easily defeated them, 54–32. King (seven points), Gates (five), and Cooper (four) played well in a supporting role. Their win set them up in the next round against the hometown favorite Chicago Bruins. Paced by Dolly King's twelve points, the Flyers went on a ten-point rally late in the second half to pull out a 48–38 win. That placed them in the semifinals against the 1941 champion Detroit Eagles. In what turned into one of the best games of the tournament, the Flyers kept their tournament run going and held the lead late in the game. The first half was a back-and-forth affair as the teams changed leads seven times. The second half continued in much the same way, and the Flyers held a 36–31 margin with five minutes remaining. At that point, Detroit made its move. Jake Ahearn scored with a hook shot from the side; then Jerry Bush followed with a long set shot and then "brought the crowd to its feet with a toss back over his head that swished through to make it 37 to 36 for the Eagles." The Eagles scored another free throw to make it a two-point lead.

The Eagles and much of the crowd thought the game was over, but Pop Gates, who led the Flyers with thirteen points, had other ideas. He "let fly with a shot that tied it up and sent it into overtime."[35] The teams traded free throws, and the Eagles held a slim 44–43 lead. A final opportunity by Gates came up short. The Flyers' amazing run through the field came to an agonizing end. Dolly King (eight points) and Tarzan Cooper (five) contributed mightily to the cause that evening.

The Grumman Flyers were not the only integrated team. Also that year, Al Price suited up for the Michigan City North Indiana Steelers. A native of Gary, Indiana, Price played the entire 1941–42 season with the Steelers, an independent team. The team then accepted an invitation to play in the World Professional Basketball Tournament. After the tournament, Price served in the military from 1942 to 1945. Upon being discharged, he headed to California, where he enrolled and later graduated in 1947 from Pepperdine University. In their opening-round match, the Steelers faced the New York Renaissance. The Steelers were outclassed from the beginning and lost, 55–37. Al Price did not score in his lone game in the World Professional Basketball Tournament. (This Al Price should not be confused with Al Price, the brother of Bernie Price, both of whom would integrate the NBL in 1942–43.)

Sonny Boswell of the Rens set a new tournament record by scoring thirty-two points, besting the mark of twenty-six by Chuck Chuckovits. The Rens, though, were on a mission to avenge their disappointing finish the previous year. As usual, Bob Douglas had high hopes for the team on the eve of the tournament: "Our boys felt that we should and could have won the title last year except for a little carelessness. They're determined not to make the same mistakes. The Rens are represented by the youngest and best team in their history."[36] Douglas was looking to keep pace with the competition as he signed the best black talent available. For the 1941–42 season, he added Sonny Boswell, Hillery Brown, and Sonny Wood. These three new stars joined a formidable lineup including Willie Smith, Puggy Bell, Zack Clayton, Charlie Isles, and Johnny Isaacs. The lineup was stacked and ready to make its move through the tournament field.

Wyatt "Sonny" Boswell was a native of Toledo, Ohio, whose professional career began in 1938–39 with the Harlem Globetrotters, for whom he played three years. He then moved to the Rens before making history as a member of the Chicago Studebakers in the NBL in 1942–43. He then returned to the Rens and bounced around over the next five years with the Globetrotters, Chicago Monarchs, Anderson Chiefs, and Dayton Mets. He finished playing in 1946–47. He played his best ball in the World Professional Basketball Tournament, where he participated in seven of the ten years. In seventeen games, he scored a total of 175 points, including a tournament record 32 in this tournament.

Next up for the Rens after Michigan City was perennial favorite Oshkosh. The All-Stars versus Rens game was considered by many experts and basketball followers to be the game of the tournament, as Leo Fischer of the *Chicago Herald American* writes: "That Oshkosh-Rens contest should be something to behold and may be the standout game of a tournament which has offered nothing but standout games." As the *Oshkosh Daily Northwestern* declared, "The Oshkosh-Rens battle tonight is one that is expected to turn out a large crowd of fans in Chicago as the teams long have been rivals." This marked the seventh year that the two teams faced each other with Oshkosh holding a 20–16 edge. The game was also a rematch of the 1939 finals in which the Rens won the inaugural tournament. This marked the fifth time the teams were facing each other this season. They played a four-game barnstorming tour in Wisconsin in November prior to the start of NBL play. Instead, this game turned into a hard-fought slugfest characterized by record-setting fouls by both clubs.[37]

Sonny Boswell played for the Chicago Studebakers during the 1942–43 season.
Courtesy of Bill Himmelman.

Writing the following day, the *Chicago Herald American's* Harry Wilson summed up the game:

> Never has this author witnessed a more fiercely contested sport event than that ding-dong game that saw a plucky Oshkosh team beat down a determined bid by the Rens, to gain the semifinal round. . . . Fifty-two fouls, twenty-seven on the Rens and twenty-five for Oshkosh, set a new title tourney record. . . . Cashing in on 24 out of 29 attempts at the charity line, Oshkosh set another tourney record. . . . Blood, sweat and tears was in evidence at the conclusion of that epic game. . . . (Who said the pros didn't play for keeps).[38]

Despite the fouls by both teams, Oshkosh jumped out to a strong start and held a 27–18 lead at halftime. Oshkosh held an eleven-point lead going into the final frame before a late spurt by the Rens closed the gap, but it could not get them over the hump. Oshkosh won, 44–38. Oshkosh's defense on Sonny Boswell proved a key in the victory. After scoring thirty-two points in the previous game, he was held to fifteen points in defeat. Despite the loss, it was the physicality of the game that most resonated. Oshkosh had a history of being physical, and this reputation carried over when they played all-black or integrated teams, as was the case in the tournament and the NBL season the following year.

The Harlem Globetrotters also entered the tournament for the fourth consecutive years. They won in 1940 and made it to the semifinals the other two years. No different than previous tournaments, their expectations this year were besting the field and claiming the title. Abe Saperstein stated, "If my boys show any semblance of the form they displayed while winning games all over the United States, Canada, and Mexico, you can put them down as the first repeater in the history of the meet. I think we have the best club in fifteen seasons."[39] In the fourteen previous seasons, the Globetrotters had won more than two thousand games. This season Saperstein incorporated two young players, Tony Peyton and Roosie Hudson, to complement the core group of Ted Strong Jr., Inman Jackson, Babe Pressley, Bernie Price, and Bill Ford. The team was loaded with a strong complement of younger and older players.

In the opening round, the Globetrotters pulled away from Hagerstown as newcomer Roosie Hudson led all scorers with fifteen points. With an easy opening-round win, the Globetrotters tightened their belts for tougher competition. Meeting them in the quarterfinals were the Sheboygan Red Skins. Again Hudson led the way with twelve points as the Globetrotters pulled out a 37–32 win.

Hudson was a great scorer. He just had a knack for finding the basket. A native of Chicago, Hudson graduated college from Morris Brown before signing with the Harlem Globetrotters in 1936–37. He played with them through 1941–42 before joining the Chicago Studebakers in the NBL in 1942–43. Afterward, he rejoined the Globetrotters before a three-year stint in the military. After the war, he played one final season, 1946–47, with the Chicago Monarchs. In this tournament, he acquitted himself well and scored forty points in four games.

He would play in several other tournaments but would not match this scoring output again.

In the semifinals, the Oshkosh All-Stars awaited them, fresh off their hard-fought victory over the Rens. The toll of the previous night's game affected the All-Stars as the Globetrotters, perhaps avenging what they saw as dirty play against the Rens the previous night, took the fight right to Oshkosh. The Globetrotters led throughout the first half as Bernie Price scored six consecutive points to contribute to that margin. Early in the second half, the lead swelled to ten before Oshkosh found its second gear in the form of Eddie Riska, who single-handedly pulled Oshkosh into the lead. Oshkosh went on to win, 48–41, despite Hudson's thirteen points.

Playing in the consolation round, the Harlem Globetrotters faced the Grumman Flyers, and the Flyers did not let the previous night's tight loss diminish their hopes. They held the lead wire to wire even as the Globetrotters made a late run to within a basket. Dolly King's sixteen points paced the team to a 43–41 win. The black players acquitted

Roosie Hudson helped integrate the National Basketball League in 1942–43 with the Chicago Studebakers. *Courtesy of Bill Himmelman.*

themselves quite well in this tournament. Pop Gates was a first-team tournament selection, and his Flyers teammate Dolly King was named to the second team. Joining King were Sonny Boswell for the Rens and Bernie Price for the Globetrotters.

The 1942–43 professional basketball season was characterized by two integrated teams in the NBL, a first in the twentieth century. One of those teams, the Chicago Studebakers, finished the NBL season and prepared to continue its history-making season in the tournament. Despite finishing the season at 8–15, the Studebakers readied themselves as they entered their first-round game against the Minneapolis Rock Spring Sparklers, who were actually from Shakopee, Minnesota, a suburb of Minneapolis. The game went back and forth throughout, and it came down to the final play.

As recounted the following day in the *Chicago Herald American*,

> Probably the most spectacular game of the day was the Minneapolis victory on a shot from mid-floor by Willie Warhol with 10 second remaining. Less than 10 seconds previous, "Duke" Cumberland had put Chicago in front by a point with a similar hair raiser, but even before the noise died down, Warhol let fly—and there was a game in the bag.[40]

The *Chicago Defender*, meanwhile, placed the blame for Chicago's loss squarely at the feet of Ted Strong Jr.

> Strong was goat, among other things. He failed to take a shot at the basket with less than three minutes to play. He might have been rushed. We will let it go at that but when [Tony] Jaros [*sic*], a Minneapolis player, stole the ball right out of his hands under the Minneapolis basket and made a field goal which tied the score 42 all, things didn't look so hot for a team that had any idea of winning the championship.[41]

Minneapolis squeaked by with a 45–44 win. Chicago's historic season had come to an end. Sadly, the Studebakers would no longer play professional basketball. Their contributions to integrating the game would become a mere footnote in basketball and sports history.

Chicago's other entry into the tournament, the Harlem Globetrotters, also enjoyed a short stay. Receiving a first-round bye, the Globetrotters roster did not resemble those teams of previous seasons. The box score indicated as much as the team consisted of James Watkins, George Ray, Goose Tatum, Bob Powell, Ziggy Marcell, and Henry Singleton. Other than Tatum, none of these individuals were household names. This was the second year for Tatum as a member of the Globetrotters and his only appearance in the tournament. He did not disappoint as he scored a game high seventeen points. His own teammates could not keep pace; the next closest scorer was Ziggy Marcell with six points. They were outclassed by the Dayton Dive Bombers, 44–34, resulting in a quick exit from the tournament.

Despite the historical significance of the Studebakers' season and the quick exit of the Globetrotters, the 1943 tournament belonged to the Washington Bears. During their stellar run to the championship, they became the third all-black team to win the tournament in its first five years. The Bears were coached by Tarzan Cooper, the first time a team in the tournament was player-coached by a black player. Bill Russell would earn more recognition as a player-coach for the Boston Celtics in the late 1960s, but in 1943, Cooper made history.

There is a misperception that the New York Renaissance was in fact the Washington Bears during World War II. In fact, they were two separate teams, operated independently. The overlap was in the number of Rens players who played at some point for both teams. The Bears were originally the Washington Bruins, owned and operated by noted black sports journalist Sam Lacy. The team was coached by Fats Jenkins and Tarzan Cooper. Hal Jackson, a Washington music man, helped organize the team. At some point during the 1941–42 season, Lacy left Washington, D.C., for Chicago. A year later, in 1941–42, the Bruins became the Bears. Jackson approached Joe Turner, owner of Turner's boxing arena, who agreed to host games. Businessman A. E. Lichtman stepped in and provided the financial backing the team needed. It appeared that Lichtman was not that interested in basketball or the team, but rather, in promoting his theater chain, which catered to a black population. He promoted the team in his theaters for a percentage of the proceeds. As a result, as long as the team was good, the better publicity helped advertise his theaters. After their sole year as the Bruins, the team played as the Bears from 1941–42 to 1946–47; their best year was 1942–43.

Pop Gates, who played on the Rens and the Bears, remembered being a Bear:

The Washington Bears was practically the same team as the Renaissance with just a different uniform. The Bears were owned by a white fellow in Washington. They started the Washington Bears around Tarzan Cooper, who had also left the Renaissance when I went to Grumman. I went to the Washington Bears later. We just played local teams around Washington. When I was there every Sunday we played two games in the Turner's Arena. Every once in a while they would get an offer to play somewhere else, but mostly it was in the Washington area. The Bears paid by the game. I was getting $40 per game and all expenses, except my transportation down there.[42]

The Washington Bears were coached by Tarzan Cooper, a great player in his own right, but this marked the first time in the history of the tournament that a team was player-coached by a black player. In his

The Washington Bears won the 1943 World Professional Basketball Tournament. *Photographs and Prints Division, Schomburg Center for Research in Black Culture, New York Public Library.*

preview article, James Enright, a writer for the *Chicago Herald American* and a well-regarded referee, wrote,

> The Bears won't lack for canny leadership as they attempt to turn the Michigan av., Armory and Stadium tourney sites into shooting galleries. Boss Bear is "Tarzan" Cooper, and if there's a smarter head in basketball anywhere it is still to be discovered. He's been through the mill for the past 14 years and has played in about every major and bush league joint in the nation. Negro basketball followers rate old "Tarzan's" pivot play on par with Dutch Dehnert, the guy generally credited with introducing it to the hardwood. [43]

The other two black teams, the Harlem Globetrotters and the New York Renaissance, were coached by Abe Saperstein and Bob Douglas, respectively, both of whom were nonplaying coaches. In this tournament, Cooper proved to be a more effective coach than player as he scored only two points in three games. His contribution was making history as a coach in the tournament.

Born in 1907, Charles "Tarzan" Cooper was a standout player in his hometown of Philadelphia. He played with the Alphas of the Southwest branch of the YMCA in Philadelphia as a young kid. After a successful career at Central High School, Cooper set out to establish a career playing professionally. In 1925–26, he joined the independent Philadelphia Panthers and began a highly successful twenty-one-year career. During the first five years, he played with a series of teams based in Philadelphia—the Panthers, Giants, and Scholastics. His play in the Philadelphia and New York area caught the eye of Bob Douglas, who signed him to join the Rens in 1928–29. As Douglas recalled on signing Cooper, "During the Depression, the Celtics and my team were the only teams with salaries, but of course they had to be cut. When I gave the contract to Cooper, he just signed it and never said a word." [44] He would be a mainstay with the Rens for the next thirteen seasons and regarded as one of the top centers in all of basketball, black or white. In that time, he earned respect from players, coaches, and fans for his tough play, smarts, and personality. Cooper was an active big man for his time; he had what today is called a high basketball IQ. In addition to rebounding and defending the basket, Cooper made his teammates better with his passing, floor spacing, and playmaking ability.

"Nicest guy in the world. He played mostly out of the pivot. He knew when you were going, when to give the ball to you, and when not to. All of the fine techniques of how to play the game, he knew."[45] Puggy Bell was a teammate of Tarzan for a number of years and well remembered his contributions decades later:

> "Tarzan" was the supreme center—aggressive, clever, elusive, tireless. Everytime he was on the court, Tarz' was doing something we could admire and learn from. His skill and effectiveness were so well known and respected that even the "big money" centers from the other teams around the country came to him to learn how to do certain things on the court. He shared himself generously. To his teammates, Tarz' was a natural leader. He always gave his best and, while he patiently helped other to learn the game and refine their skills, he was firm and demanding. He expected other players to measure up to their potential and to team standards. His leadership combined strength and gentleness and, in a quiet, soft-spoken way, he set an excellent example as a player and a man.[46]

Cooper was a character and part of the fun-loving nature of a Rens team that traveled together for months at a time. One of his teammates, Pop Gates, recalled those days with Cooper:

> Tarzan Cooper was a big man on the team. He was sitting at the very front right by the door. He guerillaed that seat. The rookies, when I came to the Renaissance, I was sitting at the very rear of the bus. If you were a rookie, "Go to the rear, rookie." The club secretary [Eric Illidge] always sat near the front, as did player-coach Fats Jenkins. But Tarzan Cooper, he had the choice seat because he was the tallest, the biggest, the baddest, and strongest and so-called best player on the team. He was at the front where all the leg room was; he could stretch out. And anything that came into the bus had to go by Tarzan Cooper first before it got to the rear. If my mother or wife or sister sent a big cake out to me, before the cake gets to me it had to go by Tarzan. He had to get his slice first.[47]

In his last season with the Rens in 1940–41, he joined the Washington Bears and spent six of the next seven years with them. He finished playing in 1945–46, and in 1976, he was inducted into the Naismith Memorial Basketball Hall of Fame. By the 1943 tournament, Cooper

Tarzan Cooper was a standout center for the New York Renaissance. © *Morgan and Marvin Smith Photographs and Prints Division, Schomburg Center for Research in Black Culture.*

had earned the respect of his teammates to be named coach. At this point in his career, his scoring was not needed as much, so he could concentrate on his coaching duties.

As Eddie Younger stated, "The media seems to believe that black basketball players started with Sweetwater Clifton. But if it weren't for the Tarzan Coopers, Hilton Slocums, Pappy Ricks and others maybe there would not have been a Sweetwater Clifton."[48]

As Bob Douglas recalled,

> He was a great player, one of the greatest. Joe Lapchick said that Cooper was the greatest center he ever saw. He was 6'4", 225, and had arms that reached the floor. When he came along, the Celtics were the greatest team and we beat them the first time we played.[49]

Dr. Roscoe Brown said, "When I was a kid, Tarzan Cooper was *the* basketball player we looked up to regardless of color. When someone did something spectacular, we'd call him Tarzan."[50]

The Bears faced three opponents in their run to the tournament championship, and none of the contests were close. There was the inevitable feeling that they were destined to win. After a first-round bye, the team faced the surprising Minneapolis Sparklers, who eked out a slim victory over the Chicago Studebakers. After a slow start, Washington poured it on to win going away, 40–21. The Bears' defense was so strong that they limited Minneapolis to six field goals for the game. As usual, Dolly King led the team with eleven points. In the semifinals, the Bears handled the surprising Dayton squad, 38–30, behind ten points each from Dolly King and Zack Clayton. Meeting them in the finals would be longtime foe Oshkosh. The game marked the fourth time in five years that Oshkosh was playing for the championship.

Despite the hype and great anticipation surrounding the contest, the game itself was one-sided. Before twelve thousand screaming fans at Chicago Stadium, the Bears got off to a quick start, held a sixteen-point margin, and were never threatened. As one writer reported the next day, "A squadron of bronze speed merchants, darting like new Thunderbolt pursuit planes in and around slow air freighters, completely outclassed the defending champions of Oshkosh and the National league."[51] Led by Johnny Isaacs's ten points, the Bears put on a show of brilliant ball-handling that left the All-Stars waving the proverbial white towel.

Johnny Isaacs enjoyed a stellar professional career that spanned three decades. Born in Panama, Isaacs and his family moved to New York when he was five years old. Growing up in Harlem, Isaacs quickly learned basketball and was playing with the Capital club team, a squad that played preliminary games to the Rens'. They became known as the Rens Jrs. Isaacs led Textile High School to the New York Public School Athletic League Championship as a senior in 1935. For Isaacs, college was not on the horizon, as he needed to earn money. "Dolly King and I came out at the same time. Dolly went to LIU but my money was short. I had to go to work."[52]

Upon graduating high school, Isaacs signed with the New York Harlem Giants for one season, 1935–36. Afterward, he graduated to the Rens, where he would spend the prime of his career along with the Washington Bears. Little did Isaacs know that Bob Douglas had been watching him when he was in high school and as a member of the Rens Jrs. Douglas sent his assistant, Frankie Richards: "The old man wants to see you. He told me, 'I've been watching you. You're the first ballplayer I've ever sent for.' I thought that was a feather in my cap."[53]

He was known as the "Wonder Boy." A well-rounded player, Isaacs drew the respect of coach Douglas, who once said, "[He] had more natural ability than any man to have ever played for me." Isaacs also had a strong personality and temperament. Arthur Grant, an opponent of Isaacs in the 1930s, recalled him on the court: "John was real mean and controversial. He was always hollering at officials. Nothing malicious but just trying to help them make decisions." Douglas stated, "You could hear Johnny's mouth from one end of the court to the other. All you could hear was his mouth—'[G]et off the ball, get your man,'—I can hear him now." Red Saracheck played against Isaacs for many years and well remembers how tough a player Isaacs was: "On the basketball court, John Isaacs was a very tough, very mean competitor. On the court, he was so tough that I hated to play against him. But off the court, you couldn't find a nicer gentleman, a nicer human being."[54]

On the road, Isaacs and his teammates faced racism. "We would walk into a white-owned restaurant, and the best they could ever do for us was let us eat, standing, in the kitchen, where no one else could see us."[55]

Isaacs also played with the Philadelphia Toppers, Long Island Grumman Flyers, Long Island Grumman Hellcats, and after the war for a series of teams in Hazelton, Orange, Brooklyn, Utica, and Saratoga. He also had the distinction of playing on the Dayton Rens when they played in the NBL in 1948–49. His playing career ended in

John Isaacs was a member of the 1939 World Professional Basketball Tournament champions, the New York Renaissance. © *Morgan and Marvin Smith Photographs and Prints Division, Schomburg Center for Research in Black Culture.*

1952–53 as he neared his fortieth birthday. He was inducted into the Basketball Hall of Fame in 2015. In addition to being on the 1939 Rens championship team, he was also instrumental in helping the Bears capture the 1943 title, averaging five points in three games. For his effort, Isaacs, along with teammate Zack Clayton, earned second-team tournament honors. Gates and King were named to the first team.

The Call from Kansas City was one of many black newspapers to cover the Bears' run to the title. So impressed was the paper with the team's performance that it sought to compare it to the 1939 Rens team.

> The Bears looked even greater than the '39 Rens. Their teamwork was well nigh perfect and their speed so blinding that the other 11 entries resembled novices. That starting team of Sonny Wood, Pop Gates, Dolly King, Johnny Isaacs, and Zack Clayton is the smoothest combination the tournament has ever seen. It's greater than any '39 Ren five out of Cooper, Smith, Gates, Fats Jenkins, Isaacs, Puggy Bell and Eyre Saitch.[56]

The Bears had now gone undefeated in forty games over a two-year period. The Bears also became the third black team to win the tournament in five years and helped make "Washington first in basketball as it is first in war and first in peace."[57]

The 1944 tournament did not field any integrated teams, although both the New York Renaissance and Harlem Globetrotters traveled to Chicago, each hoping to win their second tournament championship. Each team was on a roll heading into Chicago. As usual, the Rens captured the Cleveland tournament while the Globetrotters headed to upstate New York and won the Rochester tournament. Both were primed and ready. Each had added a new player to help offset the competition in the field.

The Rens introduced a new center, Hank DeZonie, a rugged six-foot-six-and-a-half-inch player. A native New Yorker, DeZonie excelled at Benjamin Franklin High School before heading south to Clark University in Atlanta. He stayed only one year before joining his hometown New York Rens in 1942–43. The following season, 1943–44, he signed with the Globetrotters before jumping back to the Rens in time for the tournament. Over the next four years (1944–45 to 1947–48), he would be a mainstay with the Rens, and his best years as a ballplayer would be with them.

The Globetrotters, meanwhile, added Piper Davis, but he did not see any action in the tournament. He did play for the Globetrotters for a few years during the war, traveling the country and playing 100–120 games a year, usually as center. When basketball season was over, he turned his attention to his first love, baseball. He played shortstop for the Birmingham Black Barons of the Negro Baseball League. His claim to fame would be getting a young Willie Mays ready for the majors in his lone season (1949) in the Negro Leagues.

Abe Saperstein highly touted this year's version of the Globetrotters, stating,

> This is the greatest Globetrotter team in its 17-year history. Its pass attack is even more dazzling and bewildering than ever. Our record, too, sounds almost fantastic. We established what I believe is a world record with 62 straight wins. . . . In all we have won 97 while dropping only 6. . . . That is a lot of games and a lot of wins. . . . While compiling this season's great record we broke the winning streak of the leading service teams on the West coast. . . . Such teams as Fort Lewis, March Field and Santa Anita Air Base. . . . The first two, undefeated before meeting the Trotters.[58]

The Rens and the Globetrotters were on the same side of the bracket, and eventually they met in the consolation round. The Rens' path began with a matchup against the Detroit Suffrins. Detroit proved obstinate but finally succumbed to the all-around play of the Rens. In the following round, the Rens easily defeated the Cleveland Chase Brass, 62–38, behind Dolly King's eighteen points. Also helping the cause was Sonny Wood, who tallied ten points.

Robert "Sonny" Wood led Benjamin Franklin High School to the city championship in 1941–42. Soon after winning the title, he signed with the hometown Rens and would play for the Rens, Washington Bears, and Dayton Rens over the next nine years. He was also a mainstay in the tournament, competing in six of them, and scoring ninety-six points in fifteen games. For the 1944 tournament, Wood was able to arrange a furlough from Camp Ellis in time to compete for the Rens. He made the most of it as he followed his ten points with eight in a loss to the Fort Wayne Zollner Pistons in the semifinal.

As for the Globetrotters, they faced a scare in the first round with Pittsburgh, winning by one point, 41–40, then defeating longtime rival

Oshkosh before bowing to the Brooklyn Eagles, the tournament's surprise team, in the semifinals. The matchup between Oshkosh and the Globetrotters in the quarterfinals resulted in a physical battle and an ejection, and eventually it led to the game being called. It was the only time in the tournament's history that a game was not officially completed. The *Chicago Herald American,* in its writeup of the game, noted, "The game was that between the Globetrotters and Oshkosh, and the score at the time was 41–31 in favor of the former. The two clubs have a bitter rivalry that dates back a number of years, and the intensity of their play wasn't the kind to cement cordial relations." [59]

The game was a closely played affair as the Globetrotters held a 27–26 lead with ten minutes remaining "and from then on it was about as slambang an affair as anyone ever saw. Officials Nat Messenger and Steve Barak had matters pretty much under control, but as the clock neared the finish, the bad blood cropped out."[60] It was at that point that the game got out of control.

> One fight broke out and was quelled. Play was resumed and again fists started swinging. Again things were quieted down, but once more tempers flared up and the boys began to mix. This time Managers Lon Darling and A. M. Saperstein agreed that it was time to call a halt. The score goes into the records as it was at the time.[61]

The *Chicago Defender* had a different interpretation of the game. It characterized the game as "about the worst display of sportsmanship ever witnessed in the history of the pro tournament occurred Wednesday night as the Oshkosh team went down to defeat at the hands of the Globetrotters."[62] The second half became physical as

> Oshkosh players resorted to all sorts of rough tactics. Zack Clayton was knocked unconscious twice but remained in the game. Two Oshkosh players put a flying football tackle on Roscoe Julien and Connie Mack Berry rushed from the bench in the closing minutes to go on the floor to take a poke at one of the Globetrotters. Two white spectators were arrested for going onto the playing floor to take part in the melee.[63]

With five minutes to go, the game became out of hand, and the referees lost all control.

The last five minutes was a headache for the spectators, who were disgusted. The Oshkosh players, outclassed in the fourth period when the Globetrotters rang up 14 points to Oshkosh's five, used their fists, elbows, took swings at the Globetrotters as if the game was a battle royal such as is prohibited by most boxing commissions.[64]

Whatever the differences in interpretation, the bad ending left both fans and players highly dissatisfied. This seemed to be a repeat of the previous year's matchup between the Rens and Oshkosh. Oshkosh had developed a reputation as a rough, tough team that played physical against all-black teams.

The Globetrotters' matchup against the Rens in the consolation game was just the third time in the tournament's six years that the teams faced each other. In the 1939 semifinals the Rens won, 27–23, on their way to their first tournament championship. A year later, the Globetrotters exacted revenge by winning, 37–36, in the quarterfinals on their way to the championship. Unfortunately, the championship was not at stake for either team in 1944, just pride, and the Globetrotters won, 37–29. The Rens jumped out to an early 10–7 lead, but the Globetrotters forged ahead by a point, 18–17, at intermission—a lead they would not relinquish no matter how furious a comeback the Rens waged. Wood led the Rens with eight points, and Cumberland was the game's high scorer with ten points. Sonny Wood was named to the all-tournament's first team; the Globetrotters' Bernie Price (second team) and Duke Cumberland (honorable mention) also were recognized. Both teams came agonizingly close to earning another berth in the championship round. This marked the third and final time that the two rivals faced each other in the World Professional Basketball Tournament. The Globetrotters held a 2–1 advantage.

The 1945 tournament marked a return of a team representing the Long Island Grumman company since 1942. Named the Hellcats as opposed to the Flyers, the team was integrated and featured perennial stars Pop Gates and Dolly King, who both played for Grumman in 1942. The third player was Johnny Isaacs, who essentially replaced Tarzan Cooper. On December 1, 1944, the *Long Island Daily Press* announced that Grumman was supporting a new team:

> The Hellcats will be mainly on the road this year and should be one of the greatest attractions in the pro cage ranks. During the two years

that the Grumman club functioned, it won a total of 41 games out of 48 played against the best outfits in the country. Without exception, it should be the strongest independent outfit in this area.[65]

As Harry Wilson in the *Chicago Herald American* noted in announcing the team's entry into the field,

> King is one of three famous Negro cagers with the Grumman club. "Pop" Gates and Johnny Isaacs, both former members of the New York Rens, also help make planes at the Long Island war plant, and hope to aid in bringing the world's cage title to their country.[66]

Other stars included Nat Frankel from New York University, and George Glamack from the University of North Carolina, Ossie Schectman from Long Island University, and Ed Sadowski of Seton Hall University. As opposed to previous seasons, the Grumman team would play most of their contests on the road and began their season with a Midwest swing before settling into their regular schedule. The trip to the Midwest featured stops in Dayton, Cincinnati, Indianapolis, and Erie, Pennsylvania.

Gates, a key member of the squad, remembered his time with the Flyers and their trip to Chicago:

> There was a time during the war when the Rens weren't traveling all that much, and myself and several others went to Grumman Aircraft. I was working at Grumman for a weekly salary, and we weren't getting paid for the ball games. We didn't play every day of the week; we played whenever we were able to play.
>
> At Grumman Aircraft, I worked first in a stock room. Then I became what they called a pre-flight mechanic. We played mostly at Freeport High School—probably one game per week. We went out to Chicago for the World Tournament once, maybe twice. We had some of the best players in the East—Ed Sadowski, Nat Frankel, all the big-name ballplayers. We went out there and got our ass whipped right away by a team we never heard of. Because we didn't have our show together—we had the ballplayers, but we didn't know how to run the race.[67]

Gates's recollection, although many decades after his playing career ended, was partially correct: Grumman did field a team called the Hellcats, who played in the 1945 tournament. They were whipped in the first round by the Dayton Acmes, 43–27, most likely the team they had never heard of.

The first-round game itself was unremarkable as Dayton outclassed Grumman from the outset. William McNeil (actually Bruce Hale using an assumed name) paced Dayton with fourteen points. Unfortunately, Gates, Isaacs, and King managed only five points among the three of them. One interesting side note: the team was coached by Dolly King, making it the first integrated team coached by a black player. Unfortunately, this accomplishment was not recognized by any of the major media publications and outlets covering the team or tournament. Instead, it reflected more on the World Professional Basketball Tournament and its inclusion of all-black and integrated squads throughout its ten-year run. King would have to settle for knowing he made history in March 1945.

Per previous tournaments, the Harlem Globetrotters and the New York Renaissance were entries in the field. The Globetrotters continued to add the West Coast to their basketball itinerary, and Saperstein hoped the rigorous schedule would have his team peaking at the right moment. On this particular swing through California, the Globetrotters not only entertained fans, but raised $10,000 for the war effort. The team now headed to Chicago, and Saperstein was feeling good about his chances. Saperstein touted Babe Pressley, his best player: "if we had five Pressleys no team in America could ever beat us."[68] In their lone game in the tournament, the Globetrotters faced the newest professional team, the Chicago American Gears. Despite playing with only six players, the Globetrotters hung tough and controlled much of the game. The Globetrotters managed the game's pace and led, 31–24, at halftime and 38–33 heading into the final period. The Gears started surging, but the Globetrotters hung tough throughout and led, 49–45, with less than four minutes remaining in regulation. Perhaps playing with only six players finally caught up with them, or the Gears found another level of play inside them, but over the remaining four minutes, the Gears went on an 11–1 run to close out the game. For the Globetrotters, Pressley did not play, and Saperstein could only wonder what might have been if he had.

Meanwhile, the Rens continued to have a stellar touring season and always posed a threat in the tournament. The team toured the country, and prior to heading to Chicago, the Rens made their annual stop in Cleveland to participate in the Max Rosenblum Invitational Tournament. After a third place finish in 1941, the Rens won the tournament the next three years (1942–44) and sought a fourth consecutive title in 1945. Their run ended in the finals with a loss to Newark. Despite that, the team felt confident heading into Chicago and looked to improve upon their fourth-place finish the previous year. Always a proponent of his team's chances, owner and coach Bob Douglas stated,

> You know we won the first official world cage championship in the *Herald-American*'s meet in Chicago in 1939 and the College All Star game was not inaugurated until 1940. We missed the opportunity of opposing an All-Star collegiate group in the Classic presented annually by the *Herald-American* and I have my heart set on winning this year's meet. We are working hard and intend to do it this year.
>
> My veterans "Puggy" Bell, Zack Clayton and Hank DeZonie are having their most brilliant season. Benny Garrett and Eddie Wright, a couple of newcomers from the ranks of Eastern schools, have rounded out a finely balanced scoring quintet. What really makes me enthusiastic is that "Wee" Willie Smith, for years the outstanding center of the Rens, will be using his six-foot, seven-inch height to relieve DeZonie at the pivot spot. DeZonie measures only one-half inch less than Smith. Bell and Clayton by the way have been in every one of these tournaments. We haven't been out of the final round from the start back in 1939 and we don't intend to break that record this year. [69]

In fact, Max Kase, the sports editor of the *New York Journal American*, also thought highly of the Rens and their chances: "The Rens have the best team of the 19 years of their existence. That is saying a lot too, when fans always have been of the mind that when they were watching the Rens they were seeing the best." [70]

Opening against the Indianapolis Stars, the Rens started strong and were paced by a strong front line that overwhelmed the Stars. Willie Smith (seventeen points), Puggy Bell (fifteen), Zack Clayton (fourteen), and Hank DeZonie (thirteen) led a balanced attack in a 67–59 win. Key baskets by Smith and Bell late in the game sealed the victory for the Rens. Next up were the surprising Pittsburgh Raiders. The Rens were led by five-foot three-inch Eddie Wright, whose quickness and eighteen points paced all scorers as the Rens returned to the semifinals. For the second game in a row, though, the Rens needed to withstand a late rally to hold onto victory. It finally caught up with them in the semifinals as the Fort Wayne Pistons blitzed them, 68–45, one of their worst defeats all year. Despite strong performances by Bell (sixteen points) and De-Zonie (twelve), the Rens could not contain sharp-shooting Bobby McDermott. Fort Wayne was at its peak as a team, dominating both the NBL and World Professional Basketball Tournament during the war years. In the consolation match, the Rens fell to the Chicago American Gears, 64–55, despite seventeen points apiece by Bell and Zack Clayton. Bell was named to the tournament's first team, the second time he earned the distinction (1939).

Despite finishing fourth for the second consecutive year, Douglas had concerns about his team, the talent level, and maintaining a competitive team during the war. The constant movement of players from team to team or due to military service was his greatest challenge and contributed the most to his overall concern. In an interview with Wendell Smith of the *Pittsburgh Courier*, Douglas lamented,

> We just weren't up there like we once were, because we haven't the ballplayers we had in other years. All of our top players have reached their peak, and many of them are now on the downside. It's difficult to get material too. Every time we get a new man who is any good we lose him to the Army. The teams I had from 1933 to 1940 would have walked through this tournament with ease. The only team that might have made us go all out would be Fort Wayne, but even that team would have fallen to us. Not only were those teams good, but they used their brains. They played smart ball and pulled very few boners. Now it's just the opposite. We pull a lot of boners and only seldom do we pull something smart.[71]

Susan Rayl, who has researched and written extensively about the Rens, claims that

> the Rens also lost players to new teams such as Grumman Aircraft, the Paterson Crescents, Harlem Yankees, and Washington Bears. Rens owner/manager Bob Douglas held his players to contracts but during the war he allowed them to play for other teams on nights when the Rens did not play. Douglas feared losing his top players to the military draft, as well as rival teams. In this respect, black basketball players enjoyed free agency during World War II.[72]

With the war over and thousands of veterans returning home to resume their once-promising careers that had been postponed, tournament organizers hoped for a large field in 1946. New teams entered, including the Anderson Chiefs. Located in Anderson, Indiana, the Chiefs were the brainchild of Isaac "Ike" Duffey, a meatpacking executive. Their first foray into professional basketball was as a semiprofessional team traveling the Midwest and facing top teams such as the Indianapolis Kautskys and Fort Wayne Zollner Pistons. The team fared well, but Duffey sought the brighter lights and a bigger stage, mainly in Chicago. His team was one of the final two selected to play in the 1946 World Professional Basketball Tournament. Excited to be competing, Duffey was "bringing a special train-load of rooters from the Hoosier town to see if they can't whoop it up for their pro quintet to emulate the example of the Anderson prep representative, which won the coveted high school title in Indiana a week ago."[73]

Facing the Chiefs in their first-round game were the Cleveland Allmen Transfers. The game itself was not that remarkable as Anderson won easily, 59–46. The one notable result was that both teams fielded integrated squads, the only ones in this year's tournament. Cleveland featured Willie Smith, longtime Renaissance center, who three years earlier in 1943, integrated the NBL with the Cleveland Chase Brassmen for the team's last four regular-season games. Now, he was playing with the Transfers, again for his hometown Cleveland team, and he scored seven points. Facing him was Sonny Boswell, who was competing for Anderson. Like Smith, Boswell made history in the 1942–43 NBL season as a member of the Chicago Studebakers. He tallied two points. Anderson moved on to the next round, the quarterfinals, where they faced off against the Baltimore Bullets. In a well-played affair, Baltimore edged Anderson, 69–67, as Boswell tallied fourteen points for the Chiefs.

For the first time in the history of the tournament, the Harlem Globetrotters did not participate as they were traveling with the Rochester Royals and playing a series of exhibition games. In fact, over the next two years, they would not compete in the World Professional Basketball Tournament. Instead, they focused on barnstorming the country. Their days challenging for the World Professional Basketball Tournament were over.

The Rens, meanwhile, entered the tournament playing well, having won sixty-one of sixty-five contests. The team was its usually strong self with the likes of Dolly King, Pop Gates, Sonny Wood, Puggy Bell, and Hank DeZonie. Bob Douglas was his optimistic self and declared prior to the start of the tournament, "I believe this is the best team I've ever had. Definitely we expect to make the grade this year. Between our veterans and the young fellows back from service, we're back to our prewar class."[74] He added Len Pearson, Lou Badger, and Benny Garrett to the roster, all returning from military service. Only Garrett would actually compete for the Rens.

The hype carried over to the first-round contest against an overmatched Toledo Jeeps squad that had no chance. The Rens easily manhandled them, 82–39, behind twenty-one points from Hank DeZonie and fourteen each from Pop Gates and Sonny Wood. The team set a tournament record by scoring eighty-two points, besting the previous mark of eighty points. In the next round, the Rens faced old nemesis Oshkosh, and their luck finally ran out as Oshkosh won, 50–44. The Rens dug themselves too big a hole, and a late rally fell short. Gates led the way with fifteen points, and DeZonie posted ten. It was another quick exit for the Rens much to Douglas's chagrin.

By 1947, times were changing in black basketball. The Globetrotters and the Rens were no longer the same teams they had been at the beginning of the decade. Integration was gaining a foothold in professional basketball, no matter how small the steps. The Globetrotters were focused more on traveling the world, and the Rens witnessed a lot of personnel turnover. For the second consecutive year, the Globetrotters passed on entering the tournament. The Rens, meanwhile, signed on and as was the case, Bob Douglas exuded optimism:

> It has always been my biggest regret that there was no all-star game for the winner the first year when we won the tournament. It's been my ambition ever since to get into the all-star game—and this is the team I think can make it come true.[75]

Douglas added a few new players including George Crowe, of whom he said, "he's just about the fastest man I've seen on a court in years. He's our ace and has averaged 18 points a game against all kinds of competition."[76]

A native of Franklin, Indiana, Crowe was an excellent athlete as a child. His talents led him to Indiana Central College, where he lettered in three sports—basketball, baseball, and football. After graduation, he joined the Indianapolis Pure Oils in 1943–44 before a three-year stint in the military. When he was discharged, Crowe headed to Los Angeles, where he signed on to play for the Los Angeles Red Devils and was a teammate of Jackie Robinson. He also spent time that season with the New York Rens, a team he would be with for three years, including as a member of the Dayton Rens when they played in the NBL in 1948–49. He joined New York of the ABL in 1949–50 and after a two-year hiatus, he returned for one final season in the ABL in 1952–53 with Hazelton-Saratoga. Crowe, though, also made his name as a major league baseball player from 1952–61 and was named an All-Star in 1958. With Crowe and Nat "Sweetwater" Clifton joining the Rens, Douglas's optimism was warranted. Instead, the team disappointed him in the first round, losing to the Toledo Jeeps. After falling behind by eleven points midway through the third period, the Rens waged a furious comeback that ultimately fell short. Toledo made twenty of twenty-six free throws and was able to hold on for a 62–59 victory.

In addition to the Rens, the only other black player in the field was Pop Gates, who was playing with the Tri-Cities Blackhawks. In the first round, the Blackhawks pulled away to defeat the Baltimore Bullets, 57–46. It was a tough physical affair, but led by the defensive prowess of Gates, the Blackhawks held the Bullets to only ten field goals. Gates scored seven points. In the next round, Tri-Cities fell to the Indianapolis Kautskys, 65–56, even though Gates tallied eleven points.

By 1948, the best team in professional basketball was the Minneapolis Lakers. Born out of the failure of the Detroit Gems, which lasted only one forgettable season in the NBL, the Lakers sprang up and soon dominated professional basketball. By the 1948 World Professional Basketball Tournament, Mikan and the Lakers were ready to take on all comers. The hope of containing Mikan naturally fell to Nat "Sweetwater" Clifton.

Clifton Nathaniel was born in 1922 in England, Arkansas, into a farming family. The Roaring Twenties missed that small farming community as the flooding of the Mississippi River in 1927 and then the onset of the Great Depression led his mother and aunt to relocate the family. This was during the Great Migration north, and his family headed to Chicago, where more jobs and hopefully a better life awaited them. He gravitated toward sports, particularly baseball and basketball. Eventually, he enrolled in DuSable High School and quickly made his mark. Nathaniel was a local superstar long before the term was coined. His size and his enormous hands allowed him to grab rebounds, play tight defense, and score easily on the inside. He also weighed 235 pounds, which certainly helped his cause.

As Clifton recalled,

> I started playing basketball when I was a freshman in high school. By the time I was a sophomore I was sort of like a star. I was considered a big man back then. I was already six-five when I was in high school and I only [grew] one more inch by the time I got to be a man. When I was growing up in Chicago there wasn't but two black schools in the city and you had the choice of going to either one, so I chose the one closest to my neighborhood.[77]

He was soon dominating the high school competition. Not only that, but the sportswriters jokingly said that his last name of Nathaniel was too long for their headlines. Would he mind changing it? He did and thereafter, he became Nat Clifton. Also, during this time, he earned his nickname, "Sweetwater." His new northern friends found it peculiar that he had this habit of taking soda pop bottles that had been discarded and filling them with sugar, thus creating a sweet water concoction. Thus, he became Sweetwater, sometimes known as Sweets.

In high school, he started making his name, particularly in the Stagg Tournament, named after Amos Alonzo Stagg, who was a well-regarded football coach at the University of Chicago. Stagg also had the distinction of being on the faculty of the International YMCA Training School when James Naismith invented the game in 1891. He helped promote the game in its early years. The high school tournament featured the best high school teams from around the country. In 1941, Clifton's junior year, DuSable became the first all-black team to win the tournament. The following year, he made national headlines by scoring forty-five points against Austin High School in the semifinals. Afterward, the *Chicago Daily News* sang his praises:

> The 19-year-old Clifton is without peer as a ball handler. He shoots with either hand or both. His height makes him a terrific rebounder

Nat "Sweetwater" Clifton was the first black to sign a contract in the National Basketball Association with the New York Knicks. © *Morgan and Marvin Smith Photographs and Prints Division, Schomburg Center for Research in Black Culture.*

and practically impossible to guard under the basket. But his long suit is a fancy brand of blind passes and the ability to palm the basketball with either of his ham-like hands. Yet he has a fault and it is a strange one. The big boy, although blessed with capabilities of always scoring at a high rate each game, doesn't shoot enough. Or at least he didn't before last night's walkway. "Sweetwater" has an explanation for his actions. As long as he keeps feeding the ball to teammates Morris and Randolph, excellent shots both, DuSable functions in smooth style, he explains.[78]

After such a stellar high school career, Clifton headed south to New Orleans, where he enrolled at Xavier University and played briefly before being inducted into the army.

> When I finished with high school, I went to Xavier University down in New Orleans, which was in the Southern Conference. I had a scholarship to five or six black schools like Tuskegee, Morris Brown, and Clark, but I chose Xavier because that's where the team I played with in high school went after they graduated and I wanted to keep playing with them.[79]

He also briefly played with the Harlem Globetrotters in 1942–43, a team that would exert a big influence on his professional career in the years to come. He spent three years in the army in Europe before being discharged in 1945. While in the service, he played basketball for the 369th Battalion.

> When I got out of the service and came home—it was '47—I started playing with a team called the Dayton Metropolitans. We had a bunch of college ballplayers on that team who came from Ohio State, Michigan, Purdue, Wisconsin, and schools like that. We had a good, small, semipro team. It was a mixed team, with three blacks and nine whites, a team with some good stars. We were pretty good and we beat some teams like the Lakers and the Rochester Royals when they had Bob Davies and that bunch.[80]

He spent nearly two seasons with the Dayton Mets.

> After that, I left and went to New York to play with the Rens for a while. They were located on Seventh Avenue, up near Small's Paradise, right across the street from a place called the Renaissance. We used to play upstairs. I played there about half a year and then I got with the Harlem Globetrotters. Abe Saperstein signed me to a contract. He'd heard about me, but it was kind of hard for him to catch up with me because everybody had me going all the time. I

played with them for two seasons—1947–48 and 1948–49—along with Goose Tatum and Marcus Haynes. We used to go around the country playing local teams and we'd beat them all the time.[81]

As a newcomer, Clifton earned the respect of Eric Illidge, the manager of the Rens. Wendell Smith of the *Pittsburgh Courier* interviewed Illidge for his Sports Beat column in 1948 in which Smith wrote,

Illidge says the best young player to come up recently is Sweetwater Clifton of the Dayton Mets. He's potentially the best player in the game. He is 6 feet 5 inches tall, can shoot like blazes and handles the ball like it's a golf ball. He can run and also guard. He's a wonderful ballplayer.[82]

As a player, Clifton was tough underneath the boards as DePaul coach Ray Meyer recalled, "If you brought your pivot man in, Sweetwater moved him right out. And when he was in the lane and he turned to go to the basket, anybody that was in his way went with him."[83]

Before he could focus his attention on the Globetrotters and later the NBA, Clifton was all about the Minneapolis Lakers. In what would turn out to be the tenth and final tournament, the Rens were hoping to bookend the ten years with another championship. The Rens, in their own right, presented a formidable challenge with a solid lineup of their own. Clifton was at center, flanked by George Crowe and Duke Cumberland at forwards, with Pop Gates and Sonny Wood at guards. Coming off the bench were Dolly King, Eddie Younger, and Jim Usry. It was a strong contingent that looked to offset an equally tough lineup for the Lakers with Mikan, Jim Pollard, and Herm Schaeffer. Before facing each other in a titanic matchup in the finals, the Rens dispatched Bridgeport and Tri-Cities while Minneapolis easily handled Wilkes-Barre and Anderson.

As the finals loomed, the Rens needed to devise a strategy. How do you stop Mikan? Although most observers thought the focus would be on Mikan, the Rens geared their pregame scouting and game planning to stopping Jim Pollard, the Kangaroo Kid. Coach Eric Illidge proclaimed,

The man we want . . . and the Lakers only have a two man team . . . it's Jim Pollard. Of the two he's the guy we're after and he can be stopped. George Crowe, out guard and the best in the country will do it tonight. This is one we'll win.[84]

The Lakers' Clifton, though, knew Mikan would be a challenge, as he stated:

> You can't stop Mikan, but you can slow him down. You play in front of him when you guard him. Then you can try and keep him from getting the ball. If he doesn't get the ball he can't score, or at least I never saw anybody that could.[85]

Despite the game planning, the game was a tightly contested affair. The Rens made a strong second-half surge and took the lead late in the game. The game came down to the wire as George Crowe recalled:

> I remember they had us down 18 at the half and we came back. We went one point ahead of them and Sonny Wood stole the ball and he gave it to Sweetwater Clifton and Sweetwater threw a pass behind his back and it went out of bounds. He threw that ball away and that cost us the World Championship.[86]

A chance at another title slipped through their grasp. A few more free throws by the Lakers sealed a victory. Mikan scored a game-high forty points while Clifton tallied twenty-four. For their efforts, Sweetwater was named to the tournament's first team and George Crowe to the second.

This game between the Lakers and Rens was not the only game Mikan and his teammates faced against a top black team. Earlier that season on February 19, 1948, the Minneapolis Lakers and the Harlem Globetrotters tipped off against each other in a highly publicized encounter in Chicago. Nearly eighteen thousand fans pushed through the turnstiles to witness an encounter between two of the best teams in basketball. Abe Saperstein and Minneapolis's Max Winter each believed their team was the best in the nation. What better way to prove it than to play one another?

From the beginning, the Globetrotters took the game much more seriously than did the Minneapolis Lakers. Ray Meyer, the DePaul University coach, was sitting in the stands and remembered thinking, "I was shocked, even though I knew the Trotters were a very good team. I think the Lakers took them as a joke. Then they found out they could play, and they took them serious [from then on]." As the Lakers Jim Pollard recalled, the game was "for the owners, not the players. I didn't take it seriously . . . it was a pain in the neck."[87]

The Globetrotters thought differently.

For the Globetrotters and Chicago's black community, the game proved to be a symbol of pride. As Marques Haynes noted, "The whole South Side of Chicago came out for that ball game." High expectations abounded for fans of the Globetrotters such as Timuel Black, who declared, "We wanted to see a Trotter victory—and the show. We were waiting for the show, which made the victory that much sweeter."[88]

The Lakers featured a strong lineup. In addition to Mikan and Pollard, the Lakers roster featured Herm Schaefer, Don "Swede" Carlson, Tony Jaros, Paul Napolitano, and Johnny Jorgensen.

Meanwhile, the Globetrotters had their fair share of players. Saperstein was taking no chances. He wanted to field the best team possible. For him, this was a statement game, and he wanted to win. As Marques Haynes recalled, "We had a lot of good outside shooters particularly Ermer Robinson, Wilbert King, and myself."[89] In addition, Saperstein loaded his lineup with star players such as Ted Strong, Goose Tatum, and Babe Pressley.

The game got off to a strong start with the Lakers leading, 9–2, but the Globetrotters were game planning from the start. From the Globetrotters perspective, the key part of their game planning was to focus on George Mikan and make him work for everything in the game. As the Globetrotters' Vertes Zeigler recalled,

> When we fouled him, we fouled him hard. We said, "If they're gonna call a foul, be sure to make him bleed." And that's what we did. We went to beating on him and slapping them glasses off him. . . . We were doing everything. If we'd had hatchets in our hands, he would have had scars on him—they would have taken 100 stitches, remembered Sam Wheeler.[90]

The strategy worked, and Mikan became frustrated. His temper was starting to reach the surface. Ray Meyer knew immediately this was trouble. "I was sitting at the scorer's table and Goose was really roughing up Mikan, I saw Mikan's face get real white and I thought 'Omigod, here it comes,' and Mikan leveled Tatum with a vicious elbow." The defensive shift proved a key moment in containing Mikan, who scored eighteen points in the first half but only six in the second.[91]

The Lakers led at the half, 32–23. In addition to putting two men on Mikan, the Globetrotters decided to fast-break at all times. Having played almost every night, they knew they were in great shape. The Lakers would not be able to keep up. Running at all times helped them claw back into the game in the second half. It neutralized the Lakers' size underneath the basket. As the Globetrotters made their move, one of the key figures was Marques Haynes, who would one day be known as the world's greatest dribbler.

Marques grew up playing basketball in Sand Springs, Oklahoma, and soon developed into a very good player. As Marques retells his upbringing and interest in basketball,

> My oldest brother Wendell [taught me how to dribble]. He was a great dribbler in my opinion. My youngest brother Joe, who was older than me, taught me passing. He was a great passer and guard defensively. . . . One day I was reading the *Pittsburgh Courier*, which was a black newspaper, and I saw where a fellow by the name of Pop Gates was being paid $250 to play basketball. I couldn't imagine that someone was being paid to play basketball. That's when I started concentrating a heck of a lot more on basketball.[92]

Marques eventually earned a $25 scholarship from his church to attend Langston University, where he helped the team compile a 112–3 mark during his college career. As a senior in 1946, his college squad was invited to play against the Harlem Globetrotters, and he led his team to a four-point win, which caught the eye of Abe Saperstein. After graduating college a few months later, he joined the team.

> The Hawaiian team was supposed to play the Globetrotters in Oakland, California. The Kansas City Stars were playing in the same deal. The Stars were supposed to play the first and then the Globetrotters were going to play the second game. I was on the Stars at that time. The Hawaiian team was supposed to play the Globetrotters in the main event. Somehow, they were beating the Globetrotters. Winfield Welch asked me, "Do you want to play against the team from Hawaii?" I said, "Sure." So I went on and got dressed and I took one of the Globetrotters places. As soon as I got in the game I

started firing away. I looked up and we were 10 points ahead of them. That's when I joined the Globetrotters.[93]

He was a member of the Globetrotters from 1947 to 1953, and by 1948 he was becoming a household name.

During the game, Haynes was playing his usual tough basketball game. In the third period, Haynes and Mikan collided and both ended up on the floor.

> George Mikan and I went up for a rebound. We both caught the ball at the same time. He snatched the ball and my hand slipped off of it and I fell on my back and broke it. They tried to take me out of the game but I told them I didn't want to sit on the bench and get cold. So I stayed in the ball game and finished the game.[94]

Haynes toughed it out, and the game was close and tense the rest of the way.

The Globetrotters took the lead in the third quarter only to see the Lakers pull ahead. The game was back and forth in the final period. The Lakers tied it up at fifty-nine all on a free throw. As the seconds wound down, Chicago Stadium was at a fever pitch. Haynes had the ball as the clock was ticking down. With only a few seconds left, Haynes passed the ball to Ermer Robinson, who lifted a one-handed set shot from thirty feet out that went straight through the basket. The Globetrotters had done the impossible. They beat the Lakers, 61–59. The crowd rushed onto the floor to celebrate the victory.

The last-second win for the Globetrotters was a moment that rippled through Chicago's black community. As local resident, Timuel Black proudly declared,

> It was an event of great pleasure for those of us who had grown up on the South Side . . . to see this all-black team playing this all-white team and winning. It was a great evening. We went back to our various bars or taverns and talked about it. It was more than just a victory of the Trotters; it was also a victory of the black community over the hostile white community. It was not as big, or as universal, as when Joe Louis defeated Max Schmeling, but there was a feeling of elation that gave us a sense of achievement and pride.[95]

It was a big deal to Chicago's South Side. Tim Black suggested,

Ermer Robinson hit the game-winning shot as the Harlem Globetrotters defeated the Minneapolis Lakers. *Courtesy of Bill Himmelman.*

Ted [Strong] and his teammates were playing by the rules and beating the white teams. Whether we were athletes or not, there was no point of feeling inferior. I can take your rules and beat you. I am not

saying they are good rules but they are rules and I have to abide by
them.[96]

For the Lakers it was a bitter defeat. Mikan took the pounding worse
than anyone on the Lakers, but he made no excuses.

> I'll give the Trotters credit. They knew what to do. They controlled
> the ball from start to finish and beat us. There was no monkeying
> around. He [Saperstein] had an excellent group of guys. They had
> Marques Haynes, who could dribble the ball, Goose Tatum, who was
> quite proficient as a pivot man, Babe Pressley, who guarded me, and
> a guy named Ermer Robinson who made the shot that beat us before
> twenty-one thousand at Chicago Stadium. [That was in 1949. Actual-
> ly Robinson's twenty-footer had beaten the Lakers in their previous
> game, in 1948.] There was a lot of cheering from both sides. It was a
> quite a day for everyone.[97]

Being as prideful as they were, the Lakers wanted another shot at the
Globetrotters. As Max Winter stated, "[O]ur players couldn't believe
what had happened. They were devastated." "Our players wanted a
rematch as soon as possible." A rematch was already in the works. The
two teams played the following year, and the Globetrotters won again.
Afterward, they played six more times, and all six times the Lakers came
out on top.[98]

Recalling that first game, Winter declared, "[L]ittle did Abe, or I, or
anyone else connected with it, realize that it would turn out to be one of
the most memorable basketball games of all time." As Marques Haynes
reflected, "After the first game, most people thought it was just luck.
The second game made people believe we were not only good come-
dians but good ballplayers."[99]

Indeed, the Globetrotters proved they could play and beat anyone.

3

THE NATIONAL BASKETBALL LEAGUE

December 11, 1942

The train was late arriving into Chicago, Illinois, two hours to be exact. It was carrying the Toledo Jim White Chevrolets, the National Basketball League (NBL) professional basketball entry from Toledo, Ohio. The trip was long and tiring, although it was nothing compared to the journey the team was on over the first two weeks of December 1942.

Optimism dawned on the Toledo basketball team as the 1942–43 NBL season commenced. The previous season, 1941–42, marked the first year that Toledo fielded a team in the NBL. It was not the best of seasons. In fact, it was a terrible campaign by all measure. The Toledo team finished with a 3–21 record, good for last place in the seven-team league. They scored the least points in the league, gave up the most, and generally were outmatched in all of their contests.

With World War II ongoing and America's commitments increasing since Pearl Harbor the previous year, it was a notable achievement that the league held steady with seven teams and a full season of games. That would not be the case for the 1942–43 season. The team was managed by Sid Goldberg, a local veteran of professional, semiprofessional, and independent basketball teams in Toledo. His challenge lay in finding a sponsor for the team as the league pressured him to file an application for a new franchise. The league was desperate, and Toledo had a solid track record as a city for semiprofessional and independent teams. It was only logical that Leo Fischer, the NBL commissioner, would approach Goldberg.

As Goldberg recalled,

> They were after me. They wanted Toledo and they needed teams. I paid $350 for a franchise. They also insisted on a $1,500 deposit in case of forfeits, which I couldn't raise, but I got the backing of Jim White Chevrolet. Jim White also bought us uniforms and gave us two station wagons to use. [1]

With a franchise in place, Goldberg set about filling the roster. Basketball in the 1930s and early 1940s was very local with teams comprised of players from the local region or city. For Goldberg, it was no different. He set about compiling the best team he could due to the short turnaround time until the beginning of the season. He immediately set his sights on the local talent, from which there was plenty to choose. His star player was Chuck Chuckovits, probably the finest player to hail from Toledo during World War II. He shattered all scoring records in the NBL in 1941–42 with 406 points in twenty-two games. He was joined by Bob Gerber, who succeeded him at Toledo University as the next great scorer. Pat Hintz from Toledo University joined, as well as Johnny Townsend from the University of Michigan. As one basketball writer previewed,

> Toledo will be strong inasmuch as several of the players were together last year on the Toledo [U]niversity team and should develop a smooth-working quintet. Some of them played at Toledo a year or two ago so all have worked under the same system of coaching. [2]

Goldberg, though, needed more players to round out his team. The best available talent was black players. Since its founding in 1937–38, the NBL had been an all-white league. However, the Midwest Basketball Conference (MBC), the predecessor of the NBL, integrated in 1935 when Hank Williams suited up for the Buffalo Bisons. Williams grew up in Buffalo and was a local star player before signing to play with the Buffalo Colored Bisons for the 1934–35 season. The following year, he joined the Buffalo entry in the MBC before playing one final season with the Bisons as an independent team in 1936–37. In his lone professional season, he played in fifteen games and averaged 5.5 points a contest. Since then, team owners had had no desire to integrate. By 1942, all that had changed. Goldberg needed more talent and better players. As he said,

> I went to the league and told them, "I don't know what you fellows are going to do, but if you want me to stay in I'm going to use blacks." Some of them didn't relish it, I suppose, because they thought it would bring problems. But I don't think any of them objected.[3]

With that, Casey Jones, Al Price, Shannie Barnett, and Bill Jones, all black players, became pioneers on the Toledo squad.

Three of the four grew up together in Toledo, where they played basketball recreationally and on independent and touring teams. Casey Jones enjoyed a ten-year career playing independent and professional basketball in Toledo, interrupted by one stint with the team in the NBL. He played in three of the team's four games and averaged 2.3 points.

Shannie Barnett's professional career is less well known than that of his counterparts. He grew up in East Liverpool, Ohio. In his lone season with Toledo, he scored fourteen points in four games. He played a few games with the Harlem Globetrotters in 1941–42 and he also played with the Toledo Ciralsky Meat Packers, Indiana Y Big Five, and the Brown Buddies. In 1949–50, he signed to play for the New York Comedy Kings, an independent team.

Al Price enjoyed a solid professional career during the 1940s. After a year with an independent Toledo team, Price joined the Harlem Globetrotters for a year before he signed on in the NBL. He played three games and averaged 2.7 points per game. He then returned to the Globetrotters for the rest of the decade except for one season with the Kansas City Stars.

The league began the season with five teams—Fort Wayne Zollner Pistons, Oshkosh All-Stars, Sheboygan Red Skins, Chicago Studebakers, and Toledo Jim White Chevrolets. The league and team owners all hoped they could survive the season intact, not a given with a war raging on all fronts and rationing on the home front. Of the five squads, Toledo was the biggest unknown. In an early season preview article, the *Oshkosh Northwestern* noted,

Toledo is an unknown quantity at present, not having met any of the league members in its pre-league schedule of games, but is expected to develop into a strong contender. Last year's league scoring champion, Chuck Chuckovits, formerly of Toledo University, may be lost to the team before the season closes, in the draft, but will see action at least in the early part of the season. The unstoppable Chuckovits set a new scoring record of 406 points in 22 games in the league last season, to greatly outdistance Bob McDermott, Fort Wayne, and Oshkosh's LeRoy "Lefty" Edwards, who were second and third respectively with 277 and 272. Chuckovits had 33 points in one game.[4]

With the team in tow, Goldberg embarked on the season ahead cautiously optimistic. The team traveled to Indiana and opened the season on December 9, 1942, on the road against the Fort Wayne Zollner Pistons. The game had been scheduled for the previous night, but the effects of World War II caused it to be postponed due to a "black out" of the North Side Gym, the Pistons' home venue. The *Fort Wayne News-Sentinel* detailed the postponement and Toledo's response:

Toledo willingly agreed to the postponement to help out officials here. Because the time of the blackout remained a surprise, Zollner officials were fearful that it might come at some time in the game when it would be tough on either or both quintets, as well as the fans. It is rather difficult to black out North Gym and continue play. In addition, many of the persons involved in staging pro games here are Civilian Defense work of some sort and wanted to be on the job tonight. In addition, many persons who hold season tickets or already had purchased ducats for the game tonight were in the same fix and it was deemed only fair to enable them to fulfill their duties this evening and still get to use their tickets Wednesday evening, the move being the most advisable of several possible ones suggested.[5]

With a one-day delay, the game was set to resume on December 10 at the North Side High School Gym at 8:45 p.m., preceded by an industrial league game. Although it was early in the season, Fort Wayne did not feel overconfident about its chances and showed great respect for their Toledo foe. As the *Fort Wayne News-Sentinel* declared,

But the Pistons are far from overconfident about the Toledo clash. Chuck Chuckovits, leading scorer of the loop last season and one of basketball's greatest shots, is back to worry their defense and has lots more help this year than he did last season. Big Bob Gerber, No. 1 man in the recent College All-Star voting; Johnny Townsend, former Indianapolis Kautsky player, and several former Detroit Auto Club and Toledo U. players are on the strengthened Toledo team and the Buckeyes are the team that may be throwing those monkey-wrenches into the other four's plans to attain the top spot in the loop.[6]

Despite the deference paid to Toledo and the one-day postponement, the Jim White Chevrolets were no match for the Zollner Pistons. The Pistons thoroughly whipped Toledo, 70–51. It was an ominous sign for Goldberg's squad. Toledo was without the services of Chuckovits and Townsend, both of whom were affected by that one-game postponement as coaching and officiating responsibilities respectively prohibited their participation. Toledo's high-scoring nature seemed to pass to the Pistons "in one of the most rapid scoring performances the city's pro fans have seen in a long time."[7] The game started off as a close contest as both teams got off to quick starts offensively.

The Pistons were led by Bobby McDermott, entering his prime as the finest player in the league. The *Fort Wayne News-Sentinel* wrote, "the Pistons were unable to shake off the mixed racial Toledo five (it has half white and half colored players this year like the Chicago Studebakers) until the late moments of the third period." By the end of the third quarter, the Pistons held a slim 36–32 lead. At that point, the Pistons found their second gear and ran away with the game over the final twelve minutes en route to a 70–51 victory. The bright spot for Toledo was the play of Gerber who, "warmed up to the task in the last half and gave the fans a look at the sniping that made him an outstanding college scorer at Toledo University. He got help from two long-distance snipers and former Toledo stars, Pat Hintz and Bill Jones."[8]

A highlight from that game was Bill Jones, who tallied ten points as the second-leading scorer behind Gerber. As one of four blacks on the team, Jones was a mainstay in the Toledo basketball community, playing collegiately and then professionally and semiprofessionally on teams in the Ohio area. He was a known commodity in the greater Toledo area. Finally, playing on a league-based team, Jones now had the opportunity to showcase his talent to a wider audience.

Born and raised in Toledo, Jones grew up playing basketball wherever he could find a game. He eventually enrolled at Toledo University in 1932 during some of the worst years of the Great Depression. In order to earn money for tuition and books, Jones worked the night shift at the Fort Meigs Hotel. His days were long and began with classes followed by basketball practice, then a short nap before heading out to his night job. He performed this ritual faithfully for a few years. He persevered like most people in the Depression tried to do. In those days, freshmen were ineligible to play, but he finally earned his chance as a sophomore. He played for the team in the first semester of 1933–34 but was forced to withdraw from school to help support his growing family. He worked for two years, trying to keep up his skills when time permitted, hoping one day to finish his education. Finally, he saved enough money to reenroll in school, this time for the second semester of the 1935–36 season.

By this time, the Toledo University basketball program had changed for the better, entering its golden era. The change started with the hiring of Harold Anderson as head coach and bringing in local star Chuck Chuckovits to anchor the team. With Chuckovits and Jones leading the pack, the team enjoyed two successful seasons in 1936–37 and 1937–38. In that first season, the team compiled a strong 18–4 mark and garnered national attention. However, Jones's college career was over as he had already earned three varsity letters, and school policy only permitted three varsity letters per athlete per sport.

With his college career over, Bill sought to keep playing, and he was able to latch onto some local African American squads—Toledo Brown Bombers, Joe's Toledoans, the Toledo All Stars, and the Ciralsky Packers. He traveled with them for the next several years. Bill's solid play earned him a chance to join the 1941 Toledo Jim White Chevrolets, which was, at that time, an independent integrated team playing regional games. The team did not join the NBL in 1940–41, electing to play as an independent team.

However, the team was invited to play in the 1941 World Professional Basketball Tournament in Chicago in March. It was accepted as an integrated team, and the Jim White Chevrolets fared quite well, winning its first two games against the Sheboygan Red Skins and Chicago Bruins before losing to the Oshkosh All-Stars in the semifinals. In those three games, Bill scored a total of three points. In the consolation game,

Toledo lost out to the perennial favorite, the New York Renaissance. Jones scored two points in the loss as Toledo finished in fourth place, a nice showing for an independent team. He played another year of independent ball before Sid Goldberg tapped him to join his NBL squad. Years after helping integrate the NBL, Jones spoke positively about his experience that year: "There was never any bench jockeying like in baseball. We never had problems on our own team. Players on the court for and against were fine."[9]

After that opening game loss to Fort Wayne, Toledo boarded a train and headed to Chicago to face the newest member of the league, the Chicago Studebakers. Goldberg chalked up the loss to missing two of his better players and first-game jitters. The game was set for December 11, 1942. It was a Friday night game in mid-December, the quiet time of year between Thanksgiving and Christmas. Holiday shopping had commenced. America's involvement in the war was a year old. Overshadowed by the college football season and the basketball doubleheader ninety miles north in Milwaukee—the Oshkosh All-Stars versus the Harlem Globetrotters, the Sheboygan Red Skins versus the New York Renaissance—this game would prove to be one of the most important in basketball history: it was the first on the professional level in the twentieth century between two integrated teams.

Forty years after Bucky Lew suited up in Lowell, Massachusetts, Toledo and Chicago would make history by having integrated teams play against one another. This fact did not register with anyone then, even less today. The newspapers in Oshkosh, Sheboygan, and Fort Wayne mentioned the game, but no stories discussed its importance. Even Toledo's newspaper did not deem the game significant enough to write about. In fact, the *Toledo Blade* barely covered Toledo's historic season as an integrated team. Chicago, where the game was played, barely mentioned it. The *Chicago Herald American* and *Chicago Defender* did not write about the historic nature of the contest. Only the *Chicago Daily Tribune* decided to write a preview article but made no specific mention of the black players on either team. It was as if the game did not matter.

The indifference by the press and the public reflected the secondary status of professional basketball in the country by World War II. Baseball—"America's game"—dominated print and the airwaves. Football was making great inroads in the public's consciousness, but basketball was a second-class citizen. It was still seen as rough, regional, and primitive compared to baseball and football. Beyond its local attraction, basketball had very little interest or impact on people. But professional basketball in December 1942 integrated, and it did so four years before Kenny Washington played football for the Los Angeles Rams (1946), five years before Jackie Robinson played his first major league game on April 15, 1947, and a full sixteen years ahead of the Boston Bruins signing Willie O'Ree in 1958. It was ahead of its time except in the public's imagination.

As we have seen with both Toledo and Chicago, "racial integration was born out of simple necessity."[10] Both Toledo and Chicago needed players, and the best talent available was black players. Integration happened quickly and quietly compared to other sports. The other sports integrated with one player, the lone person to take the abuse and criticism of the fans and press and, in many cases, their teammates. Basketball, however, integrated with ten players on two teams. As basketball historian Bill Himmelman points out,

> Basketball was the great melting pot of all sports for all people. Players are in shorts and shirts and bumping into one another. You do this a few times with people; you realize that there is no difference with people. Basketball was the great integrator of all sports. It did it easier and quicker than other sports.[11]

Basketball did do it easier and quicker, although basketball players were still subject to abuse both on and off the court. However, basketball had different factors than other sports working in its favor, as noted by basketball writer Bill Reynolds. Reynolds writes about the NBA's integration in 1949, but he could very easily have been writing about December 1942.

> It had been three years since Jackie Robinson had integrated baseball, but professional basketball's integration in 1950 took place almost quietly, with none of the demonstrable hate and public fervor that had accompanied Robinson's entrance into the Major Leagues. One theory was that basketball players had been to college and didn't seem to harbor the same vitriol against blacks as did many baseball players, most of whom had not gone to college. Many baseball players had also grown up in the South. Another theory was that

college basketball had long been integrated in much of the country, so most players had played against blacks before.[12]

The train carrying the Toledo players finally arrived two hours late, and the players made their way to Cicero Stadium. The delay affected both teams, and the first quarter was a sluggish affair with Chicago holding a slim 5–3 lead. Both teams found their legs and offense in the second stanza as crisp play on both ends led the Studebakers to take a 20–16 lead into halftime. In the second half, Chicago pulled away late to come away with a 42–30 win. Bernie Price led the Studebakers with ten points. With three straight wins, the Studebakers were gaining the attention of the local community and, as a result of their early success, "in order to accommodate their many friends and followers, the Studebakers will play the remainder of their home schedule at the Sixteenth and Michigan avenue armory instead of the Cicero stadium out on West Fifty-second street."[13]

In addition to a larger venue for the home games, the team attracted the attention of the *Chicago Defender*, the city's black newspaper. As basketball historian Murry Nelson states, the *Defender*'s coverage of the team marked "the first time the NBL had been covered in the top African American newspaper in the country."[14] An interesting side note in that game is that brothers Bernie Price (Studebakers) and Al Price (Jim White Chevrolets) both participated in the first integrated professional basketball game of the twentieth century. Although important, the game quietly passed as just another game on the schedule.

With the game over, Chicago moved to 3–2, riding a three-game win streak. Toledo dropped to 0–2 and faced a tough two-game road trip to Wisconsin to play Oshkosh and Sheboygan. After their lone meeting, Chicago and Toledo would go in two vastly different directions. Each of their plights would reveal a lot about the integration process. In 1943, the league did again integrate, although briefly, with Willie Smith playing the final four regular-season games with the Cleveland Chase Brassmen. It would not be until 1946 after the conclusion of World War II that the NBL would again integrate in larger numbers.

With their second loss in as many games, Goldberg rounded up his troops and headed north. First stop: Oshkosh. An inaugural member of the NBL in 1937–38, the All-Stars were in the midst of their prime years in the league. Oshkosh was considered a first-division team and a perennial contender. In the league's first three years, the All-Stars lost in the deciding game of the league championship. Finally, in 1940–41, Oshkosh won its first NBL title. It would successfully defend its title the following season. The team also won the 1941 World Professional Basketball Tournament in Chicago. Regarded by many league observers as the team to beat, Oshkosh set its sights on an unprecedented third consecutive league championship.

Oshkosh jumped out to an early 2–1 record and was eager to welcome Toledo to town. The previous season the two teams met five times, with Oshkosh winning all five contests. Four of those games were league games, and the fifth was a nonleague game held in Wisconsin. High scoring dominated all five contests as Oshkosh averaged 54.2 points whereas Toledo averaged 44.8 points per game. The draw for the Oshkosh fans was a chance to see Chuckovits, the game's best scorer. In its preview article, the *Oshkosh Daily Northwestern* extolled the scoring virtues of Chuckovits:

> While Chuckovits is admittedly one of the game's greatest "scoring machines," it has rankled Manager Lonnie Darling and the Oshkosh quintet to some extent that "Chucking Chuck" has been able to score so well against the All Stars. In the five games the Toledo ace totaled an even 100 points for a 20-point a game average and that included only 14 points in the nonleague tilt at Waupun. His best total against Oshkosh was 23 points in the game at Milwaukee. He has 22 and 20 points in the two games in Oshkosh and 21 in the game at Toledo.[15]

Oshkosh's respect for Toledo proved on the mark as Toledo controlled the tempo from the outset. Playing smart basketball and finding their groove as a team after two early-season losses, the team made up for the loss of Gerber, who was inducted into the army and sent to Camp Perry, by playing team ball. Toledo led most of the game until the final period, when Oshkosh pulled ahead for a 46–41 win. Toledo's strong play might have been the result of off-the-field incidents that they encountered upon arriving in Oshkosh. In those years, in many parts of the country, it was difficult for blacks to find lodging and food. Many times, hotels would refuse them. It was no different for basketball players, and the Toledo team faced a terrible night in Oshkosh. As Sid Goldberg recalled,

I never thought I'd encounter the problems I did there. I went into a hotel to register the team, and they said, "We don't accept blacks." So I had no place for them to sleep. The blacks couldn't even go to a hamburger place. I had to go in and get the hamburgers. The blacks had to sleep in the car. It was cold, and I remember taking the uniforms out and putting them in the car to use for blankets. I had a room, but I felt guilty so I went out and slept in the car with them. We were there for a two-game series, and the second night I finally found a place in Oshkosh. This guy had one room, and the blacks and I slept there.[16]

The team stayed together, but most likely the events stayed with the team much longer than the game. Lodging was only part of the problem. Eating was another. Restaurants would not serve them, sometimes sending them to the back of the restaurants to get their food. Asked if the black players on the team blamed him for the incident in Oshkosh, Goldberg replied,

No, they didn't blame me, because hell, I slept right with them. How could I feel right? I was no martyr, but I just didn't feel right. Hell, they couldn't even go to the hamburger place, not even through the back door. I couldn't understand it. It was not Lon Darling. He tried. I've got to hand it to him. And the crowds were good. We didn't get any guff.[17]

After Oshkosh, the team headed to Sheboygan to finish out its opening week against each of the league's teams. As Goldberg explained,

So now we go to Sheboygan for a game. A great guy, Carl Roth, ran the team there—a wonderful fellow. I called Carl and said, "I don't want what happened in Oshkosh to happen again." A minor league first baseman named Joe Hauser owned a hotel on the waterfront, and Carl called him. He told me, "Joe says you can stay in the hotel." I said, "Should I bring them in the back door?" and Joe said, "You can bring them in the front door and they stay right here." So that helped the situation. The crowds were good, and the players cooperated. I can't recall any of the black players coming to me and saying they heard the remarks that Jackie Robinson got later as the first black major leaguer. They were accepted because they were good ballplayers.[18]

With better accommodations, Toledo set out to earn its first victory of the season. Much like its game in Oshkosh, Toledo got off to a solid start and led at halftime before a strong second half start by the Red Skins put Toledo into a hole from which it could not recover. Sheboygan held on for a 38–33 win. For the second straight night, Toledo played without its best player, Chuck Chuckovits. In its preview article to the Toledo-Sheboygan game, the *Sheboygan Press* disappointedly noted,

> Toledo will bring a galaxy of stars here for the 3 o'clock Sunday afternoon game. Bad news for Red Skins fans, however, comes by special delivery; the air mail letter from Manager Sid Goldberg to the effect that the great Chuck Chuckovits may not be here. "Chuck's high school plays Friday night. I want him to come over to Oshkosh and Sheboygan Saturday and Sunday, but I don't know if he will. He made more money last year than anyone in basketball, but he's intent on making good as a coach, and while he wants me to keep his name on the list, he doesn't want to play in the first few games." [19]

In fact, Chuckovits never did play professional basketball again. Instead, he became a well-regarded basketball referee.

For Toledo it was not to be. The team played four games in five nights, all on the road. From December 9 to 13, 1942, the Toledo Jim White Chevrolets was one of two professional basketball teams that fielded an integrated team. It did so at the height of World War II, with little support and fanfare, and no recognition. Despite the odds stacked against them, the team can claim to have helped the game's growth. Goldberg met with Leo Fischer, and it was decided that the team would suspend play for the remainder of the season. The *Toledo Blade*, in one of the few articles it wrote about the team all season, declared,

> Only four teams will carry on in the current National Basketball League title race the organization said today in announcing that Toledo had been granted a "bye" for the remainder of the season. Toledo withdrew, the announcement said, because of loss of personnel to military service and transportation difficulties. The action, however, will not affect the standings since the Ohio Pros played only four games and lost once to each of the league's other clubs—Chicago, Sheboygan, and Oshkosh, Wis., and Fort Wayne, Ind. [20]

Many years later, Goldberg did not think much about his role in integrating the sport: "I was just trying to fill out a team and save my deposit."[21]

While Al Price and the Toledo Jim White Chevrolets endured a difficult and short-lived experience, Al's brother, Bernie, and his team, the Chicago Studebakers, had a much more positive experience. The country's second-largest city behind New York, Chicago bustled with a vibrant black community. On the sporting landscape, the Chicago Bruins, Cardinals, Bears, White Sox, and Cubs all drew great local interest in the myriad daily newspapers. In basketball, the Harlem Globetrotters, based in Chicago, were the Midwest's answer to the New York Renaissance. It was the Globetrotters, though, who had an impact on the league's second team integrating that year.

The Chicago Bruins were owned and operated by George Halas (Chicago Bears) and Bill Bidwell (Chicago Cardinals), who were making their mark in the NFL. The Bruins entered the fledgling NBL in 1939–40 and posted a respectable 14–14 record. That would be their high-water mark, as the next two seasons—11–13 and 8–15—saw the team regress on the court. Seeking to cut their losses, Halas and Bidwell pulled their team from the NBL. Because the league was based in Chicago, Leo Fischer badly wanted a Chicago franchise to participate. Enter the Globetrotters. The story of how the Chicago Studebakers came into being is best told by Michael Funke in an article titled "The Chicago Studebakers: How the UAW Helped Integrate Pro Basketball and Reunite Four Players Who Made History," published by the UAW:

> Studebaker was where Mike Novak, a Bruins star, got a job in 1942, after his team discontinued play. And it was outside that plant where Roosie Hudson was standing one day in 1942 while another Globetrotter, Duke Cumberland, was inside applying for a job. Hudson was invited inside by a company official who recognized him from seeing him play with the Trotters at Studebaker's plant in South Bend, Indiana. Urged to contact some other Trotters, Hudson called Bernie Price from an office phone. Price, in turn, contacted Sonny Boswell. In the meantime, Novak contacted Dick Evans and told him he could get a job at Studebaker and play ball, too. Hillery Brown, another Trotter, got wind of the plant and joined up. Tony Peyton was rooming with Duke Cumberland, and he was the last of the Trotters to join the team. Paul Sokody, who had played NBL ball

with Sheboygan, and Johnny Orr, who'd played college ball, rounded out the team. Everyone, except the security guards Evans and Novak, was a UAW Local 998 member.[22]

Thus, Mike Novak, Paul Sokody, Dick Evans, Johnny Orr were the white players; Roosie Hudson, Duke Cumberland, Bernie Price, Sonny Boswell, Tony Peyton, Ted Strong, and Hillery Brown were the former Harlem Globetrotters.

Author David Neft and his colleagues note,

> The Studebaker factory had been converted to war-industry production, so the workers there were exempt from the draft. When quite a few pro basketball players got jobs at the plant, the United Auto Workers union picked up the NBL Chicago franchise and sponsored a team. Working in the plant were Mike Novak and Dick Evans of

The Chicago Studebakers were one of two teams to integrate the National Basketball League of 1942–43. *Courtesy of the Naismith Memorial Basketball Hall of Fame.*

the Bruins, Paul Sokody of Sheboygan, and a host of Harlem Globe-trotters led by stars Sonny Boswell, Duke Cumberland, and Bernie Price. Thus, the NBL had its first racially integrated club, one that shaped up as among the strongest in the five-team field.[23]

The players worked at the factory and also participated in basketball games on the weekend. Their commitment to the Studebaker factory was evident as "this year the boys are all engaged in defense work for the Studebaker Corporation and have carried on through the basketball season without losing any time from work."[24]

The Chicago Studebakers began their season on the road in Wisconsin against the Sheboygan Red Skins. The former Harlem Globetrotters proved to be the early season draw for the team as it would be for much of the season. The *Sheboygan Press* tapped into that popularity as it previewed the game:

> On the team, in addition to [Sonny] Boswell and [Bernie] Price, are Tony Peyton and Hillery Brown and "Roosie" Hudson and Duke Cumberland all of the Harlem Globetrotters of last year and former great colored squads which were always formidable foes. These boys all know how to handle themselves on the court, can really shoot, and are expert ball-workers and passers. It is a snappy team that Chicago will put on the floor against the Red Skins.[25]

On game day, the *Sheboygan Press* stated, "All of these boys can shoot with the best of them, and when it comes to deft ball-handling and passing they don't come much better. It will be a classy team on the floor tonight."[26]

The early season hype focused on the Studebakers, but the Red Skins were the team to beat. The Studebakers fell to the Red Skins as Sheboygan played its first league game in the newly built Municipal Auditorium and Armory. The game was close for the first period as Sheboygan enjoyed a slim 13–11 lead. In the second period, Sheboygan increased its lead to 31–22. The third period was Chicago's undoing as it failed to score a field goal and managed only four free throws as Sheboygan built a comfortable 41–26 lead entering the final frame. Despite nineteen fourth quarter points and a furious comeback, Chicago had dug itself too big a hole to overcome against an experienced team. Behind Ed Dancker's sixteen points, Sheboygan won, 53–45.

Sonny Boswell and Roosie Hudson combined for twenty-seven points to lead the Studebakers.

The Studebakers continued their Wisconsin swing and rolled into Oshkosh for a Saturday evening game against the defending league champion Oshkosh All-Stars. A close game, Oshkosh pulled away for a 41–40 victory. Roosie Hudson led the way for Chicago with twelve points. Much like Toledo, Chicago faced difficulty when in Oshkosh. As Bernie Price remembers,

> They didn't like us up there, though I imagine it was because we were black; but it could have been because they were crazy about the team they had up there. And they had a good team. The fans used to shoot staples and everything at us.[27]

They also knew that some of the calls might not go their way. As Tony Peyton explained, "We knew we weren't going to get the calls from the refs with a mixed team."[28]

Their season-opening road trip concluded in Indiana against the Fort Wayne Zollner Pistons. The notion of a mixed-race team proved interesting to the Fort Wayne basketball writer, who wrote on the day of the game,

> The Studebakers sent word late Monday that they planned to start an all-Negro lineup here, this one having clicked in a 41–40 loss to the vaunted Oshkosh cagers at the Wisconsin city Saturday night as the loop campaign got under way.[29]

Certainly, the notion of starting an all-black lineup was novel in 1942, but curiously, this was not mentioned in the writeup of the Oshkosh game in the *Oshkosh Daily Northwestern*. In fact, this was not mentioned in any other article that covered the Studebakers all season. Starting an all-black lineup in 1942 did not carry the same weight or meaning as Texas Western University fielding an all-black starting five in 1966 versus the Adolph Rupp–coached University of Kentucky in the NCAA championship game. Nor did it measure up to Red Auerbach employing an all-black starting lineup for the Boston Celtics in the early 1960s.

Regardless of the lineup, the Studebakers were clearly ready to avenge two early season losses as strong defense and timely offense led them to a 54–47 win, their first of the season. Ben Tenny, the beat writer for the Zollner Pistons for the *News-Sentinel*, wrote that Chicago was "possessed of plenty height, speed galore, experience and all-around scoring ability" in defeating Fort Wayne. Tenny noted that the Studebakers played as a unit and complemented each other well, particularly

> when [Sonny] Boswell cooled off in the last half, there were plenty other former Rens and Globe Trotters to take up the sniping work and the white players of the squad, furnishing much of the size and rebound work, teamed remarkably well with their colored mates in a basketball experiment that seems sure to succeed.[30]

Fort Wayne's other newspaper, the *Journal Gazette*, wrote in its game story, "The little, speedy colored boys on the Chicago club seemed to be in great shape, and their tireless play and accurate shooting were the big factors in the Pistons' downfall, although the entire Chicago club looked good." Clearly the notion of an integrated team intrigued both Fort Wayne papers and many other observers, noting that this was a basketball experiment, but one that could be successful.[31]

Decades after Chicago's experiment, a theory gained some credence that the team was affected by racial strife and dissension. However, all of the players disputed that, which might be a product of their memories over time. Dick Evans recalled, "We were proud to be together. We admired each other." Tony Peyton concurred, noting, "We were proud of what we did. Just playing our home games in Cicero [a Chicago suburb] was groundbreaking, man, because black people weren't even allowed to walk there back then."[32]

The team got along, and the notion of playing blacks and whites together did not present a problem for the players. According to Roosie Hudson, "It did not matter if there were three black players and two whites in the game, or three whites and two blacks, we played as a team. There was no difference." The coach, Johnny Jordan, disputed any claim of racial problems, noting, "There was no strife at all and the blacks were treated well by players and fans because, you know, people knew the Globetrotters as great ballplayers. They were well received." Bernie Price agreed with this assessment: "We played all year together and didn't have any problems. The only time we had a break-up was for the World Tournament at the end of the year. I think it was a matter of egos. I don't believe it was racial."[33]

As with most teams, problems arise from players taking too many shots, not passing enough, or missing defensive assignments. It's about the basketball, not about the composition of the team. The Studebakers were not any different. Roosie Hudson believed that the problem was between Mike Novak and Sonny Boswell. "It had nothing to do with race. It was just about Sonny (Boswell) taking too many shots and not giving up the ball. That's all that was."[34] As it went, Boswell shot too much, and Novak believed that Boswell should pass the ball more often. Sonny was a good scorer who, in twenty-two games that season, tallied 229 points. His 10.4 points per game average was good for third in the league.

Although problems arose on the court, there seemed to be little dissension at the workplace in the plant. As Michael Funke wrote about one incident:

> Peyton recalls one incident in the plant when he got into a fight with a white worker who challenged his right to use a restroom. Peyton started chasing the guy through the plant. Novak, on guard duty, took up the chase, caught the man, and hauled him to a supervisor's office. It was Peyton's word against the white worker. But other workers, white and black, agreed with Peyton's version of what happened and the white worker was fired.[35]

After its first league win against Fort Wayne, the team headed home for a matchup against Oshkosh. Seeking to avenge a close loss the previous week, Chicago came out strong in front of a home crowd at Cicero Stadium, building a 12–7 lead after the first period. Behind the scoring of Bernie Price, the Studebakers' lead was 27–12 at halftime. The team went on to a 46–35 victory behind Price's fourteen points. With their first home victory under their belt, Chicago looked ahead to the next matchup against Toledo, the only team it had yet to face in the league.

After defeating Toledo to push its record to 3–2, the Studebakers set about competing for the rest of the season. Two noteworthy developments resulted from the Chicago-Toledo game. The first was that the *Chicago Defender* covered the game and would continue to follow the team on a weekly basis throughout the season. Murry Nelson notes in his history of the NBL that the *Defender*'s coverage of the Studebakers marked "the first time the NBL had been covered in the top African American newspaper in the country." The second was the growing popularity of the team. "In order to accommodate their many friends and followers, the Studebakers will play the remainder of their home schedule at the Sixteenth and Michigan avenue armory instead of the Cicero stadium out on West Fifty-second street."[36]

For the rest of the season, the Studebakers fared well and compiled an 8–15 mark. They lost in the league playoffs but accepted an invitation to play in the World Professional Basketball Tournament in Chicago. The black players on the team acquitted themselves well given that they were all good players and former Globetrotters. Roosie Hudson averaged 6.0 points; Duke Cumberland, 6.9; Bernie Price, 9.0; Sonny Boswell, 10.4; Tony Peyton, 2.4; and Hillery Brown, 4.1.

Years later, Dick Evans, one of the white players, reflected on his experience as a member of the Studebakers:

> He [Mike Novak] told me who the [former Trotters] were and we knew each other, but I don't recall the emphasis being on integration. It's just that these guys are [at Studebaker] and this is the kind of team we have. We had a lot of respect for those guys. They thought it was pretty good to play on a team like that. I never remember anybody saying, "How can you play with those guys?" because we had a lot of respect for them. And people who saw the games thought it was great. They [the black players] were just like us. Some good guys and some were wise guys. They were just like we were. We respected those guys and they showed respect for us. I had some good friends [among] the blacks and some I just got along with and some I didn't do nothing with. That's normal with any group of people, a church group or a group out of school.[37]

After the relative success of the Chicago Studebakers and the noble attempt by the Toledo Jim White Chevrolets, the NBL briefly integrated again in 1943 with Willie Smith playing four games for the Cleveland team.

Smith grew up in Cleveland and made his mark defensively and as a rebounder. In 1931–32, he joined the Cleveland Slaughter Brothers; his play and toughness caught the attention of Bob Douglas, who signed him to the Rens beginning the following year. During the 1930s, he and Tarzan Cooper became a fearsome one-two combination in the center position. Before becoming a legendary coach with UCLA, John Wooden was building a Hall of Fame career as a player in the 1930s. He faced the Rens and Smith on numerous occasions and remembered the fear Smith put into opponents: "He was the meanest player I ever saw. Whenever he got into a fight, it was over right now. I'm not ashamed to say I was scared of him."[38]

Smith continued to play for the Rens (and part of one season with the Baltimore Mets) until 1942–43, when he finally got his chance to play in a white professional league. Already thirteen years into his professional career, Smith decided to join his hometown Cleveland Chase Brassmen team for the last four regular-season games. In those four games, he scored twenty-four points, although the team finished in last place with a 3–15 record. He then played the next two years with the Rens, but after fifteen years of traveling more than one hundred games a year, Smith decided it was time to stay closer to his native Cleveland. He played for a series of independent Cleveland teams over the next two years, including the Cleveland Fifas, Allmen Transfers, Buckeyes, and later the Chicago Monarchs. He retired for one year before being lured back to join the Dayton Rens as they made history by being the first all-black team to play in a white league in 1948–49 with the NBL. In thirty-two games, he averaged four points.

For the remaining years of the war (1944–45 and 1945–46), blacks continued to play professional basketball, just not in the NBL or in its eastern counterpart, the American Basketball League (ABL). No reason was given. The tide, however, was slowly turning as would be most evident after World War II. In baseball, the twentieth-century exclusion of blacks playing in the major leagues was soon to be overturned.

In the summer of 1945, the Kansas City Monarchs of the Negro Leagues traveled to Chicago for a game showcasing their shortstop, Jackie Robinson. After the game, one of the players approached Jackie and said, "There's a man outside the clubhouse who wants to see you." Jackie went to see this person, who introduced himself: "My name's Clyde Sukeforth. I'm with the Brooklyn Dodgers. How are you feeling?"[39] As one of the Dodgers' top scouts, Sukeforth had been scouting the Negro Leagues for quite some time. He eventually settled on Robinson and invited him to meet with Branch Rickey, the Brooklyn Dodgers' general manager, in his New York office. Robinson traveled with Sukeforth to New York and met with Rickey, who offered him a

Willie Smith played for the New York Renaissance as well as the Cleveland Chase Brassmen of the National Basketball League. © *Morgan and Marvin Smith Photographs and Prints Division, Schomburg Center for Research in Black Culture.*

contract to play with the Montreal Royals, the top farm team of the Dodgers.

During this historic meeting, Robinson soon warmed to the task and began to envision himself in this new, pioneering role. At one point, he asked Rickey, "Are you looking for someone who doesn't have the courage to fight back?" Rickey responded, "No, I'm looking for someone who has the courage not to fight back." The conversation continued, and Rickey emphasized how difficult the path ahead would be:

> Jackie, I just beg two things of you: that as a baseball player you give it your utmost and as a man you give continuing fidelity to your race and to this crucial cause you symbolize. Above all, do not fight. No matter how vile the abuse, ignore it. You are carrying the reputation of a race on your shoulders. Bear it well and a day will come when every team in baseball will open its doors to Negroes.[40]

Robinson signed with the Dodgers and was assigned to Montreal, where he led the league with a .349 batting average and helped the Royals win the 1946 Little World Series. A year later, he was promoted to the Dodgers. On April 15, 1947, he became the first black player to play in the major leagues since brothers Moses and Weldy Walker suited up with Toledo in the American Association in 1884.

Football, too, was finding its way. The year 1946 was also an important year for the NFL. One of Robinson's football teammates at UCLA, Kenny Washington, was signed by the Los Angeles Rams along with Willie Strode; Bill Willis and Marion Motley both joined the Cleveland Browns. Thus, the NFL integrated with four players and two teams. In the early days of professional football in the 1920s and 1930s, the league only periodically signed black players. Thus, 1946 marked a turning point for professional football. At the same time that Washington, Strode, Willis, and Motley were making history, Jackie Robinson was playing in Montreal, hoping for a chance at the majors. Motley believed that he and his three colleagues influenced Branch Rickey's decision to promote Robinson to the parent club. In an interview for the documentary *Forgotten Four*, Joe Horrigan of the Pro Football Hall of Fame states,

> Branch Rickey was also in 1946 a part owner of the football Brooklyn Dodgers who played against the Cleveland Browns in the All-Ameri-

ca Football Conference. Branch Rickey once told Marion Motley, "Had I not had the experience of seeing you and Bill Willis play in a contact sport without incident, I might not have had the courage to bring Jackie Robinson up into the majors."[41]

Basketball was not to be excluded and decided to test the integration waters again. What led to this change? Basketball historian Murry Nelson posits this theory,

> It may have been that the signing of Jackie Robinson (who also played for a pro basketball team in California, the Red Devils) by the Dodgers to a contract with the Montreal Royals, and his Rookie of the Year performance for Montreal in the International League, was influential in the NBL owners signing black players, but that seems less compelling than the fact that African Americans had been playing regularly against top white professional teams since the Rens began in the late 1920s. These teams had been very successful and they were popular with both black and white audiences. Clearly, the black players were just as capable as the white players, but, during the war, pro league basketball was not as much of a money-maker as playing on independent black teams, so more integration did not occur.[42]

Whatever the case may be, it felt like this was the time to try again. This time upstate New York became the focal point. The person who pulled this together was Les Harrison.

A Jewish immigrant, Harrison grew up in a traditional Jewish household in Rochester, New York. His father sold fruits and vegetables while his mother tended to the household. Harrison loved playing sports; it was the way first-generation American Jews formed an American identity. Harrison played basketball in high school, but after a while he realized that his talent rested in managing a team and finding the right players to assemble a team. He managed the Rochester Seagrams, Rochester Ebers, and Rochester Wings, all semiprofessional teams from the 1920s to the 1940s. With his brother Jack, he purchased a franchise in the NBL in 1945. Harrison recalled, "I took my brother with me, even though he was a lawyer, and we went to Chicago and I joined the NBL. The first year we won the title."[43] In their first year in the league, the team defeated Sheboygan to win the championship. With a strong lineup consisting of Red Holzman, Bobby Davies, and Al

As owner of the Rochester Royals, Les Harrison helped integrate the National Basketball League in 1946. *Courtesy of Bill Himmelman.*

Cervi, the Royals were poised to unseat Fort Wayne as the league's next dynasty.

With the end of the war, the NBL was well positioned to continue to attract the best ballplayers. The 1946–47 season marked a turning point as thirteen teams signed on for the season, the most since before the war. The Eastern Division consisted of the Rochester Royals, Fort Wayne Zollner Pistons, Syracuse Nationals, Toledo Jeeps, Buffalo Bisons, Tri-Cities Blackhawks, and the Youngstown Bears. After thirteen games, the Buffalo Bisons transferred to the Tri-Cities Blackhawks franchise. The Western Division was comprised of the Oshkosh All-

Stars, Indianapolis Kautskys, Chicago American Gears, Sheboygan Red Skins, Anderson Duffey Packers, and the Detroit Gems.

The season marked another attempt by the NBL to integrate. This time four teams and a total of four players participated. Willie King played for the Detroit Gems, Bill Farrow suited up for the Youngstown Bears, Dolly King played for Rochester, and Pop Gates headed to Buffalo to pursue his professional basketball dreams.

Harrison realized he needed more talented players, so prior to the start of the season he addressed the team.

> We got together with our whole team and said we need players and I've played with them before and I feel we should accept blacks and will you guys go along with it, and they said yes. . . . I said, "Will you take a chance? We're breaking the color line. We'll have it difficult. Will you accept it?" They said "yes." [44]

With that Harrison and the Royals signed Pop Gates and Dolly King. That's the point where the story becomes more interesting: Ben Kerner, the owner of the Buffalo franchise, called Harrison. "[He] said you only need a big man, Dolly King. Why don't you sell me Pop Gates and we'll go through it together? I liked it, so I didn't sell him to him. I gave him to him, and they did play that season." [45]

"We knew it was a risk. Dolly King was a graduate of Long Island University," recalled Harrison. "We told him he would have problems and I would have problems as owner and coach. I said, 'Are you willing to take a chance?' He said. 'Absolutely.'" [46] With that, King played the season with Rochester while Gates headed to Buffalo.

Pop Gates was born to play basketball. It was his destiny to be a professional basketball player. Although he was most associated with New York his entire career, Gates was born in Decatur, Alabama, in 1917. As part of the Great Migration, Gates's parents moved their young family to New York in 1922 seeking better economic opportunities. It was the Roaring Twenties, and the Harlem Renaissance was abuzz. The confluence of art, culture, politics, and sports made Harlem a vibrant experience. It would prove to be the perfect fit for Gates. His father was a baker at Ward's Bakery in the East Bronx. Like most children during those years, Gates grew up on the streets with his friends and neighbors. His parents did not mind too much as the kids were busy, and they always knew where to find them. William Penn

Gates soon became Pop Gates, a moniker that would stay with him the rest of his life.

> I got my nickname because I played stickball with the older fellows. A guy my age thought I was older than them, so they called me "Pop." I wasn't really big, I was just like the average-sized person, trying to have a little fun playing stickball on the street. You had no cars then, so you used to play boxball, stickball, stoopball. We were always running when we bust the windows and ducked from the cops. Big Sam Lacy was the cop up there. He was a legend. He didn't take no messing around, but everybody loved Big Sam. He would crack the bat across his knee, and down the sewer it went. He even caught me sneaking on a trolley car one time and slapped my backside. Everybody had respect for the officers in the old days.[47]

Basketball was the primary sport of choice in Harlem, and soon Gates gravitated toward it. He proved to be a natural and through hard work became one of the better neighborhood players. Gates remembered,

> Basketball was big in all the community centers around the city. I started when I was 10 at the Harlem YMCA on 135th Street. I had an inspirational coach, a fellow named Al "Chake" Lind. He was a great ballplayer. He played with the Collegians, who were the amateur champions at that time.[48]

Gates also had the opportunity to watch the Harlem Renaissance, then one of the top basketball teams in the country. The close proximity he and the neighborhood had to the team no doubt played a big role in his developing a passion for basketball.

> Everybody playing basketball knew about the Renaissance. They were one of the top basketball teams in the country. I knew all the ball players when I was young. There was Pappy Ricks, who had that great carom shot off the backboard, George File, Longie Saunders, Frank Forbes. Later, I had the opportunity of playing with some of them. That was the dream of any black kid throughout the country.[49]

In a few years, his dream would become reality.

His basketball talent led him to Benjamin Franklin High School, where as a senior in 1937–38, he led his team to the city championship.

Pop Gates was an instrumental figure in the game's integration during the 1940s.
© *Morgan and Marvin Smith Photographs and Prints Division, Schomburg Center for Research in Black Culture.*

He was named first team all-city. In those days, college was not always an option. As Gates recalled,

> We didn't have any dreams of playing on major professional basketball teams like kids do today. Our thought was to play with the best high school, YMCA, or group team in our area. At that time, it was very hard to go to college because major colleges throughout the country weren't accepting blacks.[50]

For Gates, though, college beckoned, and he hopped on a bus and headed to Atlanta, Georgia, where he enrolled in Clark College. For Gates, it was not to be.

> I went to Benjamin Franklin High School in New York City. Then I went to Clark University in Atlanta, Georgia, on a basketball scholarship. Instead of playing basketball there, I played left end on their football team. I only stayed at Clark for about six months because I couldn't take the discrimination in Atlanta—riding in the back of the bus or trolley. I just couldn't adjust to that kind of life.[51]

It was not just the racism that bothered him; it was not having enough money that was a factor as well.

As Gates recalled decades later,

> coming from poor parents, and I don't want to condemn the college, but they had a very poor training table, so I more or less stayed hungry all the time. My parents did the best they could—send me $1 a month. You could buy a package of cupcakes and a container of milk. I relished that package of cupcakes and container of milk and made it last the best I could.[52]

The training table was indeed poor as "they had a training table that looked like they were spreading the eggs and the grits as thin as a dime, so I decided to return to New York."[53]

Gates was now heading to New York for a second time in his life.

> Then I contacted a fellow we used to call "Owner" [Arthur] Josephs. He had the Harlem Yankees basketball team in New York. I told him about my problem and he sent me bus fare to come back to New York. So I began to work out with the Harlem Yankees at the Harlem Bathhouse on 134th Street and Fifth Avenue. The Yankees had

Charlie Isles, Lou Badger, Lou Henderson, Benny Garrett, and a host of other people. Subsequently, Bob Douglas saw me and told Owner Josephs he'd like to have me on the team. So they worked something out and I joined the Rens. . . . I guess the Renaissance liked what they saw in a workout. They bought me for $100.[54]

With that simple transaction, Gates became a member of the Rens.

He joined the Rens at the right moment as the team was gearing up for the first World Professional Basketball Tournament in Chicago in March 1939. The Rens would go on to win that inaugural championship. In the final game, he led the Rens with twelve points. It was a huge accomplishment: the players earned the respect, if not the financial rewards, associated with winning. As Gates remembered, "When we won the championship, the prize money was $1,500 for the whole team. The owner got that money, we just got our salary."[55] Despite that, Gates had established himself as a rising player, someone to be reckoned with over the ensuing decade.

From 1939–40 until he joined the Buffalo/Tri-Cities team in 1946–47, Gates played with the New York Renaissance, Washington Bears, Long Island Grumman Flyers, Long Island Grumman Hellcats, and Chicago Monarchs. As a player, Gates had few peers. Sam Lacy, a respected journalist, recalled, "'Pop' Gates was a deadeye shotmaker. He was unerring when he drove down the left side and banked the ball in—a real bank-shot artist." His teammate Zack Clayton echoed those sentiments: "'Pop' was the greatest driver you ever saw. He could cut so hard I can still hear his sneaker squeak."[56]

Gates described the style back then: "We played a moving game, a figure-8 weave. I mostly operated backcourt. I couldn't fly through the air; we weren't dunking. Everybody just laid it up against the backboard. When we played, you had to check your man. Make him take two steps to get one." He added, "Because the ball can travel faster by air than by dribble, I was a running, cutting player. I was ambidextrous." Red Holzman, later a Hall of Fame coach of the New York Knicks, was a contemporary of Gates in the late 1940s and early 1950s. "Pop was smooth; he had great all-around ability. He could really move."[57]

During the 1940s, Gates was considered one of the best players in the country. "Back when Bobby [McDermott] and I played against each other, we were rated one-two. Bobby was a great shooter, a great com-

petitor." It was not only his play, but his demeanor, the way he con-
ducted himself, that led him to earn the respect of those who played
with and against him. In many instances, Gates was a player-coach,
earning accolades for breaking barriers in the coaching circle as well.
"They all looked up to him. He was really a playing coach out there,"
said Les Harrison. "In his decade, 'Pop' Gates was the best all-around
player in the country." As his former manager Bob Douglas said, "Pop
had a lot of ability. But he was hotheaded. Didn't take nothing from
nobody. Not even referees. . . . Nobody was better cutting to the basket
and nothing could stop him. He could shift and he was strong as the
dickens." His longtime manager, Eric Illidge, had nothing but praise for
him when interviewed in 1948: "He's a boy who played with Ricks,
Jenkins, Cooper and that gang. They taught him all the tricks of the
trade and now he's a great ballplayer. They don't come any better than
Pops."[58]

After his one season with Buffalo/Tri-Cities, Gates returned to the
Rens and was also part of the Dayton Rens team that became the first
all-black team to play in a white league, the NBL, in 1948–49. Afterward, he joined Scranton of the ABL and won a league title with them
alongside Dolly King and Eddie Younger. His coach on those Scranton
teams was Red Sarachek who, decades later, fondly recalled those days
of coaching Gates: "More than his great skill has been the manner in
which 'Pop' has always carried himself. He is a man of great stature and
pride who always led by example."[59]

As the 1940s ended, Gates had made his mark on professional basketball as one of the best all-around players and one who was instrumental in helping the game integrate. Although no longer a top-tier
player, he still had plenty in the tank, and in 1949–50 he joined the
Harlem Globetrotters and barnstormed with them until 1956–57. One
of his teammates was Marques Haynes, who remembered Gates well.
"Pop was great. He knew the game extremely well, to the extent he
could have been one of the better coaches in the game. The only reason
he wasn't considered was that he was black."[60]

Gates enjoyed an extensive career, one that was not lost on him:
"People work all their lives in order to travel. I got paid to do it. Some
people never get out of Harlem. I was fortunate to play basketball."
Years later, after a career as a New York City police officer, Gates
reflected on his obscurity in the game today: "You'd just like people to

know you were part of the game. You'd like people to know we are part of the heritage of the sport. But very few people know anything about it."

In 1989, he finally earned that recognition when he was inducted into the Naismith Memorial Basketball Hall of Fame.[61]

Buffalo rejoined the league for the first time since 1937–38, the inaugural season of the NBL. They kept their Bison name as homage to the earlier incarnation of the team. Much like that first squad, the 1946–47 team did not fare well. The team started slowly and "the competition with professional hockey, boxing and college basketball in the region was too much for the Bisons and they lost $25,000 over the first league games."[62] With a slow start, Leo and Cliff Ferris started looking at other options, one of which consisted of relocating the team to the Midwest. Milwaukee, Moline, and Minneapolis all became viable options for the brothers. Eventually, Moline won out, and the team relocated and began as the Tri-Cities Blackhawks on January 1, 1947.

As Pop Gates stated long after his playing days were over, "I was with the Tri-City Blackhawks in their very first year. They started out of Buffalo actually—the Buffalo Bisons—and they moved the franchise during the season to the Tri-City Blackhawks—Moline, Rock Island and Davenport."

> Dolly King and I were recruited up to Rochester. We used to play against Rochester all the time. We used to pick up a team and play throughout that area, so Les Harrison recruited Dolly King and me to play for the Rochester Seagrams—this would be before 1946. By this time, the National Basketball League was going down, and that's when they brought in the Rochester team, which is now called the Rochester Royals. Subsequently they started the Buffalo team, which later became the Tri-City Blackhawks, and I think through the picking of Negro ballplayers at that particular time, Les Harrison recommended me to Leo Ferris or Cliff Ferris of the Buffalo franchise. Dolly went to Rochester and I went to Buffalo, which later went to Tri-City. We started in Buffalo and moved to Tri-Cities after the season started.[63]
>
> As far as the team [Tri-Cities] was concerned, I had no problems. But our home base was Moline, and they were used to keeping blacks out of hotels. I did stay in a hotel two days. Then came one of the team owners—Cliff Ferris or Leo Ferris—and we had a very heated discussion about pulling me out of there. I said, "I want to

Pop Gates integrated the National Basketball League in 1946–47 with the Buffalo Bisons. *Photographs and Prints Division, Schomburg Center for Research in Black Culture, New York Public Library.*

stay with the team. I'm part of the team; I think I should stay with them." However, they prevailed, and I wound up being shunted to a YMCA there. Later on that season, a guy in Rock Island—he was reputed to be one of the mob people operating out of Chicago—said I could stay in a hotel he had. A certain number of ballplayers on the team said, "We're going to stay with Pop over at the Rock Island hotel." I've forgotten the name of it. There was Wilbur Schu, Don Otten and other ballplayers, maybe five of us.[64]

Gates, though, did not harbor any concerns about being the only black on a white team. He had played against and with white players for years. "I had played with white teams before. We had to scratch to make a dollar bill, so there was no apprehension. If you realized what your ability was, you knew where you stood from the git-go."[65]

For the most part, the season passed without any incident until a game on February 24, 1947, when Tri-Cities visited Syracuse. The game had playoff implications for both teams. Syracuse focused their defensive strategy at trying to limit the effectiveness of Gates, who was playing very well throughout the season. Syracuse put John "Chick" Meehan, whose physical style was known throughout the league, on him. The game was physical, and with less than five minutes remaining the two players went after a loose ball. What happened next is still a matter of interpretation, but Meehan went down; either he was pushed by Gates, or he fell. In any event, Meehan got up and confronted Gates. Gates's recollection years later:

> [He] threw me down one time, and I said, "Chick, don't do that no more!" Well, he threw me down again, so I deliberately placed myself in the pivot. When he tried again, I threw *him* down and he got up whaling. So I got mine [punch] in first before he got his in. I made him bleed. That's the reason Dolly and I only played one season.[66]

Both players received double fouls on the play. It is not clear if this fight hampered further efforts of the NBL integrating, but it did have an effect. Gates apologized, and he and Meehan always said that the incident was just competition and not based on skin color.

That season, Gates played in forty-one of the team's forty-four games and averaged 7.6 points per game, third best on the team. While Gates played in Moline, Dolly King was an integral member of the defending champions Rochester Royals. A strong presence off the bench, King averaged 4.0 points per game in forty-one games. In the finals, Rochester faced the Chicago American Gears and their rookie center, George Mikan. The finals would be a best-of-five series, beginning in Rochester. The two teams had met eight times during the season; the Gears won three of five in the regular season, and Rochester took two of three in exhibition matches. Although King gave up six inches to Mikan, he stood his ground and used his physical nature to get Mikan in foul trouble. However, over the entire game and series, Mikan proved to be too much—the Gears won 3–1 to claim the NBL title.

In addition to Gates and King, Bill Farrow of Youngstown and Willie King of Detroit earned the distinction of integrating their teams that season. A native of Chicago, Farrow enrolled at Kentucky State College, where he helped lead the team as one of the best black college teams in the country in the late 1930s. After four years (1941–45) in the military during World War II, Farrow returned home to Chicago and played two years with all-black independent teams, the Chicago Brown Bombers (1945–46) and the Chicago Collegians (1946–47). Early on with the Chicago Collegians, Farrow left to join Youngstown and help integrate the NBL. Farrow played in thirty-two games and averaged 5.7 points per game that season. Two years later, Farrow joined the Dayton Rens before ending his professional career.

Willie King was the fourth player to integrate the NBL that season. King grew up in Detroit, and in 1941–42 he joined the Harlem Globetrotters for one season before three years in the military interrupted his basketball career. After the war, King signed on with his hometown team, the Detroit Gems. He came off the bench to average 8.2 points in fourteen contests. After that season, he joined the independent Kansas City Stars before reuniting with the Harlem Globetrotters for two more years before retiring from professional basketball. Neither Farrow's nor King's teams fared well; both finished dead last in their divisions. The Youngstown Bears sat in last place in the Eastern Division with a 12–27 mark, while the Detroit Gems finished with a league worst record of 4–40. Youngstown would not field a team in the NBL, while the Detroit Gems later became the Minneapolis Lakers.

Despite the success of Pop Gates and Dolly King, the NBL did not integrate again for another two years. By this time, the NBL was a far cry from its better years. Since the end of World War II, the NBL had competition in the form of the Basketball Association of America (BAA), a league comprised of hockey owners who sought to fill the empty dates of their arenas when hockey and the ice shows were out of town. They formed their own league to challenge the NBL. They had the better markets and the larger arenas, but the NBL possessed the best players. Slowly the BAA chipped away at the market share of the NBL, raiding teams and players.

By 1948–49, the NBL was barely standing, hoping to survive one last season. In that final season, the league's Eastern Division consisted of the Anderson Duffey Packers, Syracuse Nationals, Hammond Calumet Buccaneers, Detroit Vagabond Kings, and the Dayton Rens. The Western Division was made up of the Oshkosh All-Stars, Tri-Cities Blackhawks, Sheboygan Red Skins, Waterloo Hawks, and the Denver Nuggets. In that lackluster final season, the NBL made history by having an all-black team compete in league play.

As Pop Gates recalled,

> The National Basketball League was doing badly at that particular
> time, and I think—I can't prove it, but it was told to me in a round-
> about sort of way—they put in the Dayton Rens. That's when the
> Dayton Rens went into the National Basketball League in '49. An all-
> black team. I think they thought that would help bring in more
> people. I don't think it did, because we couldn't get our salary with
> the Dayton Rens.
>
> I don't think our being there as a Negro team made that much of
> a difference. We weren't filling up the houses but we played pretty
> fair crowds. In Dayton we played in a field house that probably
> seated 8,000 people, and if we had 2,000 the few times we played
> there we were lucky. I don't think we finished the season.
>
> There was no Renaissance team after that. Consequently Saper-
> stein pitched in a roundabout way. He wanted the whole piece of the
> pie. So he buys the franchise of the New York Renaissance from Bob
> Douglas. He started his own Renaissance, and eventually he dropped
> the Renaissance so he would be the premier owner of black basket-
> ball. But he ran the Renaissance for a while and they were playing
> the preliminary games for the Harlem Globetrotters.[67]

The league's fate was largely sealed in mid-December when the Detroit
Vagabond Kings folded. The team had been doing poorly since the
beginning of the season. The main culprit in their demise was a lack of a
consistent home venue. As the *Official National Basketball League Pro
Magazine* stated,

> They [Detroit] intended to play in the Forum, a new athletic arena
> on the outskirts of Detroit, with a seating capacity of 10,000. Howev-
> er, building difficulties have delayed its completion and King Boring
> and Ernie Pabis were forced to go elsewhere. The result was that
> they never did find a suitable location, and were forced to withdraw
> from the league.[68]

As a result, the team played its home games in a variety of arenas. That,
compounded with long losing streaks, led to poor fan support. As a
result, few attended their games, leading to poor revenue at the gate. It
became unsustainable. Historian Murry Nelson noted,

> If they [the league] simply dropped the Kings and their scheduled games, it would make an even more unbalanced schedule. A better solution, it was thought by new Commissioner Doxie Moore and President Ike Duffey, was to find an existing team and convince them to enter the league, picking up the Kings' record and schedule. [69]

That is when they approached New York Renaissance owner Robert Douglas and manager Eric Illidge. The four men eventually agreed to have the Rens enter the league as the Dayton Rens. As Douglas recalled,

> In 1948, Mike Duffey, president of the white National Basketball League [he also had a club in the league, the Anderson Duffey Packers], asked us to replace the Detroit Vagabond Kings' franchise, which lasted until mid-December and then folded. We came into the league representing Dayton, Ohio, and called ourselves the Dayton Rens. The team was led by our player-coach Pop Gates, Hank De-Zonie, William "Dolly" King, and George Crowe, who later played major league baseball. [70]

Like their predecessor, the Dayton squad also faced a venue challenge as the Dayton Coliseum was already booked, so Springfield became the site of some home games. Along with Springfield, other Ohio towns that hosted the Rens were Sandusky, Lima, and Ashland, hardly a recipe for financial success or building strong fan support. Douglas recalled decades later,

> We really didn't want Dayton, Ohio, as our home court, but the league insisted. The people in Dayton just refused to attend our games. They would not accept an all-black club. Despite a lack of size, a lot of our players being over the hill, a thin bench, and DeZonie's illness, which caused him to miss the last eight games, our club— the only all-black franchise in the history of major league sports— built a competitive 14–26 record over the rest of the season. That season proved to be the last for the Rens. [71]

The Dayton Rens compiled a 14–26 record. Coached by Pop Gates, the team also featured Hank DeZonie, Sonny Wood, George Crowe, and Jim Usry. Coming off the bench were Willie Smith, Johnny Isaacs,

Pop Gates was a member of the Dayton Rens, which became the first all-black team to play in a white league, the National Basketball League, in 1948–49. *Photographs and Prints Division, Schomburg Center for Research in Black Culture, New York Public Library.*

Dolly King, Tom Sealy, and Bill Farrow. Gates earned the distinction of being the first player-coach for a black team in a white league. Not surprising, his achievement largely went unnoticed. However, the significance of an all-black team joining a white league did not go unnoticed. Wendell Smith, influential in chronicling Jackie Robinson's historic first season, wrote in the *Chicago Defender* about the Dayton Rens:

> For years, the Negro cagers have traveled the country, beating the best in the various pro leagues, but were never admitted to membership. But times insist on changing and now they are in—a Negro team representing a city of white and colored people, which is unique if nothing else. [72]

Although the Rens were finally in an all-white league (NBL), this was not their first attempt to integrate a major professional league. Two years earlier, in 1947, Bob Douglas tried again to have his team admitted to the BAA. At a league meeting in Philadelphia prior to the start of the season, the topic was placed on the agenda. Douglas was in attendance, as was his good friend Joe Lapchick. When the topic came up, the commissioner asked Lapchick for his opinion. "I may be a newcomer to professional coaching, but I support Bob Douglas's bid to play. I may lose my job for saying this, but I'd play against the Rens any goddamn day. They're the best." "How do you know that, Joe?" league official Ike Duffey asked. Lapchick then described barnstorming with the Rens during the 1920s and shared many of his memories. His opinion was not enough to sway the owners. "Financial concerns" were given as the reason. Despite his disappointment, Douglas found a silver lining in this encounter with his old friend Lapchick. "I know now there are whites who would risk everything for blacks." [73] Two years later, his Rens would be in the NBL as the Dayton Rens.

As Pop Gates summed up,

> The NBL was an excellent league at that time—the top league in the country—but we thought we were the premier team in the country. The Renaissance players didn't give a damn about the National Basketball League at that time because we thought we were their equal or better. So we weren't worried about it. We were happy to be where we were.

I think if the National Basketball League would have offered one of our guys more money than Bob Douglas offered, somebody would have gone. But we loved being with the Renaissance because we thought we were the best, and we were happy and proud to represent the Negro people and give them something they could be proud of and adhere to. And we were happy that a lot white fans loved us also.[74]

The 1948–49 season marked the last straw for the NBL as the league and the BAA merged to form the National Basketball Association (NBA) in 1949–50. The integration of the NBL would prove to be a key factor as the NBA sought to improve its talent base.

4

EARLY BLACK NBA PIONEERS

October 31, 1950

Suiting up for the game, Earl Lloyd was not thinking about making history. It was his first game as a professional basketball player, and he was both nervous and excited to be playing professionally. This was not something he had dreamed about as a kid. His team, the Washington Capitols, was facing the Rochester Royals in the Sports Arena in Rochester, New York. Only 2,148 people were in attendance that evening. The game was fairly competitive as the Rochester Royals won, 78–70. Lloyd acquitted himself well as he scored six points, tied for a game-high five assists, and led all players with ten rebounds. Neither the Rochester nor Washington papers mentioned this historic fact: Lloyd was the first black to play in an NBA game.

It was just another game on the schedule.

Lloyd recounted decades later:

> If you had to handpick a game where the first black guy would perform, you couldn't have picked a better place. In 1950 it was a little, sleepy upstate town where the schools were integrated, so people were used to seeing blacks and whites playing against each other. When people ask about that first game, they want to hear that the Ku Klux Klan was there with ropes. But believe me, that first game, it was totally and unequivocally uneventful. To add a little light to it, it was played on Oct. 31 and there is some significance to that date, that's Halloween. Maybe they thought I was a goblin or something.

You have to remember that professional baseball was our national pastime. It's very hard to get excited about something where some of the teams are playing in high school gymnasiums. The notoriety factor was just not there at that time. I think the infusion of three black players in the NBA in 1950 was received with a kind of ho-hum attitude. [1]

Although the game itself and the historical significance attached to it were glossed over, the journey getting there was anything but for Lloyd.

A native of Alexandria, Virginia, Earl Lloyd grew up in a very segregated community.

It was the cradle of segregation. Alexandria was in the '30s and '40s. All the things you heard and read, we went through it—the back of the bus and the hotels not available to you. As you reflect, you know it was humiliating and degrading, but when you were a kid, that was just the way it was. In all my formative years, I never had a conversation with a white person my age, not one. . . . In my town, the white kids had the swimming pool. We were supposed to swim in the muddy river. It was separate toilets, sit in the back of the bus, and go to an all-black school that was a in a rundown building in a bad part of town. These things had steeled me for anything I would face as an NBA player. My parents were not overly educated, and they were not people of means, so they turned us over to our coaches. They had our welfare at heart. [2]

With the local coaches as his guide, Lloyd developed into good basketball player on the eve of high school.

Lloyd starred at Parker Gray High School before enrolling at West Virginia State University, where he blossomed as a player. He led West Virginia State to two Central Intercollegiate Athletic Association (CIAA) conference and tournament championships in 1948 and 1949. He was All-Conference three times in 1948–50, and a *Pittsburgh Courier* two-time All-American in 1949–50. As a senior, he averaged fourteen points and eight rebounds. In 1947–48, his West Virginia State team was the only one undefeated in the country. For his efforts, he was named the CIAA Player of the Decade 1947–56.

As his college career was coming to a close, Lloyd had no designs on an NBA career. It was the furthest thing from his mind. "I never saw myself playing pro ball because those avenues were simply not open to

Earl Lloyd was the first African American to play in the NBA when he suited up for the Washington Capitols on October 31, 1950. *Courtesy Post-Standard, photograph by Dolph Schayes.*

me."[3] Prior to the NBA draft, there was a tournament held in Washington, D.C., in which Bones McKinney attended.

> Abe Saperstein and the Harlem Globetrotters had locks on all of the good black players, but West Virginia State had a player in the tournament Abe had overlooked. The player's name was Earl Lloyd, who was 6-6 and weighed 225 pounds and was some kind of good player. I watched Earl closely during the three days of the tournament, and the wheels started turning.[4]

That tournament led to a tryout with the Washington franchise. Joining Lloyd was Harold Hunter from North Carolina Central University. Hunter's coach, John McLendon, drove both to the tryout. According to McLendon,

> We went up to Howard University and got the gym. We ran a little two-man stuff to get the ball in their hands for about a half-hour. We started driving down to Uline and on the way down the hill, Earl said, "Wait a minute. I don't know how to switch." As soon as Earl said it, I started looking for a playground. I turned off Georgia Avenue and the first street happened to be a dead-end street.[5]

McLendon found another person to join them, and they practiced switching so Lloyd would feel comfortable. They then went to the tryout. As McKinney remembered, "I invited Earl and another black player, Harold Hunter from North Carolina College, to practice with several of the Caps players. We had an hour-long scrimmage and the best player on the floor, by far, was Earl Lloyd."[6] Lloyd's performance left a good impression in McKinney's mind, and the team drafted him in the ninth round after Boston selected Cooper. Hunter was not drafted. Instead, he was part of an NBA tryout.

Lloyd only played seven games with the Washington Capitols before being drafted again, this time into the military. When he returned from the army, the Washington franchise folded, and he was picked up by the Syracuse Nationals, a team on the rise. His focus on the floor was defending the opposing team's best scorer, which allowed Syracuse's other forward, Dolph Schayes, to play his All-NBA game. During his time with Syracuse, Lloyd became a key component of the Nats' winning the 1955 NBA title. Joining him on that team was another black

Harold Hunter had a tryout with the Washington Capitols but never played in the NBA. *Courtesy of North Carolina Central University Archives & Records.*

player, Jim Tucker, and Tucker and Lloyd became the first blacks to win an NBA championship.

During his nine-year career, he averaged 8.4 points and 6.4 rebounds per game. After his playing days, he continued in basketball and earned another "first" when in 1968 he became the first African American assistant coach with the Detroit Pistons. Three years later in 1971, he became the second African American head coach, again with the Pistons.

As the first black to play in an NBA game, Lloyd sometimes is referred to as the Jackie Robinson of basketball, but even he would be the first to admit that that comparison is stretching it, to say the least. "When you say, 'You're the Jackie Robinson of basketball,' I say, 'You do the man a tremendous disservice, because I had it so easy compared to what he had to go through.' I had no problems."[7]

The Syracuse Nationals won the 1955 NBA title with two black players, Earl Lloyd and Jim Tucker. *Courtesy Post-Standard, photograph by Frank Monell.*

Lloyd did not have the same problems as Robinson, but he did have his own set of challenges. "St. Louis, Indianapolis and Fort Wayne were tough towns. You got called a lot of names. What I learned was that if you didn't play well they didn't call you anything. So I took special pains in those towns to make sure they called me names." It was not just on the court; Lloyd faced racism and discrimination off the court as well. "You'd walk into a restaurant in Saint Louis to order food, and they'd bring it to you on a Styrofoam plate. If you were black, your order was always on the go." Eating was a challenge; so was finding a place to sleep after games.[8]

> We went to Fort Wayne, Indiana, to play the Pistons and we went to the hotel and they allowed me to sleep in the hotel, but they wouldn't allow me to eat in the hotel. Somebody asked me if that

bothered me, and I said that coming from Virginia and being born in
the late '20s and growing up in the '30s and '40s, I was shocked that
they even let me sleep in the hotel.[9]

Lloyd became the first African American to play in an NBA game merely due to scheduling. The honor could have fallen to Chuck Cooper or
Sweetwater Clifton. In fact, all three were instrumental in the NBA
integrating. Chuck Cooper was the first black player drafted when the
Boston Celtics selected him on April 25, 1950, and Nat "Sweetwater"
Clifton was the first black player to sign a contract when he signed with
the New York Knicks that summer. Years later, Lloyd reflected on what
the three achieved: "They picked three guys who were decent enough
to play in this league, gentlemen and decent human beings. There was
never any worry to my knowledge about Sweets or Chuck or me, none."
As author Ron Thomas observes, "Compared to [Jackie Robinson] the
NBA's pioneers didn't cause even a mild ripple on the calmest of lakes,
or so it seemed." Before delving into the stories of Cooper and Clifton,
it is important to understand the NBA landscape in 1950–51 and how
important the Harlem Globetrotters were to the survival of the professional game at the century's halfway mark.[10]

The 1950–51 season marked the second year of the NBA after the
merger of the National Basketball League (NBL) and the Basketball
Association of America (BAA). Basketball was not as popular as baseball
or football, and games still were played in small arenas in small towns
around the country. It had yet to make its mark nationally on a large
scale. Crowds were often small, and media coverage was uneven de-
pending on where the team played. The most popular basketball team
in the country, the one that drew the biggest crowds, was the Harlem
Globetrotters.

For many years, the Globetrotters were part of doubleheaders with
BAA teams first and then NBA teams, and their ability to draw ten
thousand plus fans helped save the financially strapped NBA during
those first few seasons. Fuzzy Levane recalled, "Abe Saperstein kept a
lot of franchise[s] alive. The Globetrotters kept Milwaukee alive; they
kept Philadelphia alive, and so on. We'd play home games on another
court, as part of a double-header, and we were guaranteed more money
that we'd get in Milwaukee, where you drew four hundred people."
Bobby Harrison, a guard with the Minneapolis Lakers, played in many

doubleheaders with the Globetrotters. "They would come in and play the feature game. The preliminary game would be an NBA game. They shared the receipts with the NBA team, so they did a lot to help the NBA survive." Fort Wayne's Carl Bennett remembered, "It [NBA integration] was delayed because of the Globetrotters. The league was convinced that the Globetrotters wouldn't play exhibitions for them and sell out their houses."[11]

Pushing back against Saperstein was a big concern for the owners. Haskell Cohen, publicity director for the NBA at that time, had a front-row seat during this time period and recalled,

> A number of the owners were worried about opening the league to blacks for two reasons. First, it would upset Abe Saperstein and the Globetrotters. In the early 1950s, the Globies were a huge draw. They played before, sometimes even after, NBA games to help with the crowds. They thought that if the NBA allowed blacks to play, then Saperstein would not play in their buildings. The second concern was that if blacks were signed, the door would be open and within a few years, black players would dominate the league. Then this would turn off the white fans. Of course, the opposite was true— black players just helped attendance.[12]

Carl Bennett served as the manager and right-hand person for Fred Zollner, the owner of the Fort Wayne Zollner Pistons. Well into the second decade of 2000, he remained the last living link to those discussions that eventually paved the way for the NBA to integrate in the summer of 1950. The winds of change, though, began a year earlier, according to Bennett.

> We had had discussions in our executive meetings a year earlier [1949]. Walter Brown [Boston], Ned Irish [New York], and myself decided to take the vote to the entire board of governors. But the rule did not pass that first year.
>
> The vote really wasn't that close the first year in 1949. Most of the resistance came from those clubs who scheduled the Harlem Globetrotters in their arenas. They didn't want to upset Abe Saperstein, who, at the time, had the exclusive market on African American talent. Scheduling the Trotters was big business back then. They were big at the box office. So no one wanted to anger Saperstein and lose their contracts with him. After all, if the NBA started bidding for

blacks, Saperstein's payroll costs would sky rocket because he'd have to pay them more to keep them on his team.

The person who deserves the real credit for getting blacks into the NBA is Ned Irish. Even back in 1949 Irish was complaining that the Knicks were having a hard time winning ball games in New York. He just wasn't attracting enough fans to Madison Square Garden. He felt he needed some quality black players to help make his club more competitive. So he approached me and some of the others about his aspirations to purchase the contract of Nat "Sweetwater" Clifton, the Globetrotters star.

Ned Irish was adamant about getting Clifton to New York. He campaigned heavily to get the vote in his favor. But the majority of the league representatives felt that the Trotters were to[o] valuable an asset to risk losing. So they turned Irish down. All season long Irish kept telling us that he couldn't stay in business without Clifton.

Ned always had a habit of doing crazy things in our meetings in order to get his point across. But this time he was really mad. He stood and pounded his fist on the table and shouted at us. "I'll tell you one thing. I want to have approved the right to have black ball-players in our league. If I can't get Sweetwater Clifton on the New York team, then New York will no longer be a part of this league." That just the way he said it. Then he turned on his heel and walked out of the room, just like that.

Everybody in the room knew that New York was the granddaddy of basketball at that time, so we all listened to him. I think Irish acted that way because he thought he could get away with it. . . . And he could, too. New York carried a lot of weight in the league. They may not have had the best team, but Madison Square Garden was a major venue for that league.[13]

So in that league meeting in 1949, Irish did his best to persuade other owners, but to no avail. He would not give up; six months later, in March 1950, the issue of integration came up again. Prior to that league meeting and the spring draft, there was discussion, and rumors were going back and forth among the coaches and owners:

"Did you hear some teams are thinking of drafting Negroes?" remarked Rochester owner Les Harrison.

"It can ruin us," retorted Philadelphia's Eddie Gottlieb.

"If the Knicks can't sign Clifton, New York will withdraw from the league," boasted Ned Irish.

"Irish isn't the only one interested in signing blacks. The Celtics intend to draft a black, too," declared Walter Brown.[14]

Another vote was taken. This time, by the slimmest of margins, the owners voted 6–5 to allow blacks to play in the NBA. The close vote and contentious debate clearly divided the owners. Listen to Carl Bennett.

> When we walked out of the meeting, Eddie Gottlieb, the owner of the Philadelphia Warriors, came up to me. He told me, "Carl, you sonuvabitch. You just ruined the league. In five years, 75 percent of the league is going to be black. We won't draw crowds. People won't come out to see them." Well, Gottlieb was right about the first part, but very wrong about the second part. In five years or so, the league indeed was 70–75 percent black. But the fans really came out to support our teams after we allowed blacks into the league. I didn't notice any dip in the league attendance. The shift didn't stop the fans from coming at all. In fact, I think they really appreciated the talents of these wonderful athletes.[15]

As Bennett went on to say, "What are you worried about? We've increased the supply of quality players. . . . How would it look if Mr. Zollner, owner of a racially mixed plant, voted against integration?"[16]

As Minneapolis's Sid Hartman remembered, "Eddie Gottlieb was sitting next to me, and he said, 'Oh-oh, Abe's gonna go crazy.' Everybody knew that Abe Saperstein would cut out all the double-headers, and in those days they couldn't get along without the double-headers."[17]

Less than two months after that historic vote, the Boston Celtics made history. With the first pick of the second round, Boston owner Walter Brown declared for all to hear, "Boston takes Charles Cooper of Duquesne."

"Walter, don't you know he's a colored boy?" said another owner.

"I don't give a damn if he's striped or plaid or polka-dot. Boston takes Charles Cooper of Duquesne." Brown knew this would impact his relationship with Saperstein and the Globetrotters playing in Boston, but Brown was adamant: "As far as I'm concerned, Abe Saperstein is out of the Boston Garden right now."[18]

With that, the Boston Celtics made history by drafting Chuck Cooper.

Sitting with Brown that day was his first-year coach, Red Auerbach, who had a front-row seat for that historic moment in the game's history.

> And he proved that one day in the spring of 1950, just after he hired me, when we drafted Chuck Cooper from Duquesne. This was just four years after Branch Rickey made history in baseball by signing Jackie Robinson. The NBA, at that time, was an all-white league.
>
> When Walter called out Cooper's name that day, one of the other owners looked at him and asked: "Are you aware of the fact that Mr. Cooper is a Negro?"
>
> "I don't care what he is," Walter shot back. "All I know is that this kid can play basketball and we want him on the Celtics."
>
> What wasn't generally known at the time, however, was that Walter was under considerable pressure from Abe Saperstein, owner of the Harlem Globetrotters, *not* to be a pioneer in breaking the color line. After all, Abe wasn't anxious to break up his own monopoly; he was getting *all* of the great black talent, the way the Montreal Canadians [*sic*] used to have exclusive claim to all of the great French-speaking skaters. Abe had a good thing going, so he wasn't at all timid about reminding Walter that the Globetrotters drew some pretty big crowds to Boston Garden, crowds Walter was in no financial position to disregard. Remember, he was losing his shirt on pro basketball at the time.
>
> Still, this was a matter of principle—a matter of conscience, if you will—and there was never any doubt in my mind as to what Walter's decision would be.
>
> "Boston takes Chuck Cooper!" he repeated.
>
> There are no flags to commemorate the occasion, but I'll always remember that as a proud moment in Boston Celtics history. [19]

Auerbach did not want to stop just with the signing of Cooper. He also had his sights on Sweetwater Clifton.

> I wanted to sign Sweetwater Clifton. I had seen him play a lot because the [Harlem] Globetrotters played games in our buildings all the time and I knew he was just the kind of guy who could help us. I found out that his contract with the Globetrotters was up and I drove out to Pennsylvania to meet with him to see if I could sign him.
>
> He [Commissioner Maurice Podoloff] told Walter Brown that he didn't want to upset the Globetrotters by signing their best player. In those days, the Globetrotters played a lot of doubleheaders with

NBA teams, and, in most cities, about the only time we'd sell out or get close to a sellout was when the Globetrotters were in town. Podoloff told Walter he was afraid [Globetrotter owner] Abe Saperstein might pull out of our deal with him if we signed Clifton. I told Walter that was nuts, where was Saperstein gonna take his team if not to NBA arenas? The deal worked well for both sides, not just for one side. But Walter didn't want to fight him on it. I was a new coach, I didn't have the kind of clout I had later, so there was nothing I could do.

A couple of weeks later, I pick up the newspaper and there's an item: CLIFTON SIGNS WITH KNICKS. I went crazy. I went in to Walter and said how could this possibly be? What happened to Podoloff not wanting to upset Saperstein? "He made a deal with Saperstein," Brown explained. "The league us going to give the Globetrotters a couple of extra appearances in [Madison Square] Garden the next couple of years, which is good for them. In return, Saperstein agreed to let Clifton go to the Knicks."

To show you what kind of guy Walter Brown was, he stepped in when Sweetwater got hurt and helped him buy a cab in Chicago. That was always what he had wanted to do when he stopped playing, drive his own cab back home in Chicago. I think he ended up owning two cabs and doing very well. But it was Walter who helped him get started. Things like that made it hard for me to stay mad at Walter.

Look, that's not what it was about for me. Where I grew up in Brooklyn, race was never an issue. Jews, blacks, Catholics—no one ever paid attention to what you were when you played ball. The only thing that mattered was if you could play. That's one of the great things about sports. When you're choosing a team—whether it's in the school yard or in the NBA—no one asks you what color you are or what religion you are. Those who do are doomed to fail on every level anyway, so who cares what they think?

My thing was always winning. If a guy was white and could play, I wanted him on my team. If he was black and could play, I wanted him on my team. But I also cared about character. Same thing held there. A bad guy is a bad guy; a good guy is a good guy. I never thought I deserved any special credit for starting five black guys. I did it for one reason: I thought it gave us the best chance to win. Period. Same with hiring Russell. It was the best thing for the team. [20]

Although Auerbach did not get Clifton, he did get Cooper, the team's target all along.

A native of Pittsburgh, Chuck Cooper was not immediately attracted to basketball. He played in the neighborhood and eventually graduated from Westchester High School.

As a youngster, I was a pretty good athlete, but I really had no intention of going out for the high school team. Apparently, the coach at Westchester High had seen me play in the schoolyard and chased after me to come out for basketball. When I joined in the ninth grade, it was the first time I'd play any organized sport.

One of the people who inspired me to seek a future in basketball was Dolly King, who was a star at Long Island University during the 1940s. He had been the subject of several national magazine articles and LIU was a national basketball power at that time. I had wanted to go there after I graduated from high school, but instead attended West Virginia State before being drafted into the Navy.

After a year-and-a half stint there, I was released just after the school year had started. My desire to go to LIU was still there and the coach, Clair Bee, had even offered me a scholarship before I went into the Navy. Being a little naive about the way things worked, I went over to Duquesne University, where Chuck Davies was coach. I knew he was friendly with Clair Bee and I hoped he'd put me in contact with him. See how naive I was?

Well, with the help of the black trainer at Duquesne, Brue Jackson, who incidentally was a longtime trainer of the Steelers also, I ended up attending Duquesne and, as a "walk-on," made the team. It was unusual for a freshman to do that. . . . Duquesne had a tradition of blacks in athletics. One of the first blacks in the National Football League went there and there was another black basketball player in the early 1930s, but I was the first black starter they had. . . .

Only in my freshman year did we have any real racial incidents. We had a game scheduled against the University of Tennessee at home and they refused to play against me. I never met them face-to-face, but from what I understand they were not aware of my presence until the last minute. We were already dressed when it was called off. There is the possibility that somebody told them I would be held out of the game. But to the credit of the school officials, they didn't back down. It didn't cause me any kind of emotional anguish. If that was what they wanted to do, let them go back to Tennessee.

Chuck Cooper became the first African American drafted in the NBA, by the Boston Celtics on April 25, 1950. *Courtesy of Duquesne University Athletics.*

As long as nobody called me "nigger," it was all right. "Nigger" automatically meant a fight!

There was another game canceled at the University of Miami. These incidents put the school on notice that they could run into situations like this and I think they tried to anticipate them. I remember a period when every time we played the game below the Mason-Dixon line, our team would be setting a precedent for a "mixed" contest. Games in some states were out of the question. Alabama, Mississippi and those other Deep South states were prime examples.

Racism wasn't limited to the South. We were playing the University of Cincinnati out in the Midwest. There was an out-of-bounds play and they were lining up to guard us. One guy shouted[,] "I got the nigger!" I walked over to him and said, "And I got your mother in my jockstrap!" He was shocked. After the game, he came over to apologize. I thought I had already said what needed to be said and I told him that. I also said, "If you can take what I said, then I can take a thousand niggers."[21]

After his college career, Cooper joined the Harlem Globetrotters before he was drafted by the Boston Celtics. It was not an experience that he entirely enjoyed.

What really disturbed me was how the Globetrotters were treated by Saperstein. When I was with the Trotters, they were playing a series of games against the College All-Stars, who were almost all white. While we all traveled in the same chartered bus, the hotel accommodations were very different. Saperstein had one of the few solid moneymakers in the game at that time. The NBA was even on thin ice at that time, yet Saperstein had his black players staying in dirty, roach-infested holes in the wall. I used to point this out to the Globetrotter players. Not only were the living conditions bad, but there was a big pay difference between the NBA players and themselves. For doing that I got the reputation as a troublemaker.[22]

His time with the Globetrotters was short. He was destined for something better: the Boston Celtics were on the horizon.

When the Celtics drafted me in the second round in 1950, I wasn't surprised. A scout for Boston named Art Spector had already talked to me about the possibility before the draft. At the time of the draft, I was on a three-week tour with the Globetrotters, so I was pretty confident about my ability to continue as a ballplayer. When I joined the Celtics, the players' attitude toward me was pretty good. Coach Auerbach and the owner, Walter Brown, made me feel at home.[23]

After being drafted by the Celtics, Cooper spoke with Brown and understood the opportunity and risk that were apparent that day:

> Thank you for having the courage to offer me a chance in pro basketball. I hope I'll never give you cause to regret it. . . . I'm convinced that no NBA team would have made the move on blacks in 1950 if the Celtics hadn't drafted me early, taking me in the second round. Seven rounds later the Washington Caps took Earl Lloyd, and a couple months later the New York Knicks bought Sweetwater Clifton's contract from the Harlem Globetrotters. But it was the case of the Caps and Knicks following the Celtics' lead. Walter Brown was the man who put his neck on the line. Walter Brown was a gentleman of backbone. Give all the credit to that man who wasn't afraid to stick his neck out all the way. He made it possible when nobody else would.[24]

During his six-year NBA career, Cooper played four years with Boston, one with the Milwaukee Hawks, and split time in his final season with St. Louis and Ft. Wayne. He averaged 6.7 points and 5.9 rebounds per game. As a pro, he became a strong or power forward, where he covered the opposing team's best scorer. His days as a leaper largely were over. His experiences in Boston and Milwaukee were very different, as he remembered,

> I had good support in terms of acceptance by my teammates and, most of all, by Red and Mr. Brown. I felt a strong relationship with them all. While with the Hawks, I had to stay in a reform school in Shreveport and I wasn't allowed to play in Baton Rouge.[25]

During his career, Cooper was not immune to incidents on the road or with opposing fans as he remembered during his lone year with Milwaukee when they were on the road in Moline, Illinois.

> One of their players called me a black bastard. I asked him what he said and he repeated it. So I pushed him in the face as hard as I could. I wanted to fight him, but I wanted him to throw the first punch. He wouldn't fight—but everyone else did. Both benches cleared and everyone started pairing off. Bob Brannum and Mel

Hutchins, a couple of muscle guys, squared off. Even the opposing coaches, Auerbach and Doxie Moore, went at it. It was quite a sight, the worst fight I remember. I was thrown out (of the game) and fined by the league. But when the commissioner, Maurice Podoloff, heard the full story, he rescinded the fine.

There were things I had to adapt to throughout my career that I wouldn't have had to if I were white. I was expected to play good, sound intensified defense and really get under the boards for the heavy dirty work. Yet, I never received the frills or extra pay of the white players. The major thing I had to adjust to upon entering the pros was the stationary pivot. In college, with my size and agility, I liked to go down low and utilize that space, but in the pros a big man in the middle would clog that area up.[26]

Cooper continued,

Injuries were a problem too. If I was hurt, they got suspicious. Auerbach, in fact, had me labeled a hypochondriac. In my four years in Boston, I never had an X-ray—lots of stitches, but never an X-ray. There were one or two white players on the Celtics that if they jammed a finger it was a cause of great concern. But then you know how strong black skin is. We don't get hurt. Ha!

Traveling around the league, I encountered all the problems any black man of that period—be he a diplomat, a porter, or a basketball player. I had to sleep in different hotels than the team in Washington and Baltimore. My teammates and the management acquiesced to this like everybody else at the time. Only later when things had changed somewhat and players with stature—like Bill Russell and Elgin Baylor—came along did conditions change. Being superstars and working in a better environment, they could boycott games if they felt things were unfair.

After four years with the Celtics and two with the Hawks, I spent another year with a team called the Harlem Magicians, sort of an offshoot of the Globetrotters. I could have stayed with them—the money was pretty good—but I was beginning to get tired of it. I also had a serious automobile accident and that helped me make the decision to stop playing.[27]

In looking back on his career, he understood its importance but also that he was no Jackie Robinson:

There was only one Jackie. When he broke baseball's color line four seasons earlier, he shouldered a terrific burden that helped all other sports. A lot of the acceptance he pioneered transferred over to all those who followed him in all sports. Besides I don't think my background and personality would have allowed me to make the kind of sacrifices Jackie did. He really went through hell and took a lot. I never could have done that. Yes, I may have helped carry on what Jackie started. But it was inevitable after he had blazed the trail. So, yes, I feel a sense of accomplishment in a very modest way and can't help but feel proud. But when I was playing, I never thought about all that. I was more preoccupied with just making the team.[28]

After his playing days ended, he became active in the parks and recreation system in Pittsburgh. His contributions to the game and its integration were finally recognized when he was inducted into the Naismith Memorial Basketball Hall of Fame in 1976.

After Cooper was selected, Sweetwater Clifton was the first black player to sign an NBA contract. Meeting one day in New York to discuss their roster for the upcoming season, Ned Irish asked his coach, Joe Lapchick, "What do you think of Sweetwater Clifton?"

"We still need a big man, and I think this fellow from the Globetrotters is the answer."

"How good would he be in our league?"

"Plenty."

"He's only 6'5" or 6'6", but he owns those long arms that reach past his knees. Clifton can help us, and I recommend we sign him."[29]

Irish went to work trying to sign Clifton to a Knicks contract.

When we last left Clifton, he was a member of the Harlem Globetrotters for two seasons in 1948–49 and 1949–50. In the summer of 1950, Saperstein sold his contract to the Knicks for $12,500. He kept $10,000 and gave the remaining $2,500 to Clifton. When he joined the Knicks, he was a twenty-nine-year-old rookie. He played with the Knicks for seven seasons until 1956–57 and then played one final year with the Detroit Pistons before his NBA career ended. In eight seasons, he averaged 10 points and 8.2 rebounds per game. He made one All-Star Game and played in fifty-three playoff teams. He still liked to play, so he joined the Harlem Stars, an independent team, for three seasons, before reuniting with Abe Saperstein when Saperstein started his short-lived American Basketball League in 1961–62. Clifton played with Chicago before rejoining the Harlem Globetrotters for two more seasons in addition to the Harlem Magicians for two additional seasons. After twenty years of traveling the country playing professional ball, Clifton finally hung up his high tops in 1964–65.

As a rookie, Clifton was already a well-established player in his own right. He had been the centerpiece of many teams, but he learned that his game was going to change once he joined the NBA. That did not sit well with him or other early black stars, who felt they had to temper their style to fit in the team. Clifton, like Chuck Cooper, felt like he had less freedom to create and score than they had in the past.

> When I first came with the Knicks I found I had to change over, you know, play in their style. They didn't want me to be fancy, or do anything like that. All the time I played there they never did get another good, black ballplayer to play with me, somebody who knew what I was doing, you understand. And that kinda held me back, 'cause you can't do something with the other guys because they played the straight way. I felt like I was sacrificing myself for some guy, and I don't think other guys would have done that.[30]

During his NBA career, Clifton was not immune to racism on the road or from opposing players and fans. Norm Drucker, an official during those years, recalled some of the tough times the black players had, including Clifton.

> When he played, the league had very few black players and many of the white players were reared in the South and had some built-in bias. I wasn't in Boston, but the referee who worked the game told me that Bob Harris made some comment to Clifton and also made a physical challenge. Clifton hit him and Harris lost several front teeth. The Boston bench started to come toward Clifton, and when Sweetwater started to meet them, they all retreated. It could have been that they didn't agree with Harris's comments, or that they used good judgment in not testing Clifton.
>
> There was an incident in St. Louis. In 1958, Walter Dukes and Sweetwater were playing for Detroit. St. Louis was not a very cordial city for the black players. Dukes went for a ball behind the basket and ended up in the first row. Suddenly, Dukes is in a fight with some fans. At this point, Clifton runs toward the stands and with his humor yells, "Walter, you take the front row, I've got the second

row." The early black players had some problems and most of these were with fans. The one city in which fans yelled obscene remarks at players was St. Louis. As the years went on and the black players started to enter the league in greater numbers, there was a steady decline of this bigotry.[31]

Clifton was not the only former New York Renaissance player looking to make history during the 1950–51 season. Hank DeZonie was the fourth black player to suit up in a professional game during that NBA season. However, he only lasted five games, leaving his contributions long overlooked and forgotten. As a child, DeZonie had two loves: "This is what I wanted to do. I aspired to be a basketball player or a lifeguard. I'd still rather go to the beach than anywhere." As he developed, DeZonie had great leaping ability and was rugged underneath the boards. As he recalled, "I got up pretty good. I'd go get it, keep it and do what I wanted with it."[32]

When we last left DeZonie, he was part of the Dayton Rens, who were making history by becoming the first all-black team to play in a white league during the 1948–49 NBL season. DeZonie then played with the New York Harlem Yankees in 1949–50 and Saratoga in 1950–51, both teams in the ABL, and he caught the attention of one of the opposing coaches, Red Sarachek. Sarachek was friendly with Ben Kerner of the Tri-Cities Blackhawks, who recommended that he sign DeZonie for the upcoming season. As Sarachek recalled,

> Kerner was not that type [who would reject a player because he was black]. I don't think he minded. He looked for a player, just like I did. It was an opportunity [for DeZonie] to go up, which was better than vagabonding with the Rens, . . . He was a good player, a tough player underneath the boards.[33]

In fact, he possessed many skills that would make him attractive to a number of NBA teams. He was strong, with great leaping ability, and a strong presence underneath the boards.

After Lloyd, Cooper, and Clifton had secured professional contracts, DeZonie finally had his opportunity. He signed with Tri-Cities and debuted on December 3 against the New York Knicks. He tallied six points but would only play in four more games that season. In five games, he scored seventeen points for 3.4 points per game average. On

December 14, eleven days after his first game, he was waived. The experience was no longer for him. He was older than many of his teammates and had spent years on the road, barnstorming and living in segregated conditions.

Reflecting on his brief stint decades later, he recalled,

> I was through. I wasn't playing. I wasn't interested. Red just thought I could play and after I got there I was past that stuff. To go in some segregated affair, forget it. This is how it was, I couldn't see it at all. Segregated from the rest of the team that was staying at a plush hotel. That would turn you inside out. The thorns of segregation left scars that were unbelievable. These [white] people don't realize what they have done to other people. It was a miserable experience because all the fun was out of the game. The accommodations, the segregation. I wasn't interested in it. I was staying in some old rooming house run by some old woman and the coach didn't know night from day. I lived better than that. Once the days in the bus were over, it was more fun playing in the schoolyard. [34]

With that brief stint, DeZonie's contributions to basketball integration faded into history. Afterward, he did return to professional basketball, playing two more years with Saratoga and Manchester of the ABL before retiring in 1952–53 after twelve years as a professional basketball player.

While the NBA integrated in its second year, 1950–51, the BAA, one of its predecessors, did not, although it did flirt with the possibility a few times. It did not appear that any of these attempts were that serious. First, in 1949 or 1950, the New York Knicks tried to sign Don Barksdale. Instead, he stayed with the Oakland Bittners in the Amateur Athletic Union (AAU). Second, it was reported that in October 1948 (for the upcoming 1948–49 season), the Chicago Stags signed six black players and offered them a contract to attend training camp. Although none of them made the team, all were part of a tryout. They included Leon Wright, Irving Ward, Henry Blackburn, George Raby, Arthur Wilson, and Leonard Jordan. [35] If true, their stay with the Stags in training camp was brief. Two other professional leagues during this time period also did not attempt to integrate. Maurice White started the ill-fated Professional Basketball League of America, which did not last even one full season in 1947–48. In that shortened, fateful season, that league did not try to integrate. The National Professional Basketball League (NPBL) did not integrate in its lone season, 1950–51.

Although the BAA did not integrate, a few of the minor basketball leagues at that time did so. The Eastern League and the ABL both integrated during this time period. It should be noted that both leagues, although professional in status, were not considered "major" like the NBA. They were weekend leagues; players would play three games and then return to work on Monday, supplementing their regular jobs with some extra money playing basketball on the weekends. From 1957 to 1961, the Eastern League integrated with Hal Lear, Dick Gaines, and Wally Choice playing for the Easton-Phillipsburg Madisons.

The ABL enjoyed some success in integrating. For some historical perspective, the first incarnation of the ABL lasted from 1925–1931 and then went dormant due to the Depression. When it returned for the 1933–34 season, it was a significantly different league in scope and operation. In its original incarnation, the ABL was considered "national" with teams in Brooklyn, Washington, D.C., Cleveland, Rochester, Fort Wayne, Boston, Chicago, Detroit, Buffalo, Baltimore, and Philadelphia. By the 1930s, the Depression forced the league to scale down its operation and keep teams close together to reduce travel expenses. Teams were confined mostly to Trenton, Brooklyn, Philadelphia, Newark, Hoboken, New Britain, New York, Kingston, Paterson, Washington, D.C., Wilmington, and Troy.

By 1946–47, the ABL was considered an unofficial minor league to the BAA. In 1947, Preston Wilcox signed with the New York Gothams, Hank DeZonie played with Trenton, and Bobby Knight was a member of the Hartford Hurricanes. During the 1948–49 season, Johnny Isaacs suited up for Brooklyn, and Bobby Knight continued with Hartford. Dolly King and Eddie Younger played for Scranton. In 1949–50, DeZonie and George Crowe were on the New York roster, Tom Sealy was with Hartford, and Pop Gates and Eddie Younger with Scranton, In 1950–51, Saratoga's roster included Hank DeZonie, Sonny Wood, Jim Usry, Charlie Isles, Clarence Bell, Eddie Younger, and Johnny Isaacs. Dolly King played for Scranton. During these years, Dolly King and Eddie Younger were also signed by the Waterbury Colonials of the New England League.

As Ron Thomas writes in his excellent book *They Cleared the Lane: The NBA's Black Pioneers,*

Overall the integration of the NBA went relatively smoothly in the 1950s and the early 1960s. Black players encountered some blatantly racist acts that even ignited a few fights, and frustrations about their roles on teams and hassles about accommodations in the South continued. But the situation in the NBA didn't come close to the racial slurs, high spikes, beanballs, and threatened boycotts that Jackie Robinson endured; and no NBA players had to face the physical intimidation (and sometimes pain) that white National Football League players inflicted on back opponents in the late 1940s and early 1950s. Football's violent nature made black players an easy target for whites who despised them. Whatever the reasons, the NBA had been a more than tolerable experience for its black players. [36]

Having too many black players on a team was a concern for owners. What would the fans think? Would this hurt attendance and ratings? There was no written rule how many black players a team could have, and it would take a number of years before teams were comfortable having more than one. As Red Auerbach noted,

> In the beginning, the more timid owners did worry about the effect of the Negro on the game and did ask themselves: how many can we have? There was a period of years when some of the owners decided that they would hold their squads to no more than two Negroes, then three, then four, then five. It wasn't anything anybody talked about; it just happened. We were all aware of it. We knew that some owners were brooding about the fact that the time was coming when they might be fielding an all-Negro team. [37]

After that first season, more blacks were signed by NBA squads. In 1951–52, Cooper was still with Boston, and Clifton was again a member of the New York Knicks. Two teams, though, integrated that season. The Baltimore Bullets signed Don Barksdale and Davage Minor while the Milwaukee Hawks added Bob Wilson.

The following season, 1952–53, there were six blacks in the league—Barksdale and Blaine Denning with Baltimore, Cooper with Boston, and Clifton with New York. Lloyd had returned from his military duties and signed with the Syracuse Nationals as his original team, the Washington Capitols, were no longer in existence. Wilson was no longer in the league; his place on the Hawks roster was taken by Minor, who moved from Baltimore to Milwaukee.

In the 1953–54 season, Clifton was still a Knick, Lloyd was in Syracuse, and Cooper was joined in Boston by Barksdale, who left Baltimore. His place in Baltimore was assumed by Ray Felix and Rollen Hans, while Milwaukee continued its revolving door of having one black on its team. Gone was Minor, who was replaced by Isaac "Rabbit" Walthour, who was signed by the Boston Celtics during the summer but never made the team.

Four first-time black players made rosters for the 1954–55 season: Jim Tucker joined Lloyd in Syracuse. Ken McBride signed with Milwaukee, which added Cooper from Boston. Philadelphia added Jackie Moore. Barksdale stayed with Boston while Felix moved from Baltimore to New York, joining Clifton. Bob Knight also joined the Knicks. Thus, for the first time, three of the five integrated teams had two black players apiece. Tucker and Lloyd became the first two black players to win an NBA championship as Syracuse won its one and only NBA championship.

In the following season, 1955–56, the Rochester Royals added three players: Ed Fleming, Dick Ricketts, and Maurice Stokes. The New York Knicks also added a third player, Walter Dukes, to join Felix and Clifton. Lloyd and Tucker stayed with Syracuse, Moore remained with Philadelphia, and Jesse Arnelle joined Cooper with the Fort Wayne Zollner Pistons. Robert Williams joined Minneapolis.

An interesting story during this period is that Marques Haynes had an opportunity to sign with the Philadelphia Warriors in 1953. According to Haynes (who turned down a $35,000 offer to play for the Philadelphia Warriors in 1953),

> Goose Tatum had left the Globetrotters and had joined my team, the Magicians. Now, if I had joined the Warriors . . . you see Saperstein thought that Goose would come back. I had bookers and I had people in all parts of the country that got games for me. This is how he was thinking. Mainly because if I would have taken that, Goose would have had no alternative but to go back and play for the Globetrotters. He was making more with me. If I had not turned it down, Goose would have been out there by himself. He wouldn't have known what to do. He didn't have the bookers or anything else.[38]

Knowing that his good friend Goose Tatum would have struggled without him and most likely would have returned to the Globetrotters under Saperstein, Haynes helped his friend's professional career rather than taking his shot at playing in the NBA. Everyone who played with and against Haynes knew he had the talent to play. As Minneapolis Lakers coach John Kundla remarked, "Marques Haynes could have played in the pros."[39]

During this period—the first six years of NBA integration—two of these early players stood out as having the potential to be the first black basketball superstars, Don Barksdale and Maurice Stokes.

A native of Berkeley, California, Don Barksdale excelled at both basketball and track. Despite his basketball interest, he was passed over for inclusion on his high school team for four years. "Dutch Rudquist, the playground director at San Pablo, finally asked the coach why I wasn't good enough to make the team. The coach told Dutch, 'I've already got one black player.'" No doubt disappointed, Barksdale learned a valuable lesson and set his sights on the bigger prize.

> I learned early in life that complaining does very little. If you were vocal in those days, you'd find yourself out in the cold. They'd walk around you. I'm not a passive man, but I am a determined person. I always found a way of getting where I was going.[40]

He finally got his chance to shine when he attended Marin Junior College for two years, 1941–43, where he led his team to two California state championships. His efforts and exploits earned him a scholarship to UCLA. He made an immediate impact, helping the Bruins defeat city rival University of Southern California (USC) for the first time in forty-two tries. He scored eighteen points in that victory. He continued to play well and eventually was drafted into the military, serving from 1944 to 1946. During that time, he held the scoring record in the military and broke the all-time single season record, 1,288 points for a 23.6 average while leading Camp Ross to a 35–2 record.

He returned from the military and immediately set his sights again on USC, where he scored thirty points against them in 1947. He finished his college career as an all-Pacific Coast Conference and became the first African American to earn consensus Helms Foundation All-America honors in 1947. During his college career, his team was cogni-

A star at UCLA, Don Barksdale became the first African American NBA All-Star in 1953. *Courtesy of UCLA Athletics.*

zant of the fact they were an integrated team and would face challenges on the road.

> UCLA was extremely careful about where they went. They had learned the hard way with Jackie [Robinson] and Kenny [Washington] where not to go and to stay away from the South if there is a black player on the team. They would not book colleges who had any type of segregation of their athletes.
>
> I graduated in December of '47 from UCLA. At that time, there were no opportunities in professional sports as the NBA had an unwritten law against admitting blacks. Although Jackie Robinson had broken the color line in baseball that year, basketball would still not accept blacks. Fortunately there were AAU [Amateur Athletic Union] basketball teams which were just about as big as the pros. In fact the AAU was bigger than the NBA at that time. The NBA only had eight or nine teams while the AAU teams were spread out all over the country. Such teams were the Denver Nuggets and the L.A. 20th Century-Fox team, the Golden State team, the Oakland Bittners, in San Francisco Stewart Chevrolets and Borlo AC, an Italian athletic club. AAU basketball was huge.[41]

Barksdale joined the Oakland Bittners; in so doing, he became the first black to break the AAU color barrier. He played with Oakland and after his first season, he was selected to the All-America AAU team. That led him to earn an invitation to the 1948 U.S. Olympic trials.

> Although it was never publicized too much, I was the first black Olympian basketball player too.
>
> I was lucky enough to be one of the two at-large AAU players through the hard work of a guy named Fred Major [Maggiori] and some other people. I made the Olympic team. I had to join the Phillips 66 team in [Bartlesville], Oklahoma. It was a little rough because there was extreme prejudice, extreme segregation. There were white and colored water fountains, different hotels and different travel arrangements. It was unbelievably ridiculous but it was the way things were in the South at that time. The ball players were all pretty good. One or two of them gave me a bad time but the majority was very supportive. The longer we were together the closer we became.
>
> I started out with a very stormy relationship with Adolph Rupp. He told me it was a pleasure coaching me in his first experience

working with a black player. More importantly, he suggested that if he could find a black player for the University of Kentucky he would. He broke the SEC color line about six years later. [42]

During the trials,

> I was staying with a black family and somebody called up and said, "If this guy is out there playing tomorrow night, he is going to get shot." It was a threat you know, and the people I was staying with were scared to death. They put me on the phone and the guy said, "I'd advise you not to go out on that court tomorrow night. If you do you are going to get shot, bang." I told a few people about the fool. I also said, "I am not going to worry about it." We played the game. They used to make the blacks people sit in the end zone and then everybody else sat around. I am out on the court and we are playing and in the first half with three minutes to go before the half. The team took a time out. The trainer came out and had a little tray with a bottle of water and a bucket and some little cups and a towel.
>
> He comes out and he is holding the tray up and Cab Renick reached the bottle and took a swig and put it back and spit in the bucket. The next guy picked up this bottle and took a swig and spit in the bucket. Now there are 12,000 to 15,000 white and about 1,000 blacks. I am the next man so here I am and I said, "Oh shit, what do I do?" I grabbed the bottle and took a swig in the bucket just like everybody. Twelve thousand people shut up and the black people must have thought, "Oh here it comes." I said, "Oh my god." I hand the bottle to Shorty Carpenter and thought, "What's he going to do with it? If he turns down the bottle. . . ." He took it and held it for one half a second and took a drink and all of a sudden it broke the whole tension. Had he not drank after me, I do not know how things would have proceeded. I have never forgotten him and I have said it a few times, "Thank god he was 6'7" and weighed 250." Nobody would mess with him anyway. He has never realized what a great service he performed on that occasion. [43]

Barksdale and his teammates made it to London for the 1948 Olympics. They earned the gold medal, and eventually he returned to the states and Oakland to resume his basketball career, where he led the Bittners to an AAU national championship. For the next three years, he was an All-American. He was a top talent, as noted in a piece written for *Ebony* magazine in 1949:

Barksdale's most amazing court forte is his agile, tricky pivot and from the bucket he can feint and fake his opponents out of their trunks. Tremendous endurance that shows in a terrific pace from whistle to whistle and as deft a pair of hands as any man that ever handled a basketball have helped establish him as a greatest cage star in the land.[44]

Barksdale recalled,

Because the NBA was a closed shop for athletes I went back to the Bittners and played. I think we fully expected that the NBA would open its doors, but they did not. It was a couple of more years before they started talking to black athletes about joining the NBA. I know that Ned Irish of New York Knicks was interested in me. By that time I had formed a beer distributorship and I was making pretty good money and playing. This is in '49 and '50 and the Bittners had gone out of business, but a team called the Blue 'N' Gold Nuggets, which was a beer company, had picked up the sponsorship. I had the distributorship for Blue 'N' Gold Beer in Oakland and started to make pretty good money at it. When they started talking to me about NBA in '50 I was not that interested, because the money they offered was less than I was making. I could have been the first black in the NBA had I listened to Ned Irish. Baltimore finally signed me in '51 at a salary that at that time was huge, $20,000 a year. It was a $60,000 contract for three years that was huge money at that time.[45]

Barksdale spent two years with Baltimore, and part of his contract included a postgame radio show. It was not without its difficult moments. One issue he encountered: his white teammates did not always pass him the ball. This was also true of the other blacks in the league.

Sweetwater should have been scoring twice what he scored—if he could have had the ball enough. I should have been scoring eight or nine more points a game, and Lloyd should have scored more, too. They had all the black players guard each other [whenever the three teams with blacks met]. We ran up and down the court and never saw the ball. Finally, the four of us got together and raised hell. They said it wasn't intentional. But it was degrading.[46]

Throughout the tough times, he could always lean on a fellow UCLA Bruin, Jackie Robinson, "Through it all, I had a great deal of inspiration.

A friend of mine, a great guy named Jackie Robinson, had talked to me, explained what I'd have to go through. He was a guiding light."[47]

Barksdale remembered,

> He told me how rough it was in the majors, how tough it was to keep his mouth shut. But that was the agreement he made with Branch Rickey when he came to the Dodgers. He had to take it. At that time, there were no black players in pro basketball, and he told me I might have to go through the same thing. It was Jackie who convinced me I could take whatever they had to dish out. I could take it so long as I could play.[48]

After two years in Baltimore, he was traded to Boston.

> Coming out of Baltimore, Boston was a dream. In Baltimore I could not go to the restaurants and eat. I had to eat at hamburger places. I could not stay at the hotel and the racism was a little bit rough. Boston by comparison was pretty good. I want to tell you this. I did not have time to be bulldozed by prejudice in a city because we were playing 70 games in a year. We were either on the road or playing at home.
>
> The only people with who we really came in contact with were fellow basketball players and a few outsiders. In Boston, I would say that the outside people were extremely hard to meet. Whether it was racism or what it was, they were just set aside. We had a coach named Red Auerbach, who kept your mind on basketball all the time. He was one of the best coaches I have ever played under. When we traveled to a place like St. Louis, there was always a problem. One of the nicest guys to ever play the game was Bob Cousy who welcomed me with open arms and made me feel at home in Boston. Another guy by the name of Johnny Most, a radio announcer, also made me welcome. He and another guy named Eddie Miller, shared an apartment with me. They were both white and I was black and there was another black kid on the team, Chuck Cooper. We did not have time to think about racism.[49]

Barksdale played well in Boston. Auerbach was glad to have picked up Barksdale for his team.

> Watching Don play basketball was like watching a ballet. He was past his prime when we got him, but you could still see the quality out

there. The league hadn't seen anyone as tall as he was who could do
the things he could do with a basketball. Tall men in those days were
gangly or big and slow. But Don was like a 6-foot-6 guard. He could
run with anyone in the league, put the ball on the floor, even dunk.[50]

Barksdale played two seasons with Baltimore and two with Boston. He
averaged eleven points and eight rebounds per game. He earned another first by becoming the first black player to play in an NBA All-Star
Game. The 1953 All-Star Game was held in Fort Wayne, Indiana, and
he played eleven minutes and scored one point.

> All we (the league's black players) would say when we got together
> was, "I'm glad one of us made that sucker." I didn't touch the ball
> much and you can't score if you don't have the ball. That happens. I
> didn't play that long. At least I got in the game.[51]

As he recalled decades later, "I didn't touch the ball much in the game,
but at least I was on the team. I was very proud of it."[52]

> In '55 I started making pretty good money in radio and decided that
> I would give up pro ball. I told Walter Brown, who owned the Boston
> Celtics and Red Auerbach that I knew a good prospect and that I
> would scout him for the Celtics. The kid's name was Bill Russell. I
> went about 15 times to see Bill. I was crazy about him and recom-
> mended him highly to the Celtics.[53]

As Barksdale's career was winding down, that of Maurice Stokes was on
the rise.

Like Chuck Cooper, Maurice Stokes grew up playing basketball in
football-crazed western Pennsylvania. He lived with his family in
Homewood and played the game as a child. He attended Westinghouse
High School and was a starter his junior and senior years.

He enrolled at Saint Francis University and single-handedly propelled the tiny college to national stardom. As a collegian, he averaged
twenty-two points and twenty-four rebounds per game. In 1955, he led
his team to the National Invitation Tournament (NIT), where they finished fourth. His outstanding efforts throughout the tournament earned
him Most Valuable Player honors. His college career over, Stokes was
bound for the NBA. Les Harrison, owner of the Rochester Royals, had
his eye on the small college player for quite some time. Like previous

black players, Stokes was approached by the Harlem Globetrotters; the NBA sought to sign him as well. This tension with Abe Saperstein still existed, although Harrison would not let that stop him from getting his man.

> Abe [Saperstein] didn't talk to me for years after that. He did a lot for the league by playing doubleheaders, with the NBA teams playing the second game, to help the gate. In fact, I had some NBA owners tell me, "Lay off Stokes. Abe had been good to us—we need him." I said, "Listen. I talked to the Stokes kid. He doesn't want to play for the Globetrotters. He wants the NBA. I want him and I'm going to sign him." So I did. [54]

Stokes joined the Rochester Royals and became an instant contributor. Rugged, strong, and a fierce rebounder, Stokes made his mark under the boards. In short, he was a rebounding machine. Stokes played two years with Rochester and one with Cincinnati. He averaged 16.4 points and 17.3 rebounds per game. He played in three All-Star Games. He was a three-time All NBA Second Team and was named Rookie of the Year in 1956. He led the NBA in rebounding in 1957.

Like other black athletes at the time, Stokes faced his share of racism while on the road with his teammates. Jack Twyman remembered one incident: "I went out with Bob Pettit and Cliff Hagan and Maurice and a couple of other guys. The guy (at the bar) said, 'We don't serve blacks' so we all got up and left. We went to another restaurant." Another teammate, Bobby Wanzer recalled, "We went out for our pregame meal and the manager came up to me and said, 'We don't serve colored people.' So we went to a Chinese restaurant instead." [55]

Stokes's NBA career was only three years before a tragic accident cut short his basketball future. On the final regular-season game of the 1958 season, Stokes fell and hit his head. He eventually was diagnosed with encephalopathy, a brain injury that causes damage to his motor control center. His teammate, Jack Twyman, became his primary caregiver, and benefits were played to raise money for his care. His died in 1970. After his injury, he never played in another NBA game.

In those three years, though, the country had its first glimpse of what a black superstar could be. Despite the short-lived careers of Stokes and Barksdale, the first wave of black basketball superstars was on the horizon.

Maurice Stokes was a star with Saint Francis University, but his professional career with the Cincinnati Royals was cut short by a brain injury. *Courtesy of Saint Francis University.*

5

THE RISE OF AFRICAN AMERICAN STARS IN THE NBA

December 26, 1964

As the Boston Celtics began the 1964–65 season, they had won six straight championships and seven of the last eight. They were the league's top team, in the midst of their historic eight consecutive titles (1959–66). They had depth, scoring, defense, rebounding, and shot blocking. They were a complete team. The 1964–65 season started well, and the Celtics continued to set the pace in the Eastern Conference. As late December arrived, starting forward Tommy Heinsohn went down with an injury. Head coach Red Auerbach needed a replacement, and he selected Willie Naulls, a solid player from UCLA. On December 26, 1964, the Celtics traveled to St. Louis to take on the Hawks. The Celtics lineup card that evening included Bill Russell, Sam Jones, K. C. Jones, Satch Sanders, and Willie Naulls. It was the first time in NBA history that a team had fielded an all-black starting five.

The Celtics started sluggish that game and fell behind by fifteen points in the early going. They fared slightly better in the second period and whittled the deficit to ten points. After regrouping at halftime, the Celtics totally dominated in the second half, outscoring the Hawks, 48–25, and winning, 97–84. Naulls stayed in the lineup, and the Celtics won the next eleven games. They would go on to win another championship, their seventh in a row.

While the Celtics' starting five during this streak was all black players, their bench was comprised of all white players. Auerbach was unaware of the historic nature of that game and of an all-black starting five. As he said,

> First of all, I had no idea that I had started five black players until a writer pointed it out to me a few weeks later. It didn't make a difference to me what color any of my players were. I was putting the five best players out on the court so that we could win. [1]

Filling out a lineup card that featured a starting five of all black players in the middle of the 1960s was most definitely not an afterthought. Society was changing in the 1960s and 1970s, and African American athletes were at the forefront of this change on the court, in the press, and in the marketing and advertising world. According to author Lew Freedman,

> Five blacks starters. At the peak of the Civil Rights movement, the world noticed. This was a seminal moment at a time when blacks were battling for equal rights and seeking to knock down barriers placed in front of them for a couple of centuries. Obviously, Auerbach recognized it was an important moment too, but he never made a big deal out of it. To him, it was all about fairness, not being a pioneer. Neither Auerbach nor his NBA contemporaries had an inkling that by 2007 the league would be 80 percent black and the comparative curiosity would be a white starting player. Still, when Auerbach died in 2006, *Boston Globe* sports columnist Bob Ryan wrote that it took "chutzpah" for Auerbach to start five blacks in the mid-1960s. [2]

Auerbach may never have thought of himself as a pioneer, but he was. According to historian David Halberstam,

> Intolerant and opinionated in many areas, on the most important question in sports in the fifties and sixties—the use of black players—he was the most tolerant and farsighted man imaginable. He immediately adapted his game to them and the quicker, more exciting game they created. [3]

With the emergence of the first wave of great African American NBA superstars, a new, more exciting brand of basketball began to emerge. Players such as Bill Russell, Wilt Chamberlain, Oscar Robertson, Elgin

Baylor, Kareem Abdul-Jabbar, and Julius Erving were forever changing the way the game was played, the role of athletes in society, and how African American athletes were perceived by white America. Each of these players elevated the game, introducing a more exciting game that later became a staple of the modern-day NBA. According to John Smallwood,

> The presence of the African-American player changed the way the NBA game was played. Because African-American athletes had been so long excluded from the structured white organizations of the game, they were not bound by the traditional approaches to basketball. The segregation of the era meant that basketball developed independently in the African-American community, separate from the more conservative style that dominated early professional leagues, such as the BAA. Since African-Americans could not play in the pro leagues, black semipro players continued with the styles they had utilized in college, which were more conducive to wide open play.[4]

Basketball in the 1960s cannot be discussed without focusing on Bill Russell. No player before or since has had such a profound effect on the game. He was a brilliant shot blocker, revolutionary in how defenses not only played but could alter a game. For Russell, however, this was not immediate. It did not occur overnight. It took years to hone his defensive talents and to develop his own philosophy as to how defenses can impact a ball game.

Russell was born in Louisiana, but his family moved to Oakland, California, because his father believed that he and his young family would have more opportunities there than in the South. Russell grew up in a housing project, a tall, gangly child. He spent time reading in the library, but basketball was not a sport that took hold with him immediately. He was cut from his junior high school team. At McClymonds High School, a similar fate seemed to await until his junior varsity coach, George Powles, stepped in. He kept him on his team and gave him $2 to join the local Boys Club. There, he would practice the game in a safe environment.

Toward the end of his high school career, Russell was not thinking of college and had no scholarship offers. In a late-season game, Hal DeJulio was scouting for the University of San Francisco and liked what he saw of Russell even though he knew Russell was still a work in progress. DeJulio arranged for a scholarship, and he soon had the chance to attend college.

While at the University of San Francisco, Russell began to develop and hone his philosophy for playing defense, rebounding, and blocking shots. Together, he and K. C. Jones would talk for hours about the geometry of basketball. As he recalled later,

> Ever since my freshman year I have looked at the game of basketball as a vertical and horizontal game. For example, jumping is a controlled asset of skill. Sometimes I jumped to touch the top of the backboard, sometimes I hardly left my feet. I have noticed that many highlight films of me show me catching so and so from behind to block his shot and get the rebound. I am always asked how I was able to do that. The answer is in merging of the horizontal and vertical games. It all starts with imagination. As a player with the ball moved down the court, I visualized the angle that I would need to block his shot. Then, trailing him, I would take a step to the left so that I would then be coming at the shooter from an angle, allowing me to block his shot with my left hand while landing to the player's side rather than on his back. Not only did it turn out to be an intimidating move, but also by arriving on the opposite side from where I'd blocked the shot, what I had done might even have seemed a little mystical.[5]

While in college, he led the University of San Francisco to two NCAA championships in 1955 and 1956. He was named the NCAA Tournament Most Outstanding Player in 1955, the UPI College Player of the Year in 1956, a two-time Helms Player of the Year in 1955 and 1956, a two-time First Team All-American in 1955 and 1956, and the West Coast Conference Player of the Year in 1956. In 1956, he was a member of the gold medal–winning basketball team in the Melbourne Olympics.

When he finally suited up for the Celtics in late December 1957, the game was never the same. Defensively, rebounding, and blocking shots, Russell forever altered how the game could be played from a defensive standpoint. As Auerbach noted,

> Nobody has ever blocked shots in the pros before Russell came along. He upset everybody. And the thing about it is that he blocked

shots with a purpose. You see today a lot of players will block a shot as hard as they can, and it goes out of bounds. Russell always tried to control the ball when he blocked it. He would block a shot and aim it towards a teammate. It was almost like a pass. Nobody else had ever done that.[6]

With Russell manning the center, the Celtics were an entirely new team. Prior to his arrival, the Celtics were a guard-dominated team, never having the needed big man to get them past the New York Knicks or Syracuse Nationals. Now with Russell, they had their big man. After a few months with Russell in the fold, the team was ready for the 1957 playoffs. The team defeated Syracuse before facing the St. Louis Hawks in the finals. The series went seven games, and Boston won an epic seventh game in double overtime, 125–123, to claim their first title and the beginning of a dynasty.

After losing the 1958 title in a rematch to St. Louis, Russell would emerge as the most dominating force in basketball, leading the Celtics to titles from 1959 to 1966. It was a run unmatched in basketball history, before or since. During his time, Russell intimidated his opponents with his shot blocking and rebounding ability. In the 1959 finals, the Celtics swept the Minneapolis Lakers in four straight contests, a series that epitomized how Russell could dominate without scoring much. Lakers coach John Kundla said,

> He's the guy who has whipped us badly psychologically. A man has it bother him when his opponents scores points. But he feels that sooner or later the guy will miss and he will start scoring. But Russell has our club worrying every second. It's getting so every one of the five men on the court thinks Russell is covering him on every play. I never sensed that a defensive player could mean so much to the game until Russell appeared.[7]

The greatest winner in team sports, Russell would go on to capture eleven championships in thirteen seasons. He appeared in twelve All-Star Games and was named the MVP in 1963. He was a five-time league MVP. In addition, he was a three-time All-NBA First Team selection and an eight-time All-NBA Second Team. Russell became the first African American to garner the league's MVP when he did so in 1958. His career scoring average was 15.1 points per game, and he grabbed a total of 12,721 rebounds. In 1969, he was named to the All-Defensive First Team and was a four-time NBA rebounding champion.

After the 1966 season, Red Auerbach finally retired, and the search was on to find a new head coach. Eventually, the choice was Russell. According to Red Auerbach,

> At the time, it hadn't even occurred to me that he would be the first black coach. Which was good because if I had announced that I was giving Russell the job and he would be the first black coach, he probably wouldn't have taken it. That's the way he was.[8]

As coach of the team, Russell spent three years as player-coach and guided the Celtics to two more championships in 1968 and 1969. He later coached the Seattle Supersonics and compiled 341 wins as an NBA head coach. In winning the 1968 and 1969 NBA championships, Russell became the first African American coach to win a professional championship.

Bill Russell was not the only big man who would come to change the game during the 1960s. Wilt Chamberlain left his mark on the NBA, and he and Russell would develop one of the greatest individual rivalries in sports. That rivalry would increase attention on the NBA and helped make it the incredibly popular game it is today. Prior to Chamberlain's arrival in the league, Russell was enjoying his three-year reign as the game's best player, having already won two titles. Fans and prognosticators thought that this might be the end of Russell. They were mistaken. According to Carl Braun, a forward on the New York Knicks and a regular competitor against both players, "This challenge by Chamberlain is going to make [Russell] better than ever. He's got a lot of pride, and nobody is going to knock him off that All-Star team without a fight."[9] Braun was right on the money. If anything, it elevated his game as well as Chamberlain's game.

Reflecting back on this rivalry, author Lew Freedman said,

> No one else in the game matched up with them in the paint. No one else possessed the same wide range of skills to give the other the supreme battle. Every great sportsman needs an equivalent rival to wring the best from his soul. Every great player needs a foil to raise his psyche to levels he did not know he could reach. That was Bill Russell to Wilt Chamberlain and vice versa, during ten-year overlap-

ping careers, during regular seasons and playoffs. That was Russell, the Celtics No. 6, and Chamberlain, the Philadelphia Warriors No. 13, scrapping for the same rebound, clawing for the same championship. They could both be great, but only one could be the champ in a single season. Either could earn the spoils of individual achievement, but only one at a time could capture the spoils of team accomplishment. Chamberlain won scoring titles and frequently outrebounded Russell, but Russell's Celtics won nine championships and Chamberlain one in their head-to-head years.[10]

Standing next to each other, Chamberlain was several inches taller. He weighed more. He was stronger, and his presence loomed larger on the court. It looked like a mismatch from the start. But it wasn't. Russell remarked,

> After I played him for the first time, I said, "Let's see. He's four or five inches taller. He's 40 or 50 pounds heavier. His vertical leap is at least as good as mine. He can get up and down the floor as well as I can. And he's smart. The real problem with all this is that I have to show up!"[11]

Show up he did, but Russell learned very quickly that it would be a challenge every time they faced each other to neutralize Wilt's dominance.

> There were players you couldn't outsmart. Wilt was one. He was really smart, which created all kinds of problems—big, strong, fast, great ability, and smart. That's a load. The nights that I got him to play lateral more than vertical, we [won] the game. No matter what it looks like or how many points he got, it doesn't make any difference. Now, if he gets 60 of them, I'm hurting.[12]

The key in this rivalry was that both Russell and Chamberlain guarded each other. The teams battled each other, and the two big men waged their own battles each time they faced off. That individual matchup was key. As Russell stated,

> People say it was the greatest individual rivalry they've ever seen. I agree with that. I have to laugh today. I'll turn on the TV and see the Knicks play the Lakers, and half the time Patrick [Ewing] isn't even guarding Shaq [O'Neal], and vice-versa. Let me assure you that if

either Wilt's or Russ'[s] coach had ever told one of them he couldn't guard the other guy, he would have lost that player forever![13]

Each player had a very different team. The Celtics featured Hall of Famers at every position. Russell's supporting cast including John Havlicek, Sam Jones, K. C. Jones, Bob Cousy, Frank Ramsey, Satch Sand-

Bill Russell and Wilt Chamberlain formed the greatest individual rivalry in basketball history. *Associated Press.*

ers, Tommy Heinsohn, and Bill Sharman. Wilt's teams had very good players but never quite at the level of the Celtics, although he played with many future Hall of Famers including Nate Thurmond, Paul Arizin, Billy Cunningham, Tom Gola, Hal Greer, Jerry West, Elgin Baylor, Chet Walker, and Guy Rodgers. The difference in supporting cast played a large role in the rivalry, particularly for Wilt and his supporters. As Wilt said in 1961,

> I respect Russell and he's my friend. But people don't understand one fact—he's with Boston. I'm with Philadelphia. He's got the greatest team in basketball around him. That's not my opinion, but fact. Bill doesn't have to carry a scoring load. If he doesn't score a point, Boston can win. Bill's out there to play defense and rebound. Now when I go to the floor for a game, I know I've got to hit forty points or so, or this team is in trouble. I must score—understand? After that I play defense and get the ball off the boards. I try to do them all, best I can, but scoring comes first. If I were with Boston, maybe I would be a different player. I don't know. Maybe it's lucky that Russell and I are where we are, but I wish people would understand that our jobs are quite different.[14]

In their careers, they met 142 times, and although Russell's team won more often, both had a healthy respect and appreciation for the other. Without the other, neither would have been as great a player.

Born in Philadelphia to a family of nine children, Chamberlain was not initially interested in sports. It was track and field that caught his attention and imagination. He excelled in track and field and left his mark on a number of individual competitions, including jumping six feet six inches in the high jump, running a 440 in 49.0 seconds and the broad jump of twenty-two feet. Despite his love of track and field, Chamberlain understood that basketball was the sport that garnered the most attention in Philadelphia, so he naturally switched to that sport. Soon enough, he was dominating that sport and the Philadelphia landscape. When he entered Overbrook High School, he stood nearly seven feet tall; and his height, strength, and ability helped the Panthers reach new heights. In his three seasons at Overbrook, he led the team to the Public League title three times and the city championship twice. In addition, he broke Tom Gola's scoring record by averaging 37.4 points. Gola eventually would be Chamberlain's teammate in the NBA.

With his high school career in the rearview mirror, Chamberlain's next stop was college. More than two hundred colleges recruited him, and eventually, he settled on the University of Kansas and Coach Phog Allen. In those days, freshmen could not play in the varsity, so he spent his first year in college playing on the freshman squad. In his first game against the varsity team, more than fourteen thousand fans showed up to watch his college debut. He scored forty-two points, grabbed twenty-nine rebounds, and blocked four shots. A legend was born.

When he finally was eligible for the varsity, Allen had retired, and Dick Harp replaced him. It was not the best relationship for Wilt. Notwithstanding that, Wilt dominated as a collegian. In his two years at Kansas, Chamberlain was a two-time First Team All-American. He led the Jayhawks to the 1957 NCAA finals, where they lost to the University of North Carolina. He was named the NCAA Final Four Most Outstanding Player. Despite his success collegiately, the game was losing its appeal for Wilt. Teams were triple-teaming him. He was fouled often. Opposing teams passed the ball for what seemed like an eternity before taking a shot at the basket. It just wasn't for Wilt anymore. He left after his junior year, joined the Harlem Globetrotters for a year, and traveled the world playing basketball. It was an important year for Wilt as a player and person. He matured and found playing basketball was fun again. Now he was ready for the NBA.

Selected by the Philadelphia Warriors as a territorial draft choice, Wilt immediately made his mark on the NBA. Strong and agile, he showed what a dominant force he could be at both ends of the floor. He became the first African American scoring champion when he averaged 37.6 points per game in 1959–60. He also averaged twenty-seven rebounds that season in becoming the Rookie of the Year and the league's Most Valuable Player. He had found his groove, and he would become a dominating force during the 1960s.

In the second year, he averaged 38.4 points and even scored seventy-eight points in one game against the Lakers. In his third year, he averaged 50.4 points and became the first player to score more than four thousand points in a season. His scoring was unprecedented as he tallied fifty-nine points twice and then sixty-seven in a game. But it was on March 2, 1962, that Wilt became a legend.

Against the New York Knicks in Hershey, Pennsylvania, with 4,124 fans in the stand, Wilt scored one hundred points. Fans rushed the court, and the feat has been memorialized in the photo of Wilt holding a handwritten sign that says one hundred. According to Harvey Pollack, the official scorer for that game, "It is a mythic game because Wilt scored exactly 100, no more, no less."[15]

Simply put, Wilt Chamberlain was a stats machine. When he retired after fourteen seasons, he held the records for most posts in a season (4,029), points in a game (100), scoring average for a season (50.4), career rebounds (23,924), rebounds in a season (2,149), single-season rebounding average (27.2), highest single season minutes average (48.5), and rebounds in a game (55). A two-time NBA champion, he was the NBA finals MVP in 1972. He was a four-time MVP, thirteen-time All-Star, once All-Star Game MVP, seven-time All-NBA First Team, three-time All-NBA Second Team, two-time All-Defensive First Team, and the Rookie of the Year in 1960. He was also a seven-time scoring champion and an eleven-time rebounding champion. As a scorer, he was without compare. He scored fifty or more points 118 times and scored forty or more points in 271 games. He led the league once in assists. He led the league in minutes played seven times. He played 47,859 career minutes, including averaging 48.5 minutes per game in 1962. Most surprisingly, in 1,045 games, he never fouled out.

Simply put, he was dominant, and he loomed large over the NBA long after he stopped playing.

While Russell and Chamberlain were rewriting the record book and creating a rivalry that would capture the public's attention, another dominant big man was waiting in the wings. In his own way, Kareem Abdul-Jabbar would leave his mark on the game long after he finished playing. Armed with the skyhook he developed in the fourth grade on the streets of New York, Abdul-Jabbar broke the record books in a twenty-year career and established himself as one of the game's most dominant players. As his longtime teammate Magic Johnson once said, "He's the most beautiful athlete in sports."[16]

Born Lew Alcindor in New York City, he was a New York sensation long before high school. He starred at Power Memorial Academy, where he led his team to a 79–2 overall record—including a seventy-one-game winning streak. His team captured three New York City Catholic championships. The "Tower from Power" had rewritten the record books for New York City high school. He was heavily recruited, but he chose John Wooden and UCLA, where he would go on to amass one of college basketball's greatest careers.

In college, he won three NCAA titles, and his UCLA teams posted an 88–2 record during those three seasons. During his three years (1967–69), he was a three-time NCAA Final Four Most Outstanding Player, two-time National College Player of the Year, and three-time First Team All-American. He became the first Naismith College Player of the Year. In 1968, his UCLA team faced Elvin Hayes's University of Houston in the first nationally televised game with fifty-two thousand plus fans in attendance in the Astrodome. Known as the "Game of the Century," Houston stopped UCLA's forty-seven-game winning streak. Despite the loss, UCLA would go on to win another title.

Selected first in the NBA draft by the Milwaukee Bucks, Alcindor dominated during his six years in Milwaukee. By his second year, he was known as Kareem Abdul-Jabbar, having changed his name while in college. The team traded for Oscar Robertson, and the Bucks won their only title in Abdul-Jabbar's second season. In 1975, he was traded to the Los Angeles Lakers, where he would continue to dominate with his grace and intelligence. Teaming with Magic Johnson, the Lakers won five titles in the 1980s. The skyhook continued to be his signature shot, one that his teammates could count on if the offense was breaking down. As his teammate Norm Nixon declared, "Whenever the fast break isn't going, there is nothing more effective than the . . . ten . . . foot . . . sky . . . hook."[17]

His skyhook has been described as the greatest offensive weapon in the history of the NBA. That shot propelled him to heights few in the game's history have ever achieved. He won six championships, one with Milwaukee and five with the Los Angeles Lakers. When he retired in 1989, his name was atop many all-time records, some of which he still holds. Those records included points (38,387), seasons played (20), points in the playoffs (5,762), MVP awards (6), minutes (57,446), games (1,560), field goals (15,837), field goal attempts (28,307), and blocked shots (3,189). His career average was 24.6 points per game. He was twice named NBA finals MVP, was a nineteen-time All-Star, ten-time All-NBA First Team, five-time All-NBA Second Team, five-time NBA All-Defensive First Team, and six-time NBA All-Defensive Second Team. He was named the Rookie of the Year in 1970, was a two-time

With his patented skyhook, Kareem Abdul-Jabbar retired with the most points in NBA history. *Steve Lipofsky, basketballphoto.com.*

NBA scoring champion, one-time rebounding champion, and four-time blocks leader.

Russell, Chamberlain, and Abdul-Jabbar helped to revolutionize the game for big men; Oscar Robertson had the same effect for the small player. Many individuals then and now regard Robertson as the best player inch for inch and pound for pound to ever have played the game. He was the first of the big guards to dominate the game. K. C. Jones, who guarded him for years as the Boston Celtics and the Cincinnati Royals battled in the Eastern Conference, had this to say about the player known as the Big O:

> Oscar made everything simple. Nobody ever wants to admit they're afraid of another player, but it was scary the things that Oscar could do to you. He had a certain presence. They call it a lot of things today, but back then it was just something that he emitted. He was a basketball player, plain and simple, and he could do it all. [18]

As a basketball player, he could do it all: score, rebound, and pass. Today, when one scores in double figures for all three categories in a game, it is a "triple-double." The triple-double was not yet a term in his day, but it surely was invented by Robertson. He averaged a triple double for the 1962–63 season (30.8 points, 12.5 rebounds, and 11.4 assists) as well as for the first five seasons of his career (30.3 points, 10.6 rebounds, and 10.4 assists). Jack McMahon, who coached him in Cincinnati for several seasons, could attest to Robertson's brilliance on the court.

> The years I had him, his stats were 10, 10, 10, 10. He'd have 10 baskets, 10 assists, 10 rebounds, 10 free throws. He'd get 30 points, 10 rebounds, 10 assists, and the amazing part about it was he could pick the quarter he would get what he needed. [19]

His ability to master all facets of the game made him a tough assignment for the defensive player. From time to time, Chet Walker would guard Robertson and remembered well the difficulties he faced.

> [I]t was extremely exhausting because Oscar was not a one-dimensional player. He presented the whole package to you. There was nothing that was predictable—great shooter, strong, played inside, played outside. When you guarded Oscar, you had to be aware of every part of the game. He was a fine defensive player—wasn't that quick but he was so smart. Once in a while he did something fancy, but he was almost the perfect ballplayer. His game was so simple that it became complex. [20]

A native of Indiana, Robertson grew up playing ball in the heartland of America, in a state where basketball is a religion. After moving from Tennessee with his family, Robertson learned to play the game in a segregated housing community in Indianapolis, and he was immediately attracted to it. Because his family did not have the money to buy a basketball, he learned to shoot with a tennis ball and rags rolled up and tied together with rubber bands. When it came time for high school, he enrolled at Crispus Attucks, an all-black school in Indianapolis. Under the direction of Coach Ray Crowe, whose brother George Crowe was a professional basketball and baseball player, Robertson blossomed as a player. His sophomore team lost in the state high school tournament to Milan, who became the 1954 Indiana State High School champions. Milan became the basis for the Hickory team in the 1986 movie *Hoosiers*. In his junior year, the team went 31–1 and won the 1955 state championship, becoming the first all-black school and first Indianapolis school to do so. The following year, the team went undefeated, 31–0, and defended their championship. He was named Indiana's Mr. Basketball, a coveted accomplishment for any schoolboy from Indiana.

His next stop was the University of Cincinnati, where he amassed one of the greatest college careers of all time. His statistics say one thing. He was a two-time Helms College Player of the Year, three-time UPI College Player of the Year, two-time United States Basketball Writers Association (USBWA) College Player of the Year, three-time *Sporting News* College Player of the Year, three-time First Team All-American, three-time NCAA Division 1 scoring leader, and a three-time First Team All-Mid-Valley Conference (MVC). He set fourteen NCAA records and nineteen school records. In 1957, his sophomore season and his first on the varsity team, he was a First Team All-American along with Elgin Baylor, Wilt Chamberlain, Guy Rodgers, and Sihugo Green. This marked the first time that the All-American team was comprised of five black players. He helped the Bearcats compile a 79–9 record that included two trips to the Final Four. Unfortunately, he was unable to lead his team to a title. Ironically, after he graduated, the Bearcats won the championship in 1961 and 1962 and came close in 1963. At the end of his college career, he was the all-time NCAA scoring leader until Pete Maravich came along. After college, he won a gold medal at the 1960 Rome Olympic Games.

Oscar Robertson was a dominant player while at the University of Cincinnati.
Associated Press.

His time in high school and college was not without racism as many of the schools that Cincinnati faced were southern schools, and road trips required him to stay in dorms apart from his teammates. It was not something he would forget.

When one measures the impact of Robertson, his statistics pale in comparison to what he could do on the court. His college coach, Ed Jucker, noted, "In his time, he was the greatest. No one was equal to him. I always called him a complete ball player, and there are not many truly complete players. But he could play any position." He could shoot, pass, play inside, play outside, and do whatever was asked of him. Pete Newell, who coached the University of California during this time period, reflected on Robertson's ability to distribute the ball to teammates. "He was such a great passer. He was so tough when he got the ball. . . .

There was no way you could stop Oscar one-on-one from penetrating and getting his shot."[21] Aside from having all the necessary tools, Robertson had an uncanny ability to control a game, dictate its flow, keep it moving, and get everyone involved. He was as fundamentally sound as they come. Kansas coach Dick Harp said,

> He had unbelievable control of a basketball game, and many times he looked like he was taking a walk in the country when he did it. He was so much in control of things. He had the size, the quickness, everything. He had all those great blessings, but among them he had great judgment about what to do with the ball.[22]

Robertson said,

> My game was just to go out and start playing. If you play hard enough, you're going to get your shots, you're going to get your rebounds and you're going to get your assist. I never put an emphasis on one area of the game, but to play successfully and win, you have to do two things—rebound and play defense. That hasn't changed throughout the history of the game.[23]

After college, Robertson was a territorial draft choice of the Cincinnati Royals, where he enjoyed a stellar career including his rookie year. In his first season (1960–61), he averaged 30.5 points, 10.1 rebounds, and 9.7 assists and won the Rookie of the Year award. He was third in the league in scoring. He was the third consecutive black player, after Elgin Baylor and Wilt Chamberlain, to win Rookie of the Year. Throughout his time with the Royals, the team was very good but could never advance past the Boston Celtics or Philadelphia Warriors. In his fourteen seasons in the pros, Robertson dominated the game like few have ever seen. Robertson was the Rookie of the Year, an MVP once, and a three-time All-Star Game MVP. He appeared in twelve All-Star Games and was a nine-time All-NBA First Team, a two-time All-NBA Second Team, and a six-time NBA assists leader. During the 1961–62 season, he averaged a triple-double for the entire season, a feat not matched until Oklahoma's Russell Westbrook did it in 2017. As Boston Celtics coach Red Auerbach noted, "Other players hurt you in one way, scoring, rebounding or playmaking, but Oscar hurt you all ways. He's the complete player."[24]

For his career, he scored 26,710 points good for a 25.7 average. When he retired, he had the career record of 9,887 assists. Late in his career, he was traded to the Milwaukee Bucks, where he teamed with Kareem Abdul-Jabbar to win the 1971 NBA title. His accomplishments on the court speak for themselves; one of his most important accomplishments off the court was the antitrust case *Robertson vs. National Basketball Association* in 1970. That case, named for Robertson because he served as the president of the NBA Players Association, eventually paved the way for free agency and higher salaries.

When one watches basketball today, it is a game far different than the one played in the NBA in the 1940s and 1950s. Today's game is played above the rim, with grace, style, and a sense of creativity unheard of decades ago. The man most responsible for introducing that style was Elgin Baylor.

Over the ensuing decades, players such as Connie Hawkins, Dr. J, Michael Jordan, and LeBron James added their own twists to how the game should be played. But the grandfather of that brand of basketball was none other than Elgin Baylor. He alone showed that basketball could be played above the rim. He elevated the game to new heights. Earl Lloyd, a pioneer in 1950 who loved watching Baylor play, once remarked,

> When you start picking forwards for an all-time team, you've got to take Elgin first. That's saying something, because I love Julius Erving. Doc can do it, but Doc doesn't have Elgin's strength. He's an axe. Rip those boards down and handle the ball on the break . . . the man was just unbelievable. [25]

A native of Washington, D.C., Baylor learned to play the game on the streets of the city, a place Celtics coach Red Auerbach proclaimed had the best basketball being played. Baylor, though, learned the game on his own; he played and experimented and developed his own style. As he once said,

> I never tried to be like anybody. I just played the game my way. I didn't know much about the NBA, and I didn't even play organized basketball until I was 15. We couldn't afford a television. I remember once, on a Sunday, we went to someone's house and I saw a playoff game on television. But I don't recall who was playing. [26]

Despite the lack of structure in much of his early development, Baylor earned a scholarship to the College of Idaho. After one season, he transferred to the University of Seattle in 1955. While in Seattle, Baylor finally saw his first NBA game and met Bill Russell. As he recalled,

> I'd met Bill in college at Corvallis, Oregon, in the Far West Regional. He was playing with a team of touring NBA all-stars and got me tickets for the game. R. C. Owens, who went on to be a great football player, was a friend of mine and he was in Seattle playing for an AAU team at the time. They needed an extra player and asked R. C. to play. He did OK, didn't embarrass himself. That was the first time I started thinking about the NBA. I got a little inspired watching R. C., because I knew I might be a little better than R. C., and he held his own with those great players.[27]

The inspiration helped, and he enjoyed a stellar career in Seattle. In 1958, he led the team to the NCAA finals, where they lost to the University of Kentucky. He was named the NCAA Final Four Most Outstanding Player. He was named an All-American in 1958 while averaging 32.5 points per game. In 1958, he also earned the Helms Foundation Player of the Year, and First Team All-American. In 1957, he was named Second Team All-American and led the NCAA in rebounding.

After college, Baylor was drafted by the Minneapolis Lakers. By 1958, the Minneapolis Lakers were a far different team than the one led by George Mikan in the early 1950s. They had fallen on hard times financially, and the product on the court was uninspiring. They needed a lift, both on the floor and at the gate, and won on both counts when they drafted Baylor. Immediately, he was a sensation, a revelation to fans who had never seen basketball played with such style and grace. As Bijan C. Bayne, Baylor's biographer, points out,

> No player before had driven so strongly to the hoop, and Baylor's powerful upper body enabled him to pull up anywhere and score, even over centers. He swooped into the lane, palming the ball away from his body in one hand. He hung in the air on his hesitation jump shot, then released the ball after the defender touched down. He snared rebounds with his strong, sure hands.[28]

In his rookie season, Baylor averaged 24.9 points and 15 rebounds in earning the Rookie of the Year. He also was named co-NBA All-Star

Game MVP with Bob Pettit. The Lakers earned a spot in the playoffs and, riding the momentum of Baylor's stellar season, made it all the way to the NBA finals, where they were dispatched by the Boston Celtics in four games. No matter. The Lakers realized they had a star on their hands.

The following season, Baylor did not suffer a sophomore slump. He averaged 29.6 points and 16.4 rebounds. After his second season in Minneapolis, the team relocated to Los Angeles and became the Los Angeles Lakers. He was joined by Jerry West, and the two formed one of the greatest one-two punches in the league. Later that season, he scored seventy-one points in a game against the New York Knicks in Madison Square Garden. In 1963, he scored sixty-one points in a playoff game against the Celtics. His first six years in the league were nothing short of miraculous in terms of his production and how he changed the game. For example, during the 1962 playoff run, Baylor scored at least thirty points each in eleven consecutive games. At the end of the 1964–65 season, Baylor injured his knee; although he made it

Elgin Baylor was the first basketball player to excel at playing above the rim.
Associated Press.

back, knee problems plagued him for the rest of his career. He retired nine games into the 1971–72 season in which the Lakers won thirty-three consecutive games and their first title in Los Angeles.

Baylor's outstanding career is reflected in the accolades and achievements he collected. The NBA Rookie of the Year in 1959, he was an eleven-time All-Star, an All-Star MVP (co-MVP with Bob Pettit in 1959), and a ten-time All-NBA First Team. He once scored seventy-one points in a game and averaged 27.4 points per game during his fourteen-year career. When he retired, he was the league's third all-time scorer. As Bayne remarks,

> Baylor was as complete a forward as has ever played the game. He combined the scoring skills of a small forward with the rebounding ability of a small forward. Though he was dwarfed by giants such as Chamberlain and Russell, he consistently knifed between them or propelled himself over them to score. Players began to emphasize body control in midair; which cannot be taught.[29]

Chick Hearn, the Lakers announcer and broadcaster for many decades, who watched Baylor during his career, reflected on what made Baylor a great player and so difficult to guard:

> He['d] go up high but he stayed up. The other guy went with him but Elgin wouldn't shoot until the guy came down. For many years I thought he was the greatest player who ever lived, and at times I still do. He was doing things in the sixties that people are getting credit for in the nineties. Dr. J with his hanging moves and spins, Elgin was doing that in the sixties. He was a tremendous athlete. The best ability I've ever seen in terms of hanging in the air.[30]

Although Baylor is most known for his scoring ability, he was also an excellent passer, which gave him a complete game that was hard to defend. Satch Sanders, who drew the unenviable task of guarding Baylor when the Celtics faced the Lakers, could attest to Baylor's underappreciated passing skills.

> He was an extraordinary passer. The rule for us whenever we played him, which is why those of us who were guarding him took such a whipping, was you never doubled him. One, because he was going to get his points no matter what; and two, his passing was uncanny. He

didn't just pass because he was doubled; he passed to the person in best position to score. Many players who are doubled swing the ball around the perimeter and hope someone else will pass to the player who can score. But Baylor had the ability to pass to the right person. In Boston the rule was "No help. We won't double-team." Which allowed him to victimize me.[31]

His legacy far exceeded his accolades. It was the style he introduced.

The next player to assume that mantle and add his signature stamp was Julius Erving.

Dr. J. was the epitome of cool. He had style, grace, and a certain way about him that made everyone want to stop and just watch the next great move he would unfurl. As a youngster on the playgrounds of East Lansing, Michigan, Ervin "Magic" Johnson followed the exploits of Dr. J., waiting to see and hear what he did next. As he recalled decades later,

> Julius Erving did more to popularize basketball than anyone else who's ever played the game. I remember going to the schoolyard as a kid, the day after one of his games would be on TV. Everyone would be saying, "Did you see The Doctor?" And we'd start trying to do those same moves. There were other big players, talented players and great players before him. But it was Dr. J who put the "Wow!" into the game.[32]

He could fly, and he made the dunk popular with fans across the country.

Julius Erving grew up in Long Island, New York, and enjoyed a nice high school career but was not sought after by colleges. He enrolled at the University of Massachusetts and played for head coach Jack Lehman. He spent two seasons in Amherst, where he averaged more than twenty points and twenty rebounds per game for his career. When he left after two years, professional basketball was split between two leagues, the well-established NBA and the upstart American Basketball Association (ABA). He joined the Virginia Squires of the ABA, where he enjoyed a great start to his professional career. His first five years were spent in the ABA, where he was a two-time ABA champion, two-time ABA Playoffs MVP, a three-time ABA MVP, a five-time ABA All-Star, a four-time All-ABA First Team, and once an All-ABA Second

Team. He earned a spot on the ABA All-Defensive First Team and ABA All-Rookie First Team once, and was an ABA Slam Dunk champion.

As a rookie with the Squires, Erving averaged 27.3 points and 15.7 rebounds and led the team to the playoffs. The following season, he improved his scoring to 31.9, but by season's end, the Squires needed to sell his contract to help the financially strapped franchise. He joined the New York Nets and helped them win two ABA titles. His dunking and artistry gave greater popularity to the ABA and elevated his profile.

At the end of the 1975–76 ABA season, the two leagues merged. The New York Nets could not afford the entrance fee into the NBA, so they were forced to sell Erving to the Philadelphia 76ers for $3 million. So, the Nets were able to enter the league, but the 76ers signed their franchise player. The Nets were never able to recover while the 76ers became a perennial contender. He earned a championship in 1983 with the Philadelphia 76ers. He was an eleven-time All-Star, a two-time All-Star Game MVP, a five-time All-NBA First Team, and a two-time All-NBA Second Team. He was the league's MVP in 1981.

Besides the accolades achieved and the championships won, Erving brought a new style and flair to the game. Erving said, "I had my own style. Call it playground, call it street ball or whatever. It was about pushing at the limits, testing my own imagination."[33] His imagination and his desire to create new moves manifested themselves as he drove to the basket, culminating in how he wanted to finish the move. Beginning in the ABA, Erving elevated the dunk to an art form beyond a mere show of power. He brought the dunk to the mainstream and made it popular among fans of all ages.

During his career, Erving had several signature moves that elevated his status and will live on in the memory of those who saw him play. In the 1976 ABA All-Star Game, paired against some outstanding dunkers in George Gervin, Larry Kenon, and Artis Gilmore, Dr. J. began one dunk by dunking two balls at once. Later in the contest, he started running from one end of the court. When he reached the other foul line, he took off, soared through the air, and dunked the ball. A year later in the 1977 NBA finals against the Portland Trailblazers, he took the ball after a made Portland basket and started running the length of the floor with the Portland team trailing him. After a few crossover dribbles, the only thing standing between him and the basket was Port-

Dr. J. redefined what it meant to play above the rim during a stellar career in the **ABA** and **NBA.** *Steve Lipofsky, basketballphoto.com.*

land center Bill Walton. As he gained momentum, he launched himself and threw down one of the most vicious dunks ever seen.

A few years later, the 76ers were back in the finals, this time against the Los Angeles Lakers. As he drove to the basket, he moved past Lakers' forward Mark Landsberger and then faced Kareem Abdul-Jabbar. In midair, with the backboard and baseline to his right and seemingly nowhere to go, Erving scored a right-handed layup even though part of his body was behind the hoop and backboard. The move defied comprehension as he made a play where one seemingly did not exist. Two years later, back again in the finals against the Lakers, Dr. J. was on a fast break, and the only defender was Lakers' Michael Cooper. He cupped the ball and started to rock it back and forth as he took off. He dunked the ball over Michael Cooper, who was ducking so as not to get hit. Lakers broadcaster Chick Hearn called it "Rock the Baby."

According to Magic Johnson, "I've seen a lot of great players, people who can do some amazing things on the court. But I've never seen anyone coming up who looks like another Julius. He was better. He was different. He was special." Erving said, "I've always tried to tell myself that the work itself is the thing, that win, lose, or draw, the work is really what counts. As hard as it was to make myself believe that sometimes, it was the only thing I had to cling to each year, that every game, every night, I did the best I could." Erving elevated the game's artistry, and a new generation of players would quickly look to assume the mantle he created.[34]

Although Russell earned the distinction as the first African American coach, that honor almost went to Earl Lloyd. After helping to integrate the league in 1949–50, Lloyd enjoyed a solid career with the Syracuse Nationals and Detroit Pistons before retiring in 1960. He stayed active in the Detroit community, and it was reported that in 1965 then Pistons General Manager Don Wattrick had designs on naming Lloyd head coach. Instead, Dave DeBusschere was named player-coach. But Lloyd became the first African American assistant coach with the Pistons (1968–70). In 1971–72, he became the coach of the Pistons, the first African American bench coach (he had already retired as a player) in league history. Nine games into the 1972–73 season he was fired with an overall record of 22–55.

Russell was not the only African American player who also served as a player-coach in the late 1960s and early 1970s. Lenny Wilkens earned

that distinction when he served as player-coach of the Seattle Supersonics from 1969–70 to 1971–72. In his three seasons as player-coach, the
team improved each year, although they failed to make the playoffs in
each of those seasons. When he was hired, Wilkens was the second
black coach in the NBA, although that fact did not seem to affect the
team at all. Tom Meschery, a player on that Seattle team, remembered,

> There were two key white guys on the team, me and Rod Thorn, and
> we had really strong leadership qualities, too. We just thought that
> [Lenny as head coach] was a fine idea. All the other players were
> younger and I don't think any of them thought anything of it. If there
> were any problems, it was that he had to play on the court and try to
> run the team, and I had to play on the court. So actually, Rod Thorn
> did a lot of bench coaching. In many ways Rod was more of Lenny's
> assistant.[35]

With the necessary support, Wilkens would develop a style that would
serve him well over the next four decades.

A native of Brooklyn, New York, Wilkens starred at Boys High
School before attending Providence College in Providence, Rhode Island. A two-time All American, Wilkens led the Friars to their first
National Invitation Tournament (NIT) appearance in 1959 and NIT
finals in 1960. He was drafted sixth overall by the St. Louis Hawks and
spent eight seasons (1960–61 to 1967–68) with the franchise before
being traded to the Seattle Supersonics, where he played for the next
four seasons (1968–69 to 1971–72). During that time, he was a three-
time NBA All-Star. In those three seasons, the team improved its win
totals each year from 36 to 38 to 47 but did not earn a playoff spot. After
two years in Cleveland as a player, he became the player-coach for the
Portland Trailblazers in 1974–75, his final season as a player in the
league. The team won thirty-eight games, good for third place in the
Pacific Division.

In fifteen seasons as a player, he was a nine-time All-Star and was
the All-Star Game MVP in 1971. He would be inducted into the Naismith Memorial Basketball Hall of Fame as a player in 1998. He would
also go on to earn a Hall of Fame career as a coach with stops in Seattle
(1977–85), Cleveland (1986–93), Atlanta (1993–2000), Toronto
(2000–2003), and finally New York (2004–5). In 1977–78, Seattle
started the season with a dismal 5–17 record. The team hired one-time

player coach Wilkens to turn the season around. That he did as he led the team to within one victory of the 1978 NBA title. The following year, with a full season under Wilkens's guidance, the Supersonics won the 1979 title. When he finally retired, he had 1,322 victories. In 1996, he coached the United States to the gold medal in the Olympics.

A year after Wilkens became a player-coach (1968–69), Al Attles earned the same distinction as player-coach of the San Francisco Warriors. With thirty games left in the season, Attles replaced George Lee and coached the team to an 8–22 record down the stretch. He was now the third African American player-coach in league history. Despite a poor record in thirty games, Attles decided to stay on as coach another season:

> The only reason I came back was I really felt good about those thirty games. The team never, ever just gave up and quit. We prepared, went to practice, we worked hard, we went into every game thinking we were going to win. I would go to bat for any of these guys. I don't think anybody looked at it from a racial standpoint. I think it's a tribute to them because it was a bad season and they never stopped trying. And if they didn't want to play for a black coach, they could have really caved in.[36]

Attles grew up in Newark, New Jersey, and his basketball playing ability led him to North Carolina A&T University. After graduation, his plan was to teach in his hometown of Newark. Instead, the Philadelphia Warriors drafted him in the fifth round, and he decided to join the team in 1960. He played his entire career for the Warriors from 1960–61 to 1970–71, including when the team relocated to San Francisco for the 1962–63 season. A tough defensive player, Attles was known as "The Destroyer" for his defensive tenacity. Twice as a member of the San Francisco Warriors, the team made the NBA finals (1964 and 1967), losing on both occasions. Attles stayed on and coached the Warriors from 1970–71 to 1982–83 (except for twenty games in the 1979–80 season). During a seven-year stretch, the Warriors were regarded as one of the best teams in the league, vying for an NBA title in six of them. In three of those seasons, the team lost in the Western Conference semifinals. Twice they lost in the Western Conference finals. However, they finally won the championship in 1975.

During the 1974–75 season, Attles engineered one of the greatest upsets in the league's history to date. After missing out on the playoffs the prior season, Attles remade the team. Future Hall of Famer Nate Thurmond was traded for Clifford Ray, Butch Beard was signed, and the team drafted Rookie of the Year Jamaal Wilkes. Attles guided the team to forty-eight regular-season wins. In the conference semifinals, the Warriors defeated the Bill Russell–coached Seattle Supersonics, 4–2, before besting the Chicago Bulls in seven games in the conference finals.

Awaiting them in the championship series were the Washington Bullets led by former Celtics guard K. C. Jones. The Bullets were heavily favored after winning sixty regular-season games. However, behind the brilliance of Rick Barry and a solid supporting cast, the Warriors pulled off the upset, winning in four games by a combined sixteen points. It was only the third time in NBA finals history that there was a sweep to crown a champion. The finals matched the first time that both NBA finals teams were coached by African Americans; each coach also employed a black assistant coach

The fact that both teams had black head coaches was not lost on the coaches themselves. According to Jones,

> What it means to me is that [NBA owners] care only what a man can do. The NBA gave a black man a chance when Bill Russell became head coach of the Celtics. Since then they've looked at whether a guy can do the job. Basketball started acting when football and baseball were just talking. [37]

Jones, Russell's teammate at the University of San Francisco, helped them win the 1955 NCAA championship. He later joined the Boston Celtics, and in his nine seasons, he helped the team win eight championships. He paired with Sam Jones to form one of the best backcourts in all of basketball. Known as a tenacious defender, K. C. Jones was later inducted into the Naismith Memorial Basketball Hall of Fame. After his playing days, Jones embarked on a coaching career, first in the college ranks at Brandeis University and Harvard University.

His former teammate Bill Sharman was head coach of the Los Angeles Lakers in 1971–72, and he hired Jones as an assistant. The team won the NBA championship in a season that included a thirty-three-game win streak. He then became the first coach of the San Diego

Conquistadors in the ABA before becoming the head coach of the Capital Bullets (later the Washington Bullets). In three years as coach, he led them to the NBA finals in 1975. One of Jones's assistant coaches on that 1975 Washington team was Bernie Bickerstaff, who later would coach Seattle, Denver, and Washington. Jones would later coach the Boston Celtics to titles in 1984 and 1986.

African American NBA coaches had much success. Russell led the Celtics to two titles. Attles, Wilkens, and Jones followed, each guiding his respective team to NBA titles. And although each of these individuals earned great success as coaches, no study of basketball and the African American influence would be complete without discussing John McLendon.

In 1961–62, McLendon became the head coach of the ABL's Cleveland Pipers. In 1961, the Harlem Globetrotters' Abe Saperstein founded the ABL, arguing that basketball was looking for something new and exciting. The league itself did not last long, 1961–63, but in that short time, it made a few lasting contributions. First, it instituted the three-point shot, one of the staples of the game today. Second, a young Connie Hawkins played in the league before embarking on his Hall of Fame NBA career. Finally, it provided the opportunity for John McLendon to become the first African American coach in any professional league.

His basketball story leads directly to the game's founder, James Naismith. Born in Hiawatha, Kansas, John McLendon first became aware of the game that would shape the rest of his life while in elementary school in Kansas City. In high school, he did not make the basketball team but served as the team's manager. After spending a year in junior college, he transferred to the University of Kansas, where he intended to major in physical education. But basketball still interested him. His father discovered that Naismith was the school's athletic director, and he encouraged his son to seek out Naismith. That he did.

When he arrived on campus, in a conversation with Naismith, McLendon said he was planning to major in physical education, he wanted to learn how to coach the game of basketball, and that Naismith would be his adviser. Naismith responded, "Who told you this?" McLendon said, "My father." So Naismith responded, "Come on in. Fathers are always right."[38]

With Naismith as his adviser and advocate, McLendon became the first black physical education student. He was unable to join the varsity—no blacks were allowed on the team, although he was able to observe Coach Phog Allen's practices. He graduated and eventually earned a graduate degree. It was his relationship with Naismith that would have the most profound effect on his life and his chosen course of study.

In reflecting on his career later in life, McLendon once said, "I did all I could do in the time frame I was in."[39] Indeed, he did.

He was a founder of the Central Intercollegiate Athletic Association (CIAA) in 1946. His coaching stops include North Carolina Central University, Hampton University, Tennessee State University, Kentucky State University, and Cleveland State University. While coaching at North Carolina Central, his team participated in the "secret game" against Duke University in which an all-black college team faced an all-white college team on a basketball court. It was held during World War II, and its existence was shrouded in secrecy for decades.

At Tennessee State, he led the team to three consecutive National Association of Intercollegiate Athletics (NAIA) titles and was a three-time NAIA coach of the year. When he was hired at Cleveland State, he was the first African American head coach of a predominantly white college. Later, he coached the Denver Nuggets of the ABA in 1969.

After his stint at Tennessee State, he was hired by the Cleveland Pipers, an Amateur Athletic Union (AAU) team set to join the National Industrial Basketball League. He became the first African American coach in the NIBL. Mike Cleary, general manager of the Pipers who hired McLendon, said,

> We didn't do John any favors. Of the white players, all of them were from below the Mason-Dixon Line. Yet, we did not have one moment of racial conflict on the team. In fairness, if there was any knock on John, it was he was so easy on the white players.[40]

In their second season, they won the NIBL title and later the AAU tournament in Denver. When the NIBL collapsed in 1961, the Pipers agreed to join the newly formed ABL. By now, the team's ownership was led by a young George Steinbrenner, who would later gain fame as the owner of baseball's New York Yankees. The team was integrated and included one of his former players, Dick Barnett, who was lured from the NBA to join the upstart ABL. Well stocked, the team won the season's first half before falling in the mid-season playoffs to Kansas City. Around that time a difference of opinion emerged between the players and Steinbrenner. McLendon sided with the players, and after much discussion, he resigned as head coach prior to the season's second half. Although he only coached for half a season, McLendon made his mark as the first African American head coach of an integrated team in a professional league.

McLendon, however, was not the only African American coach in the ABL. Ermer Robinson, a longtime player with the Harlem Globetrotters who sank the winning shot in the 1948 Harlem Globetrotters versus Minneapolis Lakers game, also served as a coach and administrator. He served as an administrator for the Chicago Majors in 1961–62. He also coached the Oakland Oaks in 1962–63. Oakland finished with

John McLendon became the first African American to coach in a professional league when he coached the Cleveland Pipers in the American Basketball League. *Cleveland Press Collection, Michael Schwartz Library, Cleveland State University.*

an 11–14 record. Robinson also served as a scout for the Oakland franchise in the ABA in 1967–68.

This time period was noted for other firsts involving African Americans and basketball. In 1968, Ken Hudson earned the distinction of becoming the first full-time African American referee in the NBA. His connection to the NBA came through Bill Russell. A native of Pittsburgh, Hudson grew up playing baseball, not basketball, in the Homewood neighborhood. He earned a name for himself on the diamond that eventually led him to accept a baseball scholarship from Central State University in Wilberforce, Ohio. While in college, Hudson needed to earn money for his room and board; as a work-study student, he began serving as a basketball referee for high school and semiprofessional teams and leagues in the Ohio area. Little did he know at the time that would become a lifelong passion, one that led him to make his mark as a pioneer in the NBA.

After he graduated in 1961, he returned home to Pittsburgh, where he started teaching elementary school and furthered his education by taking graduate courses in retail management at the University of Pittsburgh. Throughout, he continued to referee college games both because he enjoyed it and because it was a way to earn extra money.

By chance, in the mid-1960s Bill Russell watched him referee a college game and recommended to Red Auerbach that Hudson have an opportunity to referee the team's scrimmages during training camp. Auerbach agreed. After several games, he, too, was impressed by what he saw and recommended Hudson to the league. His first game was in 1968. Boston was hit by a snowstorm, and one of the referees assigned to the game was unable to make it. Hudson was called, and he agreed. His first game was nationally televised. Naturally, he was nervous, and he remembered, "Even my parents didn't know I was doing that job. They turned on the television, saw me on there and said, 'Oh my goodness, what is he doing?'"[41] Hudson did fine that first game and would spend the next four years, 1968–72, as an NBA referee. Afterward, he worked in radio, founded the Boston Shootout Tournament, and worked with Coca-Cola, the National Urban League, and the NAACP.

While Hudson made his mark on the court, another individual was earning his reputation in the front office. In 1972, Wayne Embry became the first African American general manager and team president in NBA history when he was hired by the Milwaukee Bucks. An Ohio native, Embry played basketball at Tecumseh High School, near New Carlisle. He earned Honorable Mention All-State Honors, which led him to matriculate at Miami University in Oxford, Ohio. During an excellent college career, he led the team to two conference championships and NCAA tournament appearances in 1957 and 1958. He led the Mid-American Conference in scoring and rebounding for two seasons and scored more than one thousand points and grabbed more than one thousand rebounds in his career.

A two-time honorable mention All-American in 1957–58, he was drafted in the third round in 1958 by the St. Louis Hawks, but he never played for them. Within weeks, he was traded to the Cincinnati Royals in a trade that sent Clyde Lovellette to the Hawks. The Royals were looking for a big man to replace Maurice Stokes, who recently had sustained a brain injury. In his eight seasons with the Royals, Embry was a key member of a team that was consistently in the hunt in the Eastern Conference but never quite had enough to get past the Boston Celtics or the Philadelphia 76ers.

At 6'8" and 240 pounds, Embry was a large presence with a strong all-around game. He and Robertson formed one of the league's best pick-and-rolls. After briefly retiring after the 1965–66 season, he was lured from his desk job by Bill Russell, who added him to the Celtics for the 1966–67 campaign. He played two seasons with the Celtics and won one championship. When the Milwaukee Bucks became an expansion franchise in 1968–69, he was selected by them in the draft and spent one season with Milwaukee.

As a member of the front office, Embry helped to orchestrate the trade that brought his former teammate Oscar Robertson to the Bucks. After drafting Lew Alcindor, the Bucks went on to win the 1971 NBA championship. A year later (1972) Embry became the first African American general manager in NBA history. He served with the Bucks from 1972 to 1979 and then joined the Cleveland Cavaliers in a similar capacity from 1986 to 1999. He also served one year, 2006, with the Toronto Raptors. While with Cleveland, he was a two-time NBA Executive of the Year (1992, 1998). During his time with Cleveland, he developed a consistently strong team that was one of the top squads in the Eastern Conference for much of the 1990s. His head coach during this period was Lenny Wilkens.

6

THE SHADOW OF MICHAEL JORDAN

May 7, 1989

When the playoffs began in 1989, the consensus was that the Los Angeles Lakers behind Magic Johnson and the Detroit Pistons led by Isiah Thomas would eventually meet in the NBA finals. And they did. But the playoffs' signature moment did not come in the NBA finals in June, as it typically does, but rather earlier in the playoffs in Richfield, Ohio.

On May 7, 1989, the Chicago Bulls were on the road facing the Cleveland Cavaliers in the first round of the NBA playoffs. The series was a best of five, and the two teams had split the first four games. In the regular season, the Cavaliers had swept the Bulls, 6–0. Cleveland was the third seed; the Bulls, the sixth seed. A back-and-forth game, Game 5 was tense throughout. With six seconds left, Jordan hit a shot to give the Bulls a 99–98 lead. Craig Ehlo scored on a driving layup with three seconds left to put the Cavaliers on top, 100–99. After a timeout, Jordan came down and hit the series-winning shot over Ehlo to give the Bulls a 101–100 victory.

It was the first time that Michael Jordan and the Bulls had advanced past the first round. It was also a signature moment for Jordan, who announced to everyone that he was here and would be a force to reckon with. The Shot, as it came to be known, signaled the impending dynasty of Jordan and the Bulls.

In the next round, the Bulls lost to the Pistons in six games.

When the Bulls' moment finally came, it was two years later in 1991 in the NBA finals against Magic Johnson and the Los Angeles Lakers. For much of the 1980s, the Lakers had been the game's most dominant and successful team. By the 1990s, that new dynasty would belong to the Chicago Bulls. The central figure was none other than Michael Jordan.

Born in Brooklyn, New York, Jordan grew up in Wilmington, North Carolina, and gravitated toward basketball. It took him a while to become a star in high school, having been cut previously from his high school basketball team. When he finally had his opportunity, he made the most of it and earned a scholarship to the University of North Carolina, one of college basketball's premier programs. While playing for Dean Smith at the University of North Carolina, he led the Tar Heels to a title in 1982. His shot as a freshman against the Georgetown Hoyas helped Dean Smith win his first NCAA championship. In his three seasons with the Tar Heels, he averaged 17.7 points and 5.0 rebounds per game. He was the National College Player of the Year in 1984, a two-time consensus First Team All-American, ACC Player of the Year (1984), two-time First Team All ACC, and ACC Rookie of the Year (1982). He was also a two-time USA Basketball Male Athlete of the Year.

When he was selected by the Chicago Bulls in the NBA draft, many felt Jordan would be a great player. Nobody suspected that he would transcend the game and become one of the all-time greats. In his first several years, he was a scoring machine, routinely putting up great numbers on a mediocre team. He won slam-dunk contests and routinely made the nightly news highlight reels. He was a singular talent. Air Jordan took the game to new heights. As he said in 1995, "I don't know about flying, but sometimes it feels like I have these little wings on my feet."[1]

Early in his career, even contemporaneous superstars recognized Jordan's unparalleled position. Magic Johnson said, "There's Michael Jordan and then there is the rest of us." Larry Bird, following a playoff game where Jordan dropped sixty-three points on the Boston Celtics in just his second season, said of Jordan, "God disguised as Michael Jordan." He was routinely singular in his accomplishments, but often the Bulls fell short to other more complete teams. For several years, the Bulls just could not get past the Detroit Pistons in the rugged Eastern

Conference. Like the players before him, he was paying his dues. Each spring for three years saw another tough playoff exit. Would the Bulls get better talent around Jordan to help the team advance to the next level?

During this time, he kept improving as a player. As his coach Phil Jackson said,

> The thing about Michael Jordan is he takes nothing for granted. When he first came into the league in 1984, he was primarily a penetrator. His outside shooting wasn't up to pro standards. So he put in his gym time in the offseason, shooting hundreds of shots each day. Eventually, he became a deadly three-point shooter.[2]

It was not just his offense, but his defense as well. According to Jackson,

> Playing outstanding defense didn't come automatically to him, either. He had to study his opponents, learn their favorite moves and then dedicate himself to learning the techniques necessary to stop them. He has worked extremely hard to perfect his footwork and balance.[3]

He was becoming the complete player, paying his dues, and waiting for that breakthrough. It finally came in 1990–91, when the Bulls defeated their playoff nemesis, the Detroit Pistons, to advance to the finals against the Lakers. After losing the first game, the Bulls stormed back and won the next four to win the series and their first title. Afterward, Magic Johnson sought out Jordan and congratulated him on his victory. "I saw tears in his eyes. I told him, 'You proved everyone wrong. You're a winner as well as a great individual basketball player.'"[4]

For the 1990s, the Chicago Bulls were the league's best team, winning six titles in eight years against five different teams. The only teammate to play with Jordan throughout this run was Scottie Pippen. The team was remade several times, but the constant was Jordan. In an unprecedented career, one many regard as the greatest ever, Jordan won six NBA titles. In each of those titles, he was named the finals MVP. He was a five-time NBA MVP, fourteen-time All-Star, three-time All-Star Game MVP, ten-time All-NBA First Team, All-NBA Second Team once, NBA Defensive Player of the Year once, nine-time All-Defensive First Team, Rookie of the Year, and All-Rookie First Team.

Regarded as the game's greatest player, Michael Jordan won six titles with the Chicago Bulls. *Steve Lipofsky, basketballphoto.com.*

In addition, he was a ten-time NBA scoring champion, three-time steals leader, two-time NBA Slam Dunk Contest champion, and three-time

AP Athlete of the Year. He was a member of the 1992 Dream Team gold medal–winning Olympic basketball team.

After winning his third straight title in 1992–93, Jordan retired to try his hand at baseball, playing minor league baseball for the Chicago White Sox franchise. His returned in 1994–95 for seventeen games before recommitting himself to another three-year championship run. In his first game back after being away from the game for a year and a half, he scored nineteen points against the Indiana Pacers. When he returned, he was all business. His former teammate Steve Kerr said,

> He came into camp like a man possessed. Every practice, every shooting drill was just a huge competition. It set the tone for our season. There was definitely a purpose to it. He was trying to show us what we had to do to be champions.[5]

The Bulls won another three titles, including a 72–win regular season in 1995–96. In the 1998 finals against the Utah Jazz, the Bulls were up three games to two with Game 6 in Utah. The Bulls were down one and had the ball with ten seconds remaining. Jordan dribbled the ball up the court. He dribbled right, then left, possibly pushing off Utah's Byron Russell and hitting the game-winning shot. He retired again. Jordan recognized his place in the game. In his book, *For the Love of the Game: My Story*, Jordan wrote,

> There is no such thing as a perfect basketball player, and I don't believe there is only one greatest player either. Everyone plays in different eras. I built my talents on the shoulders of someone else's talent. I believe greatness is an evolutionary process that changes and evolves era to era. Without Julius Erving, David Thompson, Walter Davis, and Elgin Baylor there would never have been a Michael Jordan. I evolved from them.[6]

In January 2000, Jordan returned as part owner and president of basketball operations for the Washington Wizards. After a year in the front office, he returned yet again to the court for two seasons with the Wizards. After retiring yet again, he was later fired by the Wizards. In 2006, he became part owner and head of basketball operations for the Charlotte Bobcats. The team later was renamed the Charlotte Hornets. He became the first billionaire NBA player in 2015.

As great as Jordan was on the court, he was equally spectacular and magnificent off it. Air Jordan, or His Airness, or MJ, as he was known, was a marketing sensation, helping grow and popularize the league worldwide. He has style and flair and often played with his tongue hanging out of his mouth. Off the court, he promoted Nike's Air Jordan sneakers beginning in 1985. Today, they remain among the best-selling, most important sneakers of all time. He starred in the 1996 film *Space Jam*. During the course of his career, he has been a pitchman for Hanes, Gatorade, Wheaties, MCI, created his Jordan Brand clothing, and owned Michael Jordan Motorsports. Like his commercials with Gatorade, everyone wants to "be like Mike." As Bulls owner Jerry Reinsdorf once said, "The trust is that for what Michael has meant to the NBA, his number 23 could very well be retired in every arena in the league."[7] Jordan's joining of sports and marketing is summed up by writer Art Thiel:

> That Jordan stimulated so many so deeply is a result of a unique confluence of events. His magnetism as well as his astonishing force of basketball will intertwined fortuitously with the invention of athletic-shoe marketing, a combination no veteran hoopster or wizened Wall Streeter could have foreseen 20 years ago. The timing coincided with an explosion of sports media, not only print and broadcast, but also advertising. The burgeoning sports-marketing wave sent his and the NBA's image around the world to millions who would not otherwise have noticed.[8]

While Michael Jordan was ascending the NBA ladder in the late 1980s, the player who had already reached the top was Magic Johnson.

From the moment that he burst onto the national scene as a sophomore at Michigan State University, Magic Johnson captivated the public. With his smile and the love he showed playing the game, Magic, as he came to be known, made playing basketball pure fun. Behind that megawatt smile was a burning desire to win. And win he did. At Michigan State, he led the Spartans to the 1979 NCAA championship and was named the NCAA Final Four Most Outstanding Player. He was a consensus First Team All-American (1979), and a Second Team All-American NABC and Third Team All-American by the AP and UPI, both in 1978. When he reached the NBA, he spent his entire career with the Los Angeles Lakers and won five titles, making the Showtime

Lakers the team of the 1980s. When he retired, he was regarded as one of the game's greatest players and one of the most dominant point guards ever to have played the game.

Magic grew up in Lansing, Michigan, with a basketball in his hands—literally. As he once described his basketball-obsessed childhood, "I practiced all day. I dribbled to the store with my right hand and back with my left. Then I slept with my basketball."[9] His basketball ability led his to play for his hometown Michigan State Spartans. In his sophomore season, he led the team to a victory over Larry Bird's Indiana State Sycamores in the most watched NCAA finals game in history. It introduced the country to the rivalry that would dominate the game over the next decade.

While in college, he honed a style that would be his trademark in the NBA. According to his college coach, Jud Heathcote,

> I'm asked a lot about what the greatest thing Earvin did. Many say passing the ball, his great court sense, the fact that he could rebound. I say the greatest things Earvin did were intangible. He always made the guys he played with better. In summer pick-up games, Earvin would take three or four non-players, and he'd make those guys look so much better and they would win, not because he was making baskets all by himself, but because he just made other players play better.[10]

Magic joined the Lakers in 1980 and quickly infused the team with his spirit. His coach during the first part of his rookie season was Paul Westhead, who remarked, "We all thought he was a movie-star player, but we found out he wears a hard hat. It's like finding a great orthopedic surgeon who can also operate a bulldozer."[11] The team was led by Kareem Abdul-Jabbar, the dominant player in the game. Magic made the team fun, and the Lakers made it to the NBA finals to face Dr. J. and the Philadelphia 76ers. It was their first trip since 1973; and with Kareem getting the ball in the right spots from Magic, the Lakers held a 3–2 lead heading into Game 6. In Game 5, Kareem badly turned his ankle. Kareem stayed home in Los Angeles and did not travel with the team to Philadelphia for Game 6.

With a one-game lead and the seventh and deciding game at home, the Lakers felt they had nothing to lose. Instead, the game turned into the Magic show as Magic Johnson dominated both ends of the floor.

Playing all positions on the court, Magic led the Lakers to a 123–107 win. As he said after that game, "What position did I play? Well, I played center, a little forward, some guard. I tried to think up a name for it, but the best I could come up with was CFG-Rover." Magic's play had everyone talking, including the defeated Sixers. Dr. J. remarked, "It was amazing, just amazing." Doug Collins, a player on that team and later an NBA coach and broadcaster, was equally effusive in his praise of Magic: "Magic was outstanding, unreal. I knew he was good, but I never realized he was great." [12]

The praise just kept coming.

Pat Riley, his coach, offered this assessment:

> The Lakers that year, even with Kareem, Norm Nixon, Jamaal Wilkes and all those guys, were not thought of as a contender. He came in and he was just a smiley from Michigan State, but he changed the face of our team forever. We didn't realize how good this guy was. But he brought this unique, special attitude about winning, and how to win at that young an age. In that Game 6, he proved his greatness as a player. To do it on the road against Dr. J without Kareem and just demand and command your team to win, was absolutely remarkable. It was one of the greatest performances that I've ever seen. Greatness is never achieved until you get to those moments where greatness is respected and given out. You can be called a great player but you are not of greatest until you play those kind of games in those kind of arenas for those kind of stakes. Magic found his greatest in Philadelphia in May of 1980. [13]

Bob Ryan, basketball writer from the *Boston Globe*, wrote,

> There didn't appear to be much left for the Magic Man to do in order to convince basketball people that he is one of the greatest winners who has ever laced up a pair of sneakers. But Magic submitted his absolute Renoir last night as he scored a career-high 42 points, hauled in 15 rebounds, accounted for seven assists and simply dominated the ballgame while seemingly playing every normal position and some that haven't been invented yet. From that first period, when he scored 13 points on five baskets that were not even distantly related, to the last period, when he brought out his hammer and bucket of nails to do the coffin-closing honors, this was Magic's Extended Moment. [14]

Magic had arrived, and the NBA took notice. Over the next nine years, the Lakers captured five titles. The 1980s were about Magic and the Lakers.

With Magic leading the show, the Lakers became Showtime; it was a style of basketball that enthralled fans from coast to coast. The Lakers got up and down the court quicker than anyone, scoring and scoring. A layup here. A dunk here. It did not matter if the fast-break started off a missed shot or a made shot, the ball always found its way into Magic's hands. He would move to the center of the court and bring the ball down court, nobody knowing where it would go. Would he pass left? Would he pass right? Would he pass it behind him to a trailing team-mate? Would he take it to the basket himself? One of his former team-mates who was on the receiving end of many of those passes, Michael Cooper, once said,

> There have been times when he has thrown passes and I wasn't sure where he was going. Then one of our guys catches the ball and scores, and I run back up the floor convinced that he must've thrown it through somebody. [15]

He made passing fun, exciting, and beautiful.

During his stellar NBA career, Johnson led the Lakers to five NBA titles. Among his accomplishments, he was a three-time finals MVP, a three-time league MVP, twelve-time All-Star, two-time All-Star Game MVP, nine-time All-NBA First Team, All-NBA Second Team once, NBA Rookie of the Year, four-time NBA assist leader, and two-time NBA steals leader. He was the first rookie to win the NBA finals MVP, in 1980. When he retired, he held the Lakers franchise record for assists and steals. He was also a member of the 1992 gold medal–winning Dream Team at the Olympics.

His career largely was defined by his rivalry with Larry Bird. Like Russell and Chamberlain in the 1960s, Johnson and Bird held sway over the game's best rivalry during the 1980s. As Bird described it,

> We did it in a way where we caught the imagination of everyone in America. People wanted to see us play against one another. . . . If you like competition you want to play against the best, and that's what we wanted to do. [16]

Magic Johnson electrified fans with his passing ability while playing for the Los Angeles Lakers. *Steve Lipofsky, basketballphoto.com.*

It was intense. It was a media circus. From the moment they met in the championship game in college, their careers would be forever intertwined. Magic said, "When the new schedule would come out each year, I'd grab it and circle the Boston games. To me it was *The Two* and other eighty." Bird said, "The first thing I would do every morning was look at the box scores to see what Magic did. I didn't care about anything else."[17]

Bird won Rookie of the Year, and Magic won his first title in 1980. Bird countered with his first championship in 1981, and in 1982 Magic led the Lakers to another title. In 1984, they met for the first time in the NBA finals and would meet three out of the next four years, with the Lakers winning two of them. In 1984, the Celtics resorted to a physical style of play that led them to a Game 7 victory.

The following year, the Lakers were focused on revenge. For the second year in a row, the two teams met. In Game 1, it looked like the Celtics would be the first team to repeat as champions since the 1968–69 Celtics, when they destroyed the Lakers on Memorial Day by a score of 148–114. Instead, the humiliation woke up the Lakers, who took control of the series. In Game 6, the Lakers finally outlasted the Celtics, 111–100, winning their first title against their hated rival and doing it in the famed Boston Garden. Lakers coach Pat Riley finally said the team was able to exorcise its demons. "All of the skeletons are out of the closet. I don't want to hear about history anymore. The history is this: This was our year. And we did it on the parquet floor. Maybe that's the ultimate test."[18]

Everyone was expecting a rematch in 1986, but the upstart Houston Rockets defeated the Lakers, and the Celtics rolled to their sixteenth title. A year later, they met again. Once again the Lakers had the Celtics' number, winning the title again. In Game 4, the Celtics had a chance to tie the series, but Magic rose to the occasion and hit a baby skyhook over Robert Parish and Kevin McHale to preserve the win. The Lakers won in six games. After their devastating Game 4 loss, Bird noted, "You expect to lose on a sky-hook. You don't expect it to be from Magic." By 1987, Magic had become the game's best player, and Bird recognized the wonderful talents of his longtime rival. "Magic is head-and-shoulders above everybody else," Larry Bird once observed in the Chicago Sun-Times. "I've never seen [anybody] as good as him."[19]

Even though many felt Bird and Magic hated each other, it was far from the truth. "I've always respected my opponents and him greatly because of the fact he was so good," Bird said. "Everybody said there was a hate element. There wasn't hate. I just had so much respect. You never let your guard down because he was so good." Johnson countered, "It made me feel good I was a thorn in his side, I'm supposed to be out there and go kick his butt. That's what my job was, and his job was to kick mine. I didn't want Larry to like me. He didn't have to like me. But we both respected each other."[20]

Long after they both stopped playing, Bird and Magic found ways to stay connected, from coauthoring a book about their careers to having a Broadway play produced about their relationship. Magic has been an advocate for HIV/AIDS prevention. "It's never been my dream to coach," Magic said. "I want to own, to be a businessman. You've got to chase your dreams."[21] Following his biggest desire in retirement, Magic has become part owner of the Lakers and is part of an investment group that purchased the Los Angeles Dodgers and Los Angeles Sparks. He runs Magic Johnson Enterprises, which oversees myriad business interests including theaters, a film studio, and a promotional company. He has become one of the most successful African American businessmen.

While Magic was able to dominate the game as a big guard, standing six feet nine and possessing extraordinary skills, Isiah Thomas was able to make his mark as one of the game's greatest small guards. The two were considered the best point guards in the 1980s.

Isiah barely stood six feet one and was fearless when it came to taking the ball to the basket. Like Magic, Thomas never shied away from taking over the game in the final minutes. As the NBA website states about Thomas's impact on the game,

> Thomas refused to let his height limit what he could do on the court. He was a dangerous shooter from any spot on the floor, a smart passer and a smooth, clever playmaker. He was also known for his full-speed, acrobatic drives into the teeth of the toughest and tallest frontcourtmen. Thomas took whatever defenses gave him, whether it was a 3-pointer, the baseline, the lane or an alley-oop opportunity. He combined intelligence, court savvy and physical gifts to attain true NBA superstardom.[22]

Big players led during much of the 1980s, but as the decade drew to a close, Thomas showed that the game's smaller players could still have an impact. A good outside shooter, Thomas proved equally adept at driving to the basket against much taller players. An opposing coach once said, "I call him the baby-faced assassin, because he smiles at you, then cuts you down."[23] Thomas was as tough as they came, largely the

One of the game's greatest guards, Isiah Thomas won two titles with the Detroit Pistons. *Steve Lipofsky, basketballphoto.com.*

result of growing up the youngest of nine children in West Chicago. He played high school ball at St. Joseph's High School, which was a ninety-minute commute for him each day. Notwithstanding that, he led the team to the state finals as a junior and became a top college prospect.

Recruiters came knocking on his door. Rick Majerus, an assistant coach at Marquette University, visited the Thomas family and tried to recruit him. As he recalled,

> You talk about abject poverty, human failing, suffering—they had all that in Isiah's neighborhood. You'd go in there and here was this young guy who's got this big smile. He was unbelievably optimistic for someone who had gone through all the misfortune that has occurred in his family. He was very focused.[24]

Everyone tried, but Thomas eventually decided on Bob Knight and Indiana University. Thomas got off to a rocky start with Coach Knight, but eventually he earned his way into his coach's good graces. As a freshman, he teamed with future NBA player Mike Woodson to win the Big Ten Conference and a trip to the Sweet Sixteen in the NCAA tournament. The following year, the two again won the conference championship, and, this time, the 1981 NCAA title. He was named the Final Four Most Outstanding Player. He was a consensus First Team All-American in 1981 and the USA Basketball Male Athlete of the Year in 1980.

Thomas was drafted by the Detroit Pistons as the second overall selection; and over his thirteen-year career, he became one the game's best guards. Although he put up impressive numbers, he was an unselfish player. Throughout the 1980s, the Pistons continually improved as a team but could not figure out how to get past the Boston Celtics during the playoffs. Their chance finally came in 1988, when they defeated the Celtics in the Eastern Conference finals and moved on to face the Los Angeles Lakers in the NBA finals. The Pistons held a 3–2 series and looked to garner their first franchise championship. In a thrilling game, Thomas scored forty-three points, including twenty-five in the third quarter, though playing on a badly sprained ankle. The twenty-five points were an NBA finals record for most points in a quarter. The Pistons lost Games 6 and 7 by a total of four points.

Notwithstanding that heartbreaker of a series, Thomas and the Pistons were ready to supplant the Celtics as the team of the East. With Mark Aguirre, Bill Laimbeer, Joe Dumars, John Salley, Rick Mahorn, Dennis Rodman, and Vinnie Johnson, the Bad Boys—as they came to be known—finally won their coveted NBA title in 1989 over the Los Angeles Lakers. A year later, they became only the sixth team in NBA history to repeat by defeating the Portland Trailblazers. Although the dynasty came to an end the following year, the Pistons had earned their place in the NBA for their grittiness and the way they played tough, hard-nosed team defense.

While a member of the Detroit Pistons, Thomas led the team to two NBA titles. He was the finals MVP in 1990. A twelve-time NBA All-Star, he was named All-Star Game MVP twice. During his career, he was a three-time All-NBA First Team, two-time All-NBA Second Team, Rookie of the Year, and assists leader in 1985. He received the J. Walter Kennedy Citizenship Award in 1987. After his playing days, Thomas became an executive with the Toronto Raptors, a commentator on television, head of the Continental Basketball Association, head coach of the Indiana Pacers and New York Knicks and the Florida International University team.

Following in the footsteps of previous great Los Angeles Lakers centers Wilt Chamberlain and Kareem Abdul-Jabbar, Shaquille O'Neal dominated the game as one of the biggest players to have suited up in the NBA.

In a nineteen-year career spanning six teams, Shaq, as he came to be known, was a central figure in the game's evolution during the 2000s. Strong, gifted, and with a disarming personality, Shaq became one of the most important big men during the new century. His strength and size, seven feet one and more than three hundred pounds, provided him a distinct advantage over many of his opponents, much like Wilt Chamberlain had experienced in the 1960s. His signature offensive move, the drop step, allowed him to power his way for an easy dunk. The dunk became a huge advantage for him and resulted in a high career field goal percentage. In addition, he possessed a right-handed jump hook shot, another offensive weapon. Blessed with power and athleticism, Shaq terrorized the NBA for much of his pro career.

Mike D'Antoni, who coached Shaq and against him, offered this assessment:

> One of the best ever. One of the best big men ever. Just good, just really, good. He changed basketball. Everything you do—if you're preparing against his team—you talk about Shaq 99 percent of the time. There are very few guys you spend the whole scouting meeting talking about, and he's one of those guys.[25]

A native of Newark, New Jersey, Shaq grew up with his mother and stepfather, a career army sergeant. The Boys and Girls Club provided him a safe place to play the game and stay off the streets. Later in his career, he often credited the Boys and Girls Club with being instrumental in keeping him off the streets and focused on extracurricular activities. His family moved often because of his stepfather's work; by high school, the family was based in San Antonio. It was then that he finally developed a national profile. At Robert G. Cole High School, Shaq led his team to a 68–1 record over a two-year span. In his senior year, his team won the state championship. Upon graduation, he enrolled at Louisiana State University, where he played for head coach Dale Brown. He was the College Player of the Year, two-time consensus National Player of the Year, and two-time SEC Player of the Year. After accomplishing his goals, he declared early for the NBA draft.

Drafted first overall by the Orlando Magic in 1992, Shaq spent the first four years of his career with the Magic. During that time, he earned Rookie of the Year, and in 1995, he led the Magic with Penny Hardaway to the NBA finals, where they lost to the defending champion Houston Rockets. As a rookie, he also was voted an All-Star starter, the first time that had happened since Michael Jordan in 1985. In 1996, he played with the Olympic basketball team at the Atlanta Olympics, where the team captured the gold medal.

A free agent after his stint with the Magic, he signed an enormous seven-year contract with the Los Angeles Lakers for $121 million. In eight seasons with the Lakers, he appeared in four NBA finals and won three consecutive titles from 2000 to 2002. He was the NBA finals MVP all three years.

He later was traded to the Miami Heat, where he captured one more title in 2006, this time with Dwyane Wade before finishing his career with the Phoenix Suns, Cleveland Cavaliers, and Boston Celtics. Overall, O'Neal won four titles and was a three-time Finals MVP. He was the league's MVP in 2000, a fifteen-time NBA All-Star, three-time All-Star Game MVP, eight-time All-NBA First Team, two-time All-NBA Second Team, and four-time All-NBA Third Team. He was a three-time All-Defensive Team, two-time scoring champion, and Rookie of the Year. He also earned FIBA World Championship MVP and was USA Basketball Male Athlete of the Year, both in 1994. Outside of basketball, O'Neal forged ahead with a highly successful career in business, continuing a trend established by earlier players. He appeared in movies, wrote books, published albums, became a media personality, and earned additional educational degrees.

During his time with the Lakers, O'Neal was paired with Kobe Bryant to form one of the most potent one-two punches in the NBA. Together, they captured three consecutive titles. However, their relationship was often tense, which led to O'Neal being traded to the Miami Heat in 2004. Notwithstanding the tension, both players achieved more when paired. Long after both retired, they reconciled; and with greater perspective, they were able to understand how dominant they were together and the impact they had playing together. As Shaq said,

> What makes us the best is that no other duo had as many outside controversies as me and you had. That's what I always say we're the enigmatic, no one could figure us out, most controversial. When it come down to step on the court, [we were] the most dominant one-two punch, little-big ever created in the game.[26]

Kobe countered,

> With you down there [in the paint], the game stops. You can't go anywhere, because the defense has come to down to get you, stops them from running out. No long rebounds. The game is always chopped up because you're drawing fouls all the time. I just would love to see how they would deal with that.[27]

For the past thirty years, the big question fans and media personalities asked is this: Who is the next Michael Jordan?

For many, the closest answer is Kobe Bryant.

As NBA writer Steve Aschburner wrote,

> At a time when the NBA was wondering "who's got next?" as it pertained to Michael Jordan, with some such as Allen Iverson, Vince Carter, Grant Hill and Tracy McGrady falling short for various reasons, Kobe Bryant was the real deal. Almost eerily so, in fact, with certain mannerisms, priorities and speech patterns that seemed to mimic Jordan's a bit too closely. But that's what the league wanted, that's what we wanted, and that's what Bryant gave us, hitting his target like no others. He didn't surpass the original, but he barged into the conversation, kept Jordan alive through the ongoing compar-

A dominating figure in the low post, Shaquille O'Neal was one of the game's greatest big men. *Steve Lipofsky, basketballphoto.com.*

isons and bridged the gap till LeBron James, Kevin Durant, Russell Westbrook and Steph Curry came along.[28]

Kobe Bryant was one of the game's transcendent figures during his twenty-year career. Bryant played his entire career with Los Angeles. During that time, he was a 5-time NBA champion, 2-time NBA finals MVP, 18-time All-Star, 4-time All-Star Game MVP, 11-time All-NBA First Team, 2-time All-NBA Second Team, 2-time All-NBA Third Team, a 9-time All-Defensive First Team, 3-time All-Defensive Team, and 2-time scoring champion. He won the Slam Dunk contest and was All-Rookie Second Team. His statistical record is beyond compare. Despite the accolades, the way he played left a more lasting impact.

Gary Vitti, the Lakers longtime trainer, was with Bryant during his entire twenty-year career. Nobody was able to observe him more than Vitti, who offered this assessment:

> Whatever you think of this kid—you love him, you hate him—there's five things you absolutely cannot take away from Kobe Bryant.
>
> The first one is talent. He had a lot of talent. He was not the most talented. And I've had this conversation with him. He would agree with me. There were other players who were more talented than him. So what was it about him that he had five rings, and some other players who were more talented ended up with none? Well, those other four things, beyond talent were, two, he worked harder than anybody else. And there's a lot of players who work hard. But he worked hard, and equally with purpose. So he worked hard with purpose. He was smart about it.
>
> The third thing was how competitive he was. He's absolutely, hands down, the most competitive human being that I've been around. And if he lost, he used the loss to come back even stronger. The fourth thing is, tough. Tough as nails. Tougher than anybody I've been around. Basically removed the words "can't" and "won't" out of his lexicon, and replaced them with "can" and "will." And the last thing was, Kobe was intellectually brilliant at basketball. He studied the game. He could tell you players way back in history, when he was a little kid, maybe before he was born, that he studied their game. And he studied the game right up until his last game.[29]

The son of Joe Bryant, a former NBA player, Kobe spent much of his early childhood in Italy as his father finished his professional career by

During a twenty-year career with the Los Angeles Lakers, Kobe Bryant won five NBA championships. *Steve Lipofsky, basketballphoto.com.*

playing in the Italian Basketball League. His school year was in Italy, and he spent his summers in the United States playing in summer leagues and testing his mettle against American players. When his father finally retired, the family moved permanently to the United States and settled in the Philadelphia area. Come high school, he garnered national attention with a stellar career at Lower Merion High School. Bryant played all four years, but his final three were spectacular. The team compiled a 77–13 mark. He was named Pennsylvania Player of the Year and instantly became a top college recruit. He was the Naismith Prep Player of the Year in 1996.

Instead of choosing college, Bryant opted to turn professional. He became only the sixth player to go directly from high school to the NBA. Drafted by the Charlotte Hornets, he was traded on draft night to the Los Angeles Lakers, where he would become the next in the line on a long list of great Lakers players.

Bryant enjoyed a stellar career, among the best of any player in NBA history. He won five titles, three paired with Shaq and two as the team's leader. He could score, pass, rebound, defend, and knock down the key shot when needed. He once scored eighty-one points in a game, second only to Wilt Chamberlain's one hundred. He retired as the third-leading scorer in NBA history.

But there were times when Bryant proved a difficult teammate and a player who did not always accept coaching. There was a time when he was not very popular in Los Angeles, but as his career ended, his legacy on the court was well intact. As Fran Blinebury declared,

> A single-minded, ferocious competitor with a penchant for the dramatic and a fearlessness in the face of any situation. For all the talent and the breathtaking exploits, he'll also be remembered as a virtuoso talent who could never truly enjoy playing with the rest of the kids. [30]

Fearless and an assassin on the court, Bryant established himself as someone who wanted the ball in the closing seconds. His goal was to put the final nail in the coffin and demoralize an opponent. He may have been one of the toughest players in NBA history. As Lang Whitaker concluded,

> Kobe was the greatest player of his generation, as well as the fiercest competitor of his generation, and perhaps the most mentally tough player to ever play the game. Did he shoot too much? Did he not get along with teammates or coaches? Maybe, but in the reflection of

history, those things won't be as important to remember when recalling what made Kobe, Kobe.[31]

As the 2000s dawned, fans sought the next great player. LeBron James quickly became that player.

Following in the footsteps of Kevin Garnett, Kobe Bryant, and Tracy McGrady, who all jumped directly from high school to the professional ranks, LeBron James was an instant success on the NBA level. He scored twenty-five points in his first NBA game. With a body built for the ruggedness of the NBA, LeBron made the transition; and in a fifteen-year career as of this publication, he continued to excel and change the way the game is played.

A native of Akron, Ohio, LeBron James was a star at St. Vincent–St. Mary High School, where he earned Mr. Basketball Ohio three times, was the McDonald's All-American Game MVP, the Naismith Prep Player of the Year, and two-time Mr. Basketball USA.

Selected first by his hometown Cleveland Cavaliers in 2003, James quickly made his mark on the NBA. During his first stint with the Cavaliers, he averaged 27.8 points, 7 rebounds, 7 assists, and 1.7 steals per game. As a free agent, he decided to "take his talents to South Beach" and join the Miami Heat as part of The Decision. Along with Dwayne Wade and Chris Bosh, James led the Heat to two NBA finals. After four years, he returned to Cleveland and helped his hometown team win the championship, the first in NBA history. He has appeared in seven straight NBA finals. He is also only the seventh player to score thirty thousand points in his career.

One the game's greatest players, James excels on both ends of the floor. As former Chicago Bulls player Scottie Pippen noted,

> No guy on the basketball court is a threat to score with LeBron James out there. Not only will LeBron dominate from the offensive end as well, but he's also doing it on the defensive end, which really makes him the complete package.[32]

His ability to make tough shots consistently makes him tough to defend and a player who wants the ball in the closing seconds. During the 2017–18 playoffs, James was single-handedly carrying Cleveland. As his teammate Kevin Love states, "He does it at both ends every single night. That's why he's the best player in the world."[33]

James is still adding to a career already considered one of the greatest. He is a four-time NBA champion, three-time NBA finals MVP, four-time League MVP, fourteen-time NBA All-Star, three-time All-Star MVP, eleven-time All-NBA First Team, two-time All-NBA Second Team, five-time NBA All-Defensive First Team, once NBA All-Defense Second Team, NBA Rookie of the Year, NBA scoring champion, two-time AP Athlete of the Year, recipient of the J. Walter Kennedy Citizenship Award, and USA Basketball Male Athlete of the Year in 2012.

Even as great change and innovation came to the game over the past thirty years from the players' side, the game witnessed another milestone: Robert Johnson became the first African American majority owner of an NBA franchise when he purchased the Charlotte Bobcats in 2002. In 2010, he sold his majority interest to Michael Jordan. As he said at the time,

> The best decision I made since acquiring the Bobcats was to convince my friend Michael to become an investor in the Bobcats and to appoint him as managing member of basketball operations. As the new majority owner of the Bobcats, his dedication will be stronger now more than ever. [34]

Johnson became the first African American billionaire and has spent his career as an entrepreneur, investor, philanthropist, and businessman. He was the cofounder of Black Entertainment Network (BET), which later was sold to Viacom. BET became the first African American–owned company traded on the New York Stock Exchange. He is also the founder of RLJ Companies, an asset management company, which includes interests in financial services, sports and entertainment, automobile dealerships, and business interests. He sits on the board of the Smithsonian Institution's National Museum of African American History and Culture.

Today, the game continues to evolve and transform itself in ways that could not be imagined decades ago. New stars such as Stephen Curry, Kevin Durant, Russell Westbrook, and James Harden, among others, have taken the game to new heights. Their commitment, creativity, and determination have continued to push the game in new, more exciting directions. It is hoped that the road paved by the likes of Bucky Lew, Pop Gates, the New York Renaissance, Harlem Globetrot-

LeBron James has won four **NBA MVP** titles during his career. *Associated Press.*

ters, Dolly King, Chicago Studebakers, Earl Lloyd, Chuck Cooper, and Sweetwater Clifton, among many others, will not be lost on the players of today or tomorrow. As Kevin Garnett, a future Hall of Famer, stated,

> We live a great life. We make great money and I don't think you'll hear anybody bickering about the money or the opportunities that basketball has created. So, if anything, the Bill Russells, the Wilt Chamberlains, the Oscar Robertsons, the Magic Johnsons, the Kareems were the guys who laid the foundation for guys like myself, [Allen] Iverson, Antawn Jamison, Stephon Marbury, or Shaq—the great players you see now. We're stepping in the same footprint and are creating our own at the same time. That's just how history goes, and the opportunity we have now will be vastly greater for others down the line.[35]

NOTES

I. EARLY BLACK PROFESSIONAL BASKETBALL

1. "P.A.C. Lost," *Lowell Courier-Citizen*, November 7, 1902, n.p.
2. Gerry Finn, "Bucky Lew First Negro in Pro Basketball," *Springfield Union*, April 2, 1958, 27.
3. Tatsha Robertson, "Echoes of the Underground Railroad," *Boston Globe*, February 22, 1999, A12.
4. Robertson, "Echoes of the Underground Railroad," A12.
5. Kay Lazar, "The Fight for Bucky Lew's Name: Lowell Native Broke Pro Basketball Color Barrier, But He's Not Recognized," *Lowell Sun*, Summer 1997, 7.
6. www.probasketballencyclopedia.com.
7. Lazar, "The Fight for Bucky Lew's Name"; Caroline Louise Cole, "Recalling How Black Star Broke Barriers in 1902," *Boston Globe*, NorthWest Weekly, February 16, 1997, 6.
8. Ron Thomas, *They Cleared the Lane: The NBA's Black Pioneers* (Lincoln: University of Nebraska Press, 2002), 6.
9. Finn, "Bucky Lew First Negro in Pro Basketball," 27.
10. Cole, "Recalling How Black Star Broke Barriers in 1902," 6.
11. www.probasketballencyclopedia.com; Thomas, *They Cleared the Lane*, 6.
12. www.probasketballencyclopedia.com.
13. Lazar, "The Fight for Bucky Lew's Name," 6.
14. Cole, "Recalling How Black Star Broke Barriers in 1902," 6.
15. Cole, "Recalling How Black Star Broke Barriers in 1902," 6.

16. Cole, "Recalling How Black Star Broke Barriers in 1902," 6; Lazar, "The Fight for Bucky Lew's Name," 7.

17. "Black Sports Hall of Fame Taps Henderson," *Ledger-Enquirer East Alabama TODAY*, November 7–8, 1973, n.p. Edwin Henderson Hall of Fame File, Naismith Memorial Basketball Hall of Fame.

18. Text courtesy of www.ivyleaguesports.com, "Agents of Change" by Eddie Lentz, February 7, 2005.

19. "African American Professional Pioneer Edwin Bancroft Henderson," *The Horizon, A Publication of National African American Fitness and Health Association* 1, no. 1 (Spring 1996): n.p. Edwin Henderson Hall of Fame File, Naismith Memorial Basketball Hall of Fame.

20. "Black Sports Hall of Fame Taps Henderson."

21. "Black Sports Hall of Fame Taps Henderson."

22. "African American Professional Pioneer Edwin Bancroft Henderson."

23. Edna and Art Rust Jr., *Art Rust's Illustrated History of the Black Athlete* (Garden City, NY: Doubleday, 1985), 298; Fredrick McKissack Jr., *Black Hoops: The History of African Americans in Basketball* (New York: Scholastic Press, 1999), 48; Nelson George, *Elevating the Game: Black Men and Basketball* (New York: Harper Collins, 1992), 34–35.

24. Rust and Rust, *Art Rust's Illustrated History of the Black Athlete*, 298.

25. Rust and Rust, *Art Rust's Illustrated History of the Black Athlete*, 298–99.

26. Rust and Rust, *Art Rust's Illustrated History of the Black Athlete*, 299.

27. Rust and Rust, *Art Rust's Illustrated History of the Black Athlete*, 299–300.

28. Thomas, *They Cleared the Lane*, 7; Robert W. Peterson, *Cages to Jump Shots: Pro Basketball's Early Years* (New York: Oxford University Press, 1990), 98.

29. "In '38, Dance Floor Was Champs' Arena," William Gates Collection, Schomburg Center for Research in Black Culture; Arthur Ashe, *A Hard Road to Glory: A History of the African-American Athlete 1619–1918*, vol. 1. 3 vols. (New York: Amistad, 1988), 10.

30. Peterson, *Cages to Jump Shots*, 98.

31. Ashe, *A Hard Road to Glory*, 10 and 12.

32. McKissack, *Black Hoops,* 59.

33. Kareem Abdul-Jabbar with Raymond Obstfeld, *On the Shoulders of Giants: My Journey through the Harlem Renaissance* (New York: Simon & Schuster, 2007), 160 and 168.

34. Thomas, *They Cleared the Lane*, 8; Jim Myers, "Black Pioneers Not on 'Hall' Roster," *USA Today*, October 12, 1988, 7C.

35. Peterson, *Cages to Jump Shots,* 100.

36. Rust and Rust, *Art Rust's Illustrated History of the Black Athlete*, 300.

37. Nelson George, *Elevating the Game: Black Men and Basketball* (New York: HarperCollins, 1992), 39; Joe Gergen, "Place in Hoop Hall is Gates' Rightful Reward," William Gates Collection, Schomburg Center for Research in Black Culture.

38. Abdul-Jabbar, *On the Shoulders of Giants*, 159.

39. Peterson, *Cages to Jump Shots*, 11–12.

40. Ashe, *A Hard Road to Glory*, 13.

41. Rust and Rust, *Art Rust's Illustrated History of the Black Athlete*, 304.

42. Peterson, *Cages to Jump Shots*, 96.

43. Rust and Rust, *Art Rust's Illustrated History of the Black Athlete*, 300.

44. Rust and Rust, *Art Rust's Illustrated History of the Black Athlete*, 304; Thomas, *They Cleared the Lane*, 9.

45. Ashe, *A Hard Road to Glory*, 10; McKissack, *Black Hoops*, 58.

46. Abdul-Jabbar, *On the Shoulders of Giants*, 160.

47. McKissack, *Black Hoops*, 58.

48. Abdul-Jabbar, *On the Shoulders of Giants*, 163; Gergen, "Place in Hoop Hall is Gates' Rightful Reward."

49. Todd Gould, *Pioneers of the Hardwood: Indiana and the Birth of Professional Basketball* (Bloomington: Indiana University Press, 1998), 26–27.

50. Gould, *Pioneers of the Hardwood*, 26.

51. John Devaney, *The Story of Basketball* (New York: Random House, 1976), 32; Gould, *Pioneers of the Hardwood*, 25; Abdul-Jabbar, *On the Shoulder of Giants*, 162.

52. McKissack, *Black Hoops*, 53; Ashe, *A Hard Road to Glory*, 9; George, *Elevating the Game*, 35–36; Chris Broussard, "Pioneer with Early Black Pro Team Looks Back," *New York Times*, February 15, 2004, http://www.nytimes.com/2004/02/15/sports/inside-the-nba-pioneer-with-early-black-pro-team-looks-back.html.

53. Gould, *Pioneers of the Hardwood*, 26.

54. McKissack, *Black Hoops*, 57.

55. Gould, *Pioneers of the Hardwood*, 27.

56. Peterson, *Cages to Jump Shots*, 96–97.

57. Gould, *Pioneers of the Hardwood*, 25–26.

58. Bill Yancey letter to Lee Williams, Robert L. Douglas Hall of Fame File, Naismith Memorial Basketball Hall of Fame, n.d.

59. George, *Elevating the Game*, 37.

60. Nat Holman letter to the Basketball Hall of Fame Honors Committee, June 25, 1969. Robert L. Douglas Hall of Fame File, Naismith Memorial Basketball Hall of Fame.

61. Rust and Rust, *Art Rust's Illustrated History of the Black Athlete*, 300.

62. Rust and Rust, *Art Rust's Illustrated History of the Black Athlete*, 303.

63. Peterson, *Cages to Jump Shots*, 107.

64. Thomas, *They Cleared the Lane*, 10; Myers, "Black Pioneers Not on 'Hall' Roster," 7C.

2. THE WORLD PROFESSIONAL BASKETBALL TOURNAMENT

1. Wendell Smith, "Smitty's Sport Spurts," *Pittsburgh Courier*, February 11, 1939, 17.

2. Smith, "Smitty's Sport Spurts."

3. John Schleppi, *Chicago's Showcase of Basketball: The World Tournament of Professional Basketball and the College All-Star Game* (Haworth, NJ: St. Johann Press, 2008), 5.

4. www.aafla.org/SportsLibrary/NASSH_Proceddings/NP1989/NP1989Zd.pdf.

5. *Pittsburgh Courier*, April 1, 1939, 16.

6. Ben Green, *Spinning the Globe: The Rise, Fall, and Return to Greatness of the Harlem Globetrotters* (New York: HarperCollins, 2005), 108–9.

7. Green, *Spinning the Globe*, 109.

8. Kareem Abdul-Jabbar, with Raymond Obstfeld, *On the Shoulders of Giants: My Journey Through the Harlem Renaissance* (New York: Simon & Schuster, 2007), 171.

9. Leo Fischer, "Pro Cagers in Semifinals," *Chicago Herald American*, March 27, 1939, 15.

10. Abdul-Jabbar, *On the Shoulders of Giants*, 171–72; Ron Thomas, *They Cleared the Lane: The NBA's Black Pioneers* (Lincoln: University of Nebraska Press, 2002), 10.

11. Leo Fischer, "Rens Capture U.S. Pro Cage Tourney," *Chicago Herald American*, March 29, 1939, 24.

12. Abdul-Jabbar, *On the Shoulders of Giants*, 169.

13. Frederick McKissack Jr., *Black Hoops: The History of African Americans in Basketball* (New York: Scholastic Press, 1999), 63.

14. Abdul-Jabbar, *On the Shoulders of Giants*, 173.

15. Green, *Spinning the Globe*, 134; Susan Rayl, "The New York Renaissance Professional Black Basketball Team, 1923–1950," PhD dissertation, 1996, 286.

16. Sherman L. Jenkins, *Ted Strong Jr.: The Untold Story of an Original Harlem Globetrotter and Negro League All-Star* (Lanham, MD: Rowman & Littlefield, 201), 34.

17. Jenkins, *Ted Strong Jr.*, 35.

18. Jenkins, *Ted Strong Jr.*, 35.

19. Jenkins, *Ted Strong Jr.*, 42.

20. "Court Mourns Passing of Great 'Pappy' Ricks," *Pittsburgh Courier*, February 22, 1941, 16.

21. Dennis Gildea, *Hoop Crazy: The Lives of Clair Bee and Chip Hilton* (Fayetteville: University of Arkansas Press, 2013), 134 and 139.

22. Gildea, *Hoop Crazy*, 140.

23. St. Clair Bourne, "Big Sepian Invasion," *Amsterdam News*, September 24, 1938, 6.

24. Rochester Royals Yearbook, 1946. In the possession of the author.

25. Douglas Stark, *When Basketball Was Jewish: Voices of Those Who Played the Game* (Lincoln: University of Nebraska Press, 2017), 123.

26. Leo Fischer, "Oshkosh vs. Detroit for Pro Title!," *Chicago Herald American*, March 19, 1941, 23.

27. http://www.orangehoops.org/Sadat_Singh.htm; Luke Cyphers, "Syracuse's Lost Hero: Wilmeth Sidat-Singh," *Post Standard*, April 25, 2001, E3; Sean Kirst, "Ahead of His Time: Wilmeth Sidat-Singh's Basketball Legend," *Post Standard*, December 27, 1994, D8.

28. http://www.orangehoops.org/Sadat_Singh.htm; Cyphers, "Syracuse's Lost Hero"; Kirst, "Ahead of His Time."

29. http://www.orangehoops.org/Sadat_Singh.htm.

30. Kirst, "Ahead of His Time."

31. Leo Fischer, "Globetrotters Enter Pro Cage Meet," *Chicago Herald American*, February 2, 1941, 15.

32. Jenkins, *Ted Strong Jr.*, 43.

33. Green, *Spinning the Globe*, 151.

34. Fay Young, "Globe Trotters Advance in World Pro Tourney," *Chicago Defender*, March 14, 1942, 21.

35. Leo Fischer, "Oshkosh and Eagles Win," *Chicago Herald American*, March 11, 1942, 25.

36. Leo Fischer, "Sixteen Teams Eye World's Cage Laurels," *Chicago Herald American*, March 2, 1942, 17–18.

37. Leo Fischer, "Rens Test Oshkosh Tonight," *Chicago Herald American*, March 9, 1942, 17; "Stars Meet Rens in Pro Cage Contest Tonight," *Oshkosh Daily Northwestern*, March 9, 1942, 12.

38. Harry Wilson, "Oshkosh Victory Cage Stunner," *Chicago Herald American*, March 10, 1942, 14.

39. Fischer, "Sixteen Teams Eye World's Cage Laurels," 17.

40. Leo Fischer, "Trotters, Dayton Top Cage Tonight," *Chicago Herald American*, March 15, 1943, 21.

41. "Studebakers out of Pro Cage Meet," *Chicago Defender*, March 20, 1943, 21.

42. Pop Gates interview, Robert Peterson Collection, Naismith Memorial Basketball Hall of Fame.

43. James Enright, "Basketball's Best: '39 Cage Champs Back, But as Bears,'" *Chicago Herald American*, March 10, 1943, 24.

44. Aaron C. Elson, "The Forgotten Superstar," *New York Post*, June 10, 1974, 47.

45. Bob Kuska, *Hot Potato: How Washington and New York Gave Birth to Black Basketball and Changed America's Game Forever* (Charlottesville: University of Virginia Press, 2004), 177.

46. Clarence Bell letter to Lee Williams, August 16, 1976. Charles Cooper File, Naismith Memorial Basketball Hall of Fame.

47. Thomas, *They Cleared the Lane*, 9.

48. Elson, "The Forgotten Superstar," 47.

49. Elson, "The Forgotten Superstar," 47.

50. Elson, "The Forgotten Superstar," 47.

51. "Bears Pro Basketball Champions," *The Call*, March 26, 1943, 10.

52. Susan Rayl, "Holding Court: The Real Renaissance Contribution of John Isaacs," *Journal of Sports History* (Spring 2011): 7.

53. Rayl, "Holding Court: The Real Renaissance Contribution of John Isaacs," 7.

54. Nelson George, *Elevating the Game: Black Men and Basketball* (New York: HarperCollins, 1992), 40; Rayl, "Holding Court." 8; Vincent M. Mallozzi, "A Living Wonder of the Harlem Renaissance: John Isaacs, a 1930's Barnstormer, Was Surprised to Find Himself in a Sneaker Ad, 'They Didn't Know I was Still Alive,'" *New York Times*, March 9, 1997, 8.

55. Vincent C. Mallozzi, "John Isaacs, Star for Rens Basketball, Dies at 93," *New York Times*, February 4, 2009, A21.

56. "Bears Pro Basketball Champions," *The Call*, 10.

57. 1943 World Professional Basketball Tournament program. In the possession of the author.

58. Harry Wilson, "World Cage Briefs: Best of the Trotters," *Chicago Herald American*, March 8, 1944, 18.

59. "Rens, Zollners, Eagles, Trotters in Cage Race," *Chicago Herald American*, March 23, 1944, 18.

60. "Rens, Zollners, Eagles, Trotters in Cage Race," 18.

61. "Rens, Zollners, Eagles, Trotters in Cage Race," 18.

62. "Trotters Take Rens, 37–29, for 3rd Place as Zollners Top Pro Cagers," *Chicago Defender*, April 1, 1944, 9.

63. "Trotters Take Rens, 37–29, for 3rd Place as Zollners Top Pro Cagers," 9.

64. "Trotters Take Rens, 37–29, for 3rd Place as Zollners Top Pro Cagers," 9.

65. "Grumman Five Is Returning to Pro Picture," *Long Island Daily Press*, December 1, 1944, 20.

66. Harry Wilson, "Grumman Returned for World Cage Try," *Chicago Herald American*, February 27, 1945, 12.

67. Pop Gates interview.

68. Keith Brehm, "Globe Trotters Bid for World Cage Role," *Chicago Herald American*, March 2, 1945, 26.

69. Harry Wilson, "Famous Rens Third to Enter World Cage," *Chicago Herald American*, February 20, 1945, 12.

70. Wilson, "Famous Rens Third to Enter World Cage," 12.

71. *Pittsburgh Courier*, March 31, 1945, 12.

72. Susan Rayl, "A War Begins from Rens to Bears: Player Revolving and Free Agency in Black Basketball in the Early 1940s," *North American Society for Sports History, Proceedings and Newsletter* 1997, 60.

73. Keith Brehm, "Of World Cage Play," *Chicago Herald American*, March 23, 1946, 23.

74. Leo Fischer, "Rens Enter World Cage," *Chicago Herald American*, March 3, 1946, 27.

75. Leo Fischer, "New York Rens Enter World Pro Cage Tourney," *Chicago Herald American*, March 16, 1947, 35.

76. Fischer, "New York Rens Enter World Pro Cage Tourney," 35.

77. Charles Salzberg, *From Set Shot to Slam Dunk: The Glory Days of Basketball in the Words of Those Who Played It* (Lincoln: University of Nebraska Press, 1987), 131.

78. Salzberg, *From Set Shot to Slam Dunk*, 131.

79. Salzberg, *From Set Shot to Slam Dunk*, 131.

80. Salzberg, *From Set Shot to Slam Dunk*, 132.

81. Salzberg, *From Set Shot to Slam Dunk*, 132–33.

82. Wendell Smith, "Wendell Smith's Sport Beat," *Pittsburgh Courier*, February 14, 1948, 16.

83. "Ex-Trotter, NBA Star Sweetwater Clifton Dead." Sweetwater Clifton clipping file, Naismith Memorial Basketball Hall of Fame, n.d.

84. Edgar C. Greene, "Rens' Plan is to Stop . . . Pollard," *Chicago Herald American*, April 11, 1948, 11.

85. Greene, "Rens' Plan Is to Stop . . . Pollard," 11.

86. Thomas, *They Cleared the Lane*, 8–9.

87. Green, *Spinning the Globe*, 203 and 209.

88. Green, *Spinning the Globe*, 203 and 214.

89. Green, *Spinning the Globe*, 205.

90. Green, *Spinning the Globe*, 205.

91. Green, *Spinning the Globe*, 205.

92. Marques Haynes, Voices of Oklahoma, University of Tulsa Oklahoma Center for the Humanities, 5–6.

93. Haynes, Voices of Oklahoma, 11–12.

94. Haynes, Voices of Oklahoma, 12.

95. Green, *Spinning the Globe*, 209–10.

96. Jenkins, *Ted Strong Jr.*, 91.

97. Michael Schumacher, *Mr. Basketball: George Mikan, the Minneapolis Lakers, and the Birth of the NBA* (New York: Bloomsbury, 2007), 124; Thomas, *They Cleared the Lane*, 11.

98. Green, *Spinning the Globe*, 209–10.

99. Green, *Spinning the Globe*, 210; Schumacher, *Mr. Basketball*, 124.

3. THE NATIONAL BASKETBALL LEAGUE

1. Robert W. Peterson, *Cages to Jump Shots: Pro Basketball's Early Years* (New York: Oxford University Press, 1990), 129.

2. "Gerber, Chuckovits to Be Here with Toledo," *Oshkosh Daily Northwestern*, December 11, 1942, 15.

3. Peterson, *Cages to Jump Shots*, 130.

4. "Stars, 'Skins to Play Twin Bill at Milwaukee Friday," *Oshkosh Northwestern*, December 7, 1942, 13.

5. "Zollner Piston-Toledo Clash Is Postponed until Wednesday," *Fort Wayne News-Sentinel*, December 8, 1942, 21.

6. "Pistons Seek .500 Loop Standing at Expense of Toledo Five," *Fort Wayne News-Sentinel*, December 9, 1942, 26.

7. "Toledo Five 70–51 Victim of Zollners," *Fort Wayne News-Sentinel*, December 10, 1942, 32.

8. "Toledo Five 70–51 Victim of Zollners," 32.

9. Douglas Stark, "Paving the Way: The National Basketball League," *Basketball Digest*, February 2001, 76.

10. Todd Gould, *Pioneers of the Hardwood: Indiana and the Birth of Professional Basketball* (Bloomington: Indiana University Press, 1998), 116.

11. Bill Himmelman, interview by the author, Norwood, NJ, August 2007.

12. Bill Reynolds, *Rise of a Dynasty: The '57 Celtics, the First Banner, and the Dawning of a New America* (New York: New American Library, 2010), 129–30.

13. "Studebakers Turn Toledo Back, 42–30," *Chicago Defender*, December 19, 1942, 21.

14. Murry R. Nelson, *The National Basketball League: A History, 1935–1949* (Jefferson, NC: McFarland, 2009), 117.

15. "Chuckovits Will Play Here Saturday Night," *Oshkosh Daily Northwestern*, December 9, 1942, 13.

16. Peterson, *Cages to Jump Shots*, 130.

17. Sid Goldberg interview, Robert Peterson Collection, Naismith Memorial Basketball Hall of Fame.

18. Peterson, *Cages to Jump Shots*, 130.

19. "Redskins Drub Rens, 65–47," *Sheboygan Press*, December 12, 1942, 10.

20. "Toledo Out of Pro Loop," *Toledo Blade*, December 23, 1942, 19.

21. Sid Goldberg interview.

22. Michael Funke, "The Chicago Studebakers: How the UAW Helped Integrate Pro Basketball and Reunite Four Players Who Made History," n.d. Naismith Memorial Basketball Hall of Fame.

23. David S. Neft, Roland T. Johnson, Richard M. Cohen, and Jordan A. Deutsch, *The Sports Encyclopedia: Pro Basketball* (New York: Grosset & Dunlap, 1975), 36.

24. 1943 World Professional Basketball Tournament program. In the possession of the author.

25. "Invaders to Give Team Real Fight," *Sheboygan Press*, November 24, 1942, 12.

26. "Redskins Open League Season Tonight: New Team Has Lots of Class," *Sheboygan Press*, November 25, 1942, 18.

27. Peterson, *Cages to Jump Shots*, 131.

28. Funke, "The Chicago Studebakers."

29. "Chicago Studebakers Oppose Pistons in Opening Contest," *News-Sentinel*, December 1, 1942, 11.

30. Ben Tenny, "Pistons, Beaten in Home Opener, Go on Road Trip," *News-Sentinel*, December 2, 1942, 22.

31. Gould, *Pioneers of the Hardwood*, 117.

32. Funke, "The Chicago Studebakers."

33. Funke, "The Chicago Studebakers"; Peterson, *Cages to Jump Shots*, 131.

34. Peterson, *Cages to Jump Shots*, 131.

35. Funke, "The Chicago Studebakers."

36. Nelson, *National Basketball League*, 117; "Studebakers Turn Toledo Back, 42–30," *Chicago Defender*, December 19, 1942, 21.

37. Ron Thomas, *They Cleared the Lane: The NBA's Black Pioneers* (Lincoln: University of Nebraska Press, 2002), 13.

38. John Devaney, *The Story of Basketball* (New York: Random House, 1976), 32.

39. Roger Kahn, *Rickey & Robinson: The True, Untold Story of the Integration of Baseball* (New York: Rodale, 2014), 103.

40. Kahn, *Rickey & Robinson*, 107.

41. Gretchen Atwood, *Lost Champions: Four Men, Two Teams, and the Breaking of Pro Football's Color Line* (New York: Bloomsbury, 2016), 225.

42. Nelson, *National Basketball League*, 163–64.

43. Douglas Stark, *When Basketball Was Jewish: Voices of Those Who Played the Game* (Lincoln: University of Nebraska Press, 2017), 23.

44. Thomas, *They Cleared the Lane*, 14.

45. Thomas, *They Cleared the Lane*, 14–15.

46. Ron Thomas, "King, Gates First Black Pros. Two Pre-NBA Pioneers," *San Francisco Chronicle*, February 17, 1987, 52.

47. Jeff Kisseloff, "Following the Bouncing Ball," *New York Post*, May 28, 1989, 38.

48. Kisseloff, "Following the Bouncing Ball," 38.

49. Kisseloff, "Following the Bouncing Ball," 38.

50. Bob Kuska, *Hot Potato: How Washington and New York Gave Birth to Black Basketball and Changed America's Game Forever* (Charlottesville: University of Virginia Press, 2004), 167.

51. Edna and Art Rust Jr., *Art Rust's Illustrated History of the Black Athlete* (Garden City, NY: Doubleday, 1985), 303.

52. Thomas, *They Cleared the Lane*, 8.

53. Kisseloff, "Following the Bouncing Ball."

54. Rust and Rust, *Art Rust's Illustrated History of the Black Athlete*, 303; Dave Anderson, "Pop Gates Earned His Grits," *New York Times*, February 19, 1989, http://www.nytimes.com/1989/02/19/sports/sports-of-the-times-pop-gates-earned-his-grits.html.

55. Kisseloff, "Following the Bouncing Ball."

56. Jim Myers, "Black Pioneers Not on 'Hall' Roster," *USA Today*, October 12, 1988, 7C.

57. Anderson, "Pop Gates Earned His Grits"; Thomas, *They Cleared the Lane*, 9.

58. Anderson, "Pop Gates Earned His Grits"; Joe Gergen, "Place in Hoop Hall Is Gates' Rightful Reward," William Gates Collection, Schomburg Center for Research in Black Culture; Nelson George, *Elevating the Game: Black Men and Basketball* (New York: HarperCollins, 1992), 39; Wendell Smith, "Wendell Smith's Sport Beat," *Pittsburgh Courier*, February 14, 1948, 16.

59. Bernie "Red" Sarachek letter, William Gates scrapbooks, Schomburg Center for Research in Black Culture.

60. Thomas, "King, Gates First Black Pros. Two Pre-NBA Pioneers."

61. Gergen, "Place in Hoop Hall is Gates' Rightful Reward"; Thomas, "King, Gates First Black Pros. Two Pre-NBA Pioneers."

62. Nelson, *National Basketball League*, 164.

63. Pop Gates interview, Robert Peterson Collection, Naismith Memorial Basketball Hall of Fame.

64. Peterson, *Cages to Jump Shots*, 13.

65. Thomas, "King, Gates First Black Pros. Two Pre-NBA Pioneers."

66. Arthur Ashe, *A Hard Road to Glory: A History of the African-American Athlete 1619–1918*, vol. 1. 3 vols. (New York: Amistad, 1988), 22.

67. Pop Gates interview.

68. *Official National Basketball League Pro Magazine*, 8, as quoted in Nelson, *National Basketball League*, 164.

69. Nelson, *National Basketball League*, 206.

70. Rust and Rust, *Art Rust's Illustrated History of the Black Athlete*, 301.

71. Rust and Rust, *Art Rust's Illustrated History of the Black Athlete*, 301.

72. *Chicago Defender*, December 11, 1948, 13.

73. Gus Alfieri, *Lapchick: The Life of a Legendary Player and Coach in the Glory Days of Basketball* (Guilford, CT: Lyons Press, 2006), 143 and 151.

74. Peterson, *Cages to Jump Shots*, 101.

4. EARLY BLACK NBA PIONEERS

1. Mark Rosner, "Integrating the NBA: It Happened Oct. 31, 1950, When Earl Lloyd of the Washington Capitols Stepped on the Court in Rochester, N.Y." *Austin American-Statesmen*, November 12, 2000, C1 and C11.

2. Ann Cerhart, "A Player Who Stands Tall: A Basketball Pioneer: Still Scoring Points with Fans," *Washington Post*, February 10, 2001, C4; Pat Farabaugh, *An Unbreakable Bond: The Brotherhood of Maurice Stokes and Jack Twyman* (Haworth, NJ: Haworth Press, 2014), 12.

3. Cerhart, "Player Who Stands Tall."

4. Bethany Bradsher, *Bones McKinney: Basketball's Unforgettable Showman* (Houston: Whitecap Media, 2014), 103.

5. Ron Thomas, "Breaking the NBA Color Barrier: It's Easy to Forget There Was a Time When the Now 75 Percent Black League Was 100 Percent White," *Sporting News 1990–91 Pro Basketball Yearbook*, 34.

6. Bradsher, *Bones McKinney*, 104.

7. Bradsher, *Bones McKinney*, 102.

8. Chris Broussard, "Pro Basketball: 3 Pioneers Hailed for Breaking Color Line," *New York Times*, November 1, 2000, http://www.nytimes.com/2000/11/01/sports/pro-basketball-3-pioneers-hailed-for-breaking-color-line.html; Farabaugh, *An Unbreakable Bond*, 101.

9. Mark Rosner, "Integrating the NBA."

10. Frank Foster, *Sweetwater: A Biography of Nathaniel "Sweetwater" Clifton* (Anaheim, CA: BookCaps, 2014), 63; Ron Thomas, *They Cleared the Lane: The NBA's Black Pioneers* (Lincoln: University of Nebraska Press, 2002), 3.

11. Michael Schumacher, *Mr. Basketball: George Mikan, the Minneapolis Lakers, and the Birth of the NBA* (New York: Bloomsbury, 2007), 119 and 124.

12. Farabaugh, *An Unbreakable Bond*, 10.

13. Todd Gould, *Pioneers of the Hardwood: Indiana and the Birth of Professional Basketball* (Bloomington: Indiana University Press, 1998), 175–77.

14. Gus Alfieri, *Lapchick: The Life of a Legendary Player and Coach in the Glory Days of Basketball* (Guilford, CT: Lyons Press, 2006), 144; Farabaugh, *An Unbreakable Bond*, 10.

15. Gould, *Pioneers of the Hardwood*, 177.

16. Alfieri, *Lapchick*, 144; Farabaugh, *An Unbreakable Bond*, 10.

17. Schumacher, *Mr. Basketball*, 174.

18. Schumacher, *Mr. Basketball*, 175.

19. Red Auerbach with Joe Fitzgerald, *Red Auerbach: On & Off the Court* (New York: Bantam Books, 1986), 198.

20. John Feinstein and Red Auerbach. *Let Me Tell You a Story: A Lifetime in the Game* (New York: Little, Brown, 2004), 299–303.

21. Edna and Art Rust Jr., *Art Rust's Illustrated History of the Black Athlete* (Garden City, NY: Doubleday, 1985), 312; Farabaugh, *An Unbreakable Bond*, 9.

22. Rust and Rust, *Art Rust's Illustrated History of the Black Athlete*, 313.

23. Rust and Rust, *Art Rust's Illustrated History of the Black Athlete*, 313.

24. Farabaugh, *An Unbreakable Bond*, 10–11; George Sullivan, "The Celtics, Chuck Cooper and the Struggling N.B.A.," *New York Times*, April 27, 1980, 2S.

25. George Sullivan, "The Celtics, Chuck Cooper and the Struggling N.B.A.," 2S.

26. Farabaugh, *An Unbreakable Bond*, 11–12; Rust and Rust, *Art Rust's Illustrated History of the Black Athlete*, 313.

27. Rust and Rust, *Art Rust's Illustrated History of the Black Athlete*, 313–14.

28. George Sullivan, "Remember . . . The Celtics broke the NBA's color barrier in 1950 by drafting a Duquesne All-America named Chuck Cooper. He earned a niche in basketball history by surviving racism, humiliation and loneli-

ness in blazing the train in a league now 68 percent black." *Boston Globe*, April 3, 1977, 88.

29. Alfieri, *Lapchick*, 147.

30. Charles Salzberg, *From Set Shot to Slam Dunk: The Glory Days of Basketball in the Words of Those Who Played It* (Lincoln: University of Nebraska Press, 1987), 135–36.

31. Salzberg, *From Set Shot to Slam Dunk*, 197–98.

32. Peter Vescey, "That Was Ren, This Is Now," *New York Post*, May 2, 2004, 55.

33. Thomas, *They Cleared the Lane*, 46.

34. Vescey, "That Was Ren, This Is Now."

35. Nelson George, *Elevating the Game: Black Men and Basketball*. New York: HarperCollins, 1992, 67.

36. Thomas, *They Cleared the Lane*, 133.

37. Farabaugh, *An Unbreakable Bond*, 106.

38. Marques Haynes, Voices of Oklahoma, University of Tulsa Oklahoma Center for the Humanities, 15.

39. Schumacher, *Mr. Basketball*, 123.

40. Charles Bricker, "The Don Barksdale Story: Breaking the Color Line in the NBA," *San Jose Mercury News*, n.d., n.p. Don Barksdale nomination file, Naismith Memorial Basketball Hall of Fame.

41. An Olympian's Oral History: Don Barskdale, LA84 Foundation, October 2007, 5 and 8.

42. An Olympian's Oral History: Don Barskdale, LA84 Foundation, October 2007, 5 and 10.

43. An Olympian's Oral History: Don Barskdale, LA84 Foundation, October 2007, 6–7.

44. "Don Barksdale: As an Amateur, Coast Cage Star Will Make More Money Than Any Basketball Player This Winter," *Ebony* 5, no. 2 (December 1949).

45. An Olympian's Oral History: Don Barksdale, LA84 Foundation, 12.

46. Ron Thomas, "The Forgotten Milestone: Barksdale Was NBA's 1st Black All-Star During Time of Segregation," n.d. Don Barksdale nomination file; Brian Higgins, "Basketball Trailblazer and Much More Bay Area Top 50 of the Century 38 Don Barksdale," April 14, 1999, Sports 5, Don Barksdale nomination file.

47. Carolyn White, "League's First Black All-Star Reaps Rewards 40 Years Later," *USA Today*, February 18, 1993, 6C.

48. Bricker, "Don Barksdale Story."

49. An Olympian's Oral History: Don Barksdale, LA84 Foundation, 13.

50. Bricker, "The Don Barksdale Story."

51. Farabaugh, *An Unbreakable Bond*, 95.
52. Thomas, "The Forgotten Milestone."
53. An Olympian's Oral History: Don Barksdale, LA84 Foundation, 14.
54. Farabaugh, *An Unbreakable Bond*, 78.
55. Farabaugh, *An Unbreakable Bond*, 101.

5. THE RISE OF AFRICAN AMERICAN STARS IN THE NBA

1. www.interbasket.net/news/10999/2013/02/back-in-time-1964-65-boston-celtics-made.
2. Lew Freedman, *Dynasty: The Rise of the Boston Celtics* (Guilford, CT: Lyons Press, 2008), 180–81.
3. Pat Farabaugh, *An Unbreakable Bond: The Brotherhood of Maurice Stokes and Jack Twyman* (Haworth, NJ: Haworth Press, 2014), 104.
4. Jan Hubbard, ed., *The Official NBA Encyclopedia* (New York: Doubleday, 2000), 59.
5. James Johnson, *The Dandy Dons: Bill Russell, K. C. Jones, Phil Woolpert, and One of College Basketball's Greatest and Most Innovative Teams* (Lincoln: University of Nebraska Press, 2009), 40–41.
6. Hubbard, *The Official NBA Encyclopedia*, 60.
7. Clif Keane, "Russell's Rebounds Give Boston Edge," *Boston Globe*, April 9, 1959, 39.
8. Farabaugh, *An Unbreakable Bond*, 105–6.
9. Hubbard, *The Official NBA Encyclopedia*, 30.
10. Freedman, *Dynasty*, 125.
11. Hubbard, *The Official NBA Encyclopedia*, 33.
12. Ron Thomas, *They Cleared the Lane: The NBA's Black Pioneers* (Lincoln: University of Nebraska Press, 2002), 186.
13. Hubbard, *The Official NBA Encyclopedia*, 31.
14. Gary M. Pomerantz, *Wilt, 1962: The Night of 100 Points and the Dawn of a New Era* (New York: Random House, 2005), 125.
15. Hubbard, *The Official NBA Encyclopedia*, 185.
16. Hubbard, *The Official NBA Encyclopedia*, 231.
17. Hubbard, *The Official NBA Encyclopedia*, 231.
18. Hubbard, *The Official NBA Encyclopedia*, 250.
19. Thomas, *They Cleared the Lane*, 205.
20. Thomas, *They Cleared the Lane*, 206.
21. Hubbard, *Official NBA Encyclopedia*, 174.
22. Hubbard, *The Official NBA Encyclopedia*, 174.
23. Hubbard, *The Official NBA Encyclopedia*, 249–50.

24. Bijan C. Bayne, *Sky Kings: Black Pioneers of Professional Basketball* (New York: Franklin Watts, 1997), 112.

25. Thomas, *They Cleared the Lane*, 190.

26. Hubbard, *The Official NBA Encyclopedia*, 233.

27. Hubbard, *The Official NBA Encyclopedia*, 233.

28. Bayne, *Sky Kings*, 99.

29. Bayne, *Sky Kings*, 104.

30. Thomas, *They Cleared the Lane*, 188.

31. Thomas, *They Cleared the Lane*, 190.

32. Hubbard, *The Official NBA Encyclopedia*, 238.

33. Hubbard, *The Official NBA Encyclopedia*, 238.

34. Hubbard, *The Official NBA Encyclopedia*, 150 and 238.

35. Thomas, *They Cleared the Lane*, 217.

36. Thomas, *They Cleared the Lane*, 223.

37. Art Spander, "Quiet Coaches—Attles, Jones," *San Francisco Chronicle*, May 22, 1975, 59.

38. Milton S. Katz, *Breaking Through: John B. McLendon, Basketball Legend and Civil Rights Pioneer* (Fayetteville: University of Arkansas Press, 2007), 11.

39. Thomas, *They Cleared the Lane*, 163.

40. Katz, *Breaking Through*, 115.

41. www.post.gazette.com/news/obituaries/2012/05/17/Obituary-Kenneth-Samuel-Hudson.

6. THE SHADOW OF MICHAEL JORDAN

1. Hubbard, Jan, ed., *The Official NBA Encyclopedia* (New York: Doubleday, 2000), 21.

2. Hubbard, *The Official NBA Encyclopedia*, 21–22

3. Hubbard, *The Official NBA Encyclopedia*, 22.

4. Hubbard, *The Official NBA Encyclopedia*, 134.

5. Hubbard, *The Official NBA Encyclopedia*, 22.

6. http://www.nba.com/history/legends/profiles/michael-jordan.

7. Hubbard, *The Official NBA Encyclopedia*, 22–23.

8. Hubbard, *The Official NBA Encyclopedia*, 23.

9. http://www.nba.com/history/legends/profiles/magic-johnson.

10. Hubbard, *The Official NBA Encyclopedia*, 156.

11. http://www.nba.com/history/legends/profiles/magic-johnson.

12. Hubbard, *The Official NBA Encyclopedia*, 156.

13. Hubbard, *The Official NBA Encyclopedia*, 83.

14. Bob Ryan, *Scribe: My Life in Sports* (New York: Bloomsbury, 2014), 95.

15. http://www.nba.com/history/legends/profiles/magic-johnson.

16. https://www.npr.org/templates/story/story.php?storyId=120053152.

17. Hubbard, *The Official NBA Encyclopedia*, 32–33.

18. Hubbard, *The Official NBA Encyclopedia*, 146.

19. Hubbard, *The Official NBA Encyclopedia*, 142; http://www.nba.com/history/legends/profiles/magic-johnson.

20. http://articles.latimes.com/2012/apr/12/sports/la-sp-ln-la-magic-johnson-on-larry-bird-were-mirrors-of-each-other-20120412.

21. http://www.nba.com/history/legends/profiles/magic-johnson.

22. http://www.nba.com/history/legends/profiles/isiah-thomas.

23. http://www.nba.com/history/legends/profiles/isiah-thomas.

24. http://www.nba.com/history/legends/profiles/isiah-thomas.

25. http://www.nba.com/lakers/history/shaq.

26. https://www.washingtonpost.com/news/early-lead/wp/2018/02/17/i-owe-you-an-apology-shaquille-oneal-explains-why-he-loves-kobe-bryant-years-after-feud/?noredirect=on&utm_term=.9bca98db9ac3.

27. https://www.washingtonpost.com/news/early-lead.

28. http://hangtime.blogs.nba.com/2015/11/30/blogtable-what-will-kobes-legacy-be/?ls=nba:specialssplit4.

29. http://www.nba.com/article/2017/12/18/morning-tip-heart-will-kobe-bryant-unmeasured.

30. http://hangtime.blogs.nba.com/2015/11/30.

31. http://hangtime.blogs.nba.com/2015/11/30.

32. https://www.brainyquote.com/quotes/scottie_pippen_844332?src=t_lebron_james.

33. www.nytimes.com/2018/04/26/sports/basketball/nba-playoffs-lebron-james-cavaliers.html.

34. www.cnbc.com/2018/02/26/what-to-know-about-robert-johnson-americas-first-black-billionaire.html.

35. Ron Thomas, *They Cleared the Lane: The NBA's Black Pioneers* (Lincoln: University of Nebraska Press, 2002), 249.

BIBLIOGRAPHY

Abdul-Jabbar, Kareem, and Peter Knobler. *Giant Steps: The Autobiography of Kareem Abdul-Jabbar*. New York: Bantam, 1983.

———, with Mignon McCarthy. *Kareem*. New York: Random House, 1990.

———, with Raymond Obstfeld. *On the Shoulders of Giants: My Journey Through the Harlem Renaissance*. New York: Simon & Schuster, 2007.

Alfieri, Gus. *Lapchick: The Life of a Legendary Player and Coach in the Glory Days of Basketball*. Guilford, CT: Lyons Press, 2006.

Anderson, Lars, and Chad Millman. *Pickup Artists: Street Basketball in America*. New York: Verso, 1998.

Ashe, Arthur. *A Hard Road to Glory: A History of the African-American Athlete 1619–1918*, vol. 1. 3 vols. New York: Amistad, 1988.

Auerbach, Arnold "Red," and Joe Fitzgerald. *Red Auerbach: An Autobiography*. New York: Putnam, 1977.

Auerbach, Red, with Joe Fitzgerald. *On and Off the Court*. New York: Macmillan, 1985.

Bayne, Bijan C. *Elgin Baylor: The Man Who Changed Basketball*. Lanham, MD: Rowman & Littlefield, 2015.

———. *Sky Kings: Black Pioneers of Professional Basketball*. New York: Franklin Watts, 1997.

Bird, Larry, and Earvin Magic Johnson, with Jackie MacMullan. *When the Game Was Ours*. New York: Mariner Books, 2010.

Bjarkman, Peter C. *Boston Celtics Encyclopedia*. Chicago: Sports Publishing, 2002.

Black Fives Foundation. "The Hidden Story: Rens Break Pre-NBA Color Barrier, 1948," December 18, 2007.

Boyd, Todd. *Young, Black, Rich, and Famous: The Rise of the NBA, the Hip Hop Invasion, and the Transformation of American Culture*. New York: Doubleday, 2003.

Bradsher, Bethany. *Bones McKinney: Basketball's Unforgettable Showman*. Houston: Whitecap Media, 2014.

Caponi-Tabery, Gena. *Jump for Joy: Jazz, Basketball & Black Culture in 1930s America*. Amherst: University of Massachusetts Press, 2008.

Chamberlain, Wilt. *A View from Above*. New York: Villard Books, 1991.

———, and David Shaw. *Wilt: Just Like Any Other 7-Foot Black Millionaire Who Lives Next Door*. New York: Macmillan, 1973.

Cherry, Robert. *Wilt: Larger Than Life*. Chicago: Triumph Book, 2004.

Christgau, John. *Tricksters in the Madhouse: Lakers vs. Globetrotters, 1948*. Lincoln: University of Nebraska Press, 1999.

Connelly, Michael. *Rebound! Basketball, Busing, Larry Bird, and the Rebirth of Boston*. Minneapolis: Voyageur Books, 2008.

Cousy, Bob, with John Devaney. *The Killer Instinct*. New York: Random House, 1975.

———, with Al Hirshberg. *Basketball Is My Life*. Englewood Cliffs, NJ: Prentice Hall, 1957.

———, with Edward Linn. *The Last Loud Roar*. Englewood Cliffs, NJ: Prentice Hall, 1964.

———, and Bob Ryan. *Cousy on the Celtic Mystique*. New York: McGraw-Hill, 1988.

Ellsworth, Scott. *The Secret Game: A Wartime Story of Courage, Change, and Basketball's Lost Triumph*. New York: Little, Brown, 2015.

Embry, Wayne, with Mary Schmitt Boyer. *The Inside Game: Race, Power, and Politics in the NBA*. Akron, OH: University of Akron Press, 2004.

Entine, Jon. *Taboo: Why Black Athletes Dominate Sports and Why We're Afraid to Talk about It*. Westport, CT: Greenwood Press, 1994.

Erving, Julius, with Karl Taro Greenfeld. *Dr. J: The Autobiography*. New York: HarperLuxe, 2013.

Farabaugh, Pat. *An Unbreakable Bond: The Brotherhood of Maurice Stokes and Jack Twyman*. Haworth, NJ: Haworth Press, 2014.

Feinstein, John, and Red Auerbach. *Let Me Tell You a Story: A Lifetime in the Game*. New York: Little, Brown, 2004.

Fitzpatrick, Frank. *And the Walls Came Tumbling Down: Kentucky, Texas Western, and the Game That Changed American Sports*. New York: Simon & Schuster, 1999.

Foster, Frank. *Sweetwater: A Biography of Nathaniel "Sweetwater" Clifton*. Anaheim, CA: BookCaps, 2014.

Freedman, Lew. *Dynasty: The Rise of the Boston Celtics*. Guilford, CT: Lyons Press, 2008.

George, Nelson. *Elevating the Game: Black Men and Basketball*. New York: HarperCollins, 1992.

Gildea, Dennis. *Hoop Crazy: The Lives of Clair Bee and Chip Hilton*. Fayetteville: University of Arkansas Press, 2013.

Goudsouzian, Aram. *King of the Court: Bill Russell and the Basketball Revolution*. Berkeley: University of California Press, 2010.

Graham, Tom, and Rachel Graham Cody. *Getting Open: The Unknown Story of Bill Garrett and the Integration of College Basketball*. New York: Atria Books, 2006.

Green, Ben. *Spinning the Globe: The Rise, Fall, and Return to Greatness of the Harlem Globetrotters*. New York: HarperCollins, 2005.

Grundman, Dolph. *Dolph Schayes and the Rise of Professional Basketball*. Syracuse, NY: Syracuse University Press, 2014.

Heinsohn, Tommy, and Joe Fitzgerald. *Give 'em the Hook*. New York: Prentice Hall, 1988.

———, with Leonard Lewin. *Heinsohn, Don't You Ever Smile? The Life and Times of Tommy Heinsohn and the Boston Celtics*. Garden City, NY: Doubleday, 1976.

Hubbard, Jan, ed. *The Official NBA Encyclopedia*, 3rd ed. New York: Doubleday, 2000.

Isaacs, Neil D. *All the Moves: A History of College Basketball*. Philadelphia: Lippincott, 1975.

———. *Vintage NBA: The Pioneer Era, 1946–1956*. Indianapolis: Masters Press, 1996.

Jenkins, Bruce. *A Good Man: The Pete Newell Story*. Berkeley, CA: Frog, 1999.

Johnson, Claude. *Black Fives: The Alpha Physical Culture Club's Pioneering African American Basketball Team, 1904–1923*. Greenwich, CT: Black Fives Publishing, 2012.

Johnson, Earvin "Magic," with William Novak. *My Life*. New York: Fawcett, 1993.

Johnson, James W. *The Dandy Dons: Bill Russell, K. C. Jones, Phil Woolpert, and One of College Basketball's Greatest and Most Innovative Teams*. Lincoln: University of Nebraska Press, 2009.

Jones, K. C., with Jack Warner. *Rebound: The Autobiography of K. C. Jones and an Inside Look at the Champion Boston Celtics*. Boston: Quinlan, Press, 1986.

Katz, Milton S. *Breaking Through: John B. McLendon, Basketball Legend and Civil Rights Pioneer*. Fayetteville: University of Arkansas Press, 2007.

Koppett, Leonard. *24 Seconds to Shoot: The Birth and Improbably Rise of the NBA*. New York: Macmillan, 1968.

Kuska, Bob. *Hot Potato: How Washington and New York Gave Birth to Black Basketball and Changed America's Game Forever*. Charlottesville: University of Virginia Press, 2004.

Lane, Jeffrey. *Under the Boards: The Cultural Revolution in Basketball*. Lincoln: University of Nebraska Press, 2007.

Lazenby, Roland. *The Lakers: A Basketball Journey*. New York: St. Martin's Press, 1993.

———. *Michael Jordan: The Life*. New York: Back Bay Books, 2015.

———. *The NBA Finals: A Fifty-Year Celebration*. Indianapolis: Masters Press, 1996.

———. *The Show: The Inside Story of the Spectacular Los Angeles Lakers in the Words of Those Who Lived It*. New York: McGraw-Hill, 2006.

———. *Showboat: The Life of Kobe Bryant*. New York: Little, Brown, 2016.

Lloyd, Earl, and Sean Kirst. *Moonfixer: The Basketball Journey of Earl Lloyd*. Syracuse, NY: Syracuse University Press, 2011.

Mallozzi, Vincent M. *Doc: The Rise and Rise of Julius Erving*. Hoboken, NJ: Wiley, 2009.

McKissack, Fredrick, Jr. *Black Hoops: The History of African Americans in Basketball*. New York: Scholastic Press, 1999.

Neft, David S., Roland T. Johnson, Richard M. Cohen, and Jordan A. Deutsch. *The Sports Encyclopedia: Pro Basketball*. New York: Grosset & Dunlap, 1975.

Nelson, Murry R. *The National Basketball League: A History, 1935–1949*. Jefferson, NC: McFarland, 2009.

O'Neal, Shaquille, and Jackie MacMullan. *Shaq Uncut: My Story*. New York: Grand Central Publishing, 2011.

Peterson, Robert W. *Cages to Jump Shots: Pro Basketball's Early Years*. New York: Oxford University Press, 1990.

Pluto, Terry. *Loose Balls: The Short, Wild Life of the American Basketball Association*. New York: Simon & Schuster, 1992.

———. *Tall Tales: The Glory Years of the NBA, in the Words of the Men Who Played, Coached, and Built Pro Basketball*. Lincoln, NE: Bison Books, 2000.

Pomerantz, Gary M. *Wilt, 1962: The Night of 100 Points and the Dawn of a New Era*. New York: Random House, 2005.

Rayl, Susan. "The New York Renaissance Professional Black Basketball Team, 1923–1950." PhD dissertation, Pennsylvania State University, 1996.

Reynolds, Bill. *Cousy: His Life, Career, and the Birth of Big-Time Basketball*. New York: Simon & Schuster, 2005.

———. *Rise of a Dynasty: The '57 Celtics, The First Banner, and the Dawning of a New America*. New York: New American Library, 2010.

Rhoden, William C. *Forty Million Dollar Slaves: The Rise, Fall, and Redemption of the Black Athlete*. New York: Crown, 2004.

Robertson, Oscar. *The Big O: My Life, My Times, My Game*. Lincoln, NE: Bison Books, 2010.

Rosen, Charley. *The First Tip-Off: The Incredible Story of the Birth of the NBA*. New York: McGraw-Hill, 2009.

Russell, Bill, and Taylor Branch. *Second Wind: The Memoirs of an Opinionated Man*. New York: Random House, 1979.

———, as told to William McSweeny. *Go Up for Glory*. New York: Berkley Books, 2010.

———, with Alan Steinberg. *Red and Me: My Coach, My Lifelong Friend*. New York: HarperCollins, 2009.

Rust, Edna, and Art Rust Jr. *Art Rust's Illustrated History of the Black Athlete*. Garden City, NY: Doubleday, 1985.

Ryan, Bob. *Scribe: My Life in Sports*. New York: Bloomsbury, 2014.

Salzberg, Charles. *From Set Shot to Slam Dunk: The Glory Days of Basketball in the Words of Those Who Played It*. Lincoln: University of Nebraska Press, 1987.

Schleppi, John. *Chicago's Showcase of Basketball: The World Tournament of Professional Basketball and the College All-Star Game*. Haworth, NJ: St. Johann Press, 2008.

Shaughnessy, Dan. *Ever Green: The Boston Celtics: A History in the Words of Their Players, Coaches, Fans and Foes, from 1946 to the Present*. New York: St. Martin's Press, 1990.

———. *Seeing Red*. Cincinnati: Adams Media, 1995.

Sullivan, George. *A Picture History of the Boston Celtics*. Indianapolis: Bobbs-Merrill, 1982.

Taylor, John. *The Rivalry: Bill Russell, Wilt Chamberlain, and the Golden Age of Basketball*. New York: Ballantine Books, 2005.

Thomas, Isiah, and Matt Dobek. *Bad Boys: An Inside Look at the Detroit Pistons' 1988–89 Championship Season*. Dallas: Master's Press, 1989.

Thomas, Ron. *They Cleared the Lane: The NBA's Black Pioneers*. Lincoln: University of Nebraska Press, 2002.

West, Jerry, with Jonathan Coleman. *West by West: My Charmed, Tormented Life*. New York: Little, Brown, 2011.

Whalen, Thomas J. *Dynasty's End: Bill Russell and the 1968–69 World Champion Boston Celtics*. Boston: Northeastern University Press, 2005.

Wideman, John Edgar. *Hoop Roots: Basketball, Race, and Love*. Boston: Houghton Mifflin, 2001.

Wiggins, David K. *Glory Bound: Black Athletes in a White America*. Syracuse, NY: Syracuse University Press, 1997.

———, ed. *Out of the Shadows: A Biographical History of African American Athletes*. Fayetteville: University of Arkansas Press, 2006.

———, and Patrick B. Miller. *The Unlevel Playing Field: A Documentary History of the African American Experience in Sport*. Urbana: University of Illinois Press, 2005.

Wilkens, Lenny, with Terry Pluto. *Unguarded: My Forty Years Surviving in the NBA*. New York: Simon & Schuster, 2010.

Windhorst, Brian, and Dave McMenamin. *Return of the King: LeBron James, the Cleveland Cavaliers and the Greatest Comeback in NBA History*. New York: Grand Central Publishing, 2018.

INDEX

AAU. *See* Amateur Athletic Union
ABA. *See* American Basketball
  Association
Abdul-Jabbar, Kareem, 179–181; injury
  and, 209
ABL. *See* American Basketball League
abolitionists, 4
accidents, 151
achievements, 185, 189; Embry and,
  200–201; Johnson, E., and, 211;
  Jordan, M., and, 204, 205; Wilkens
  and, 194
advocacy, 214
African Americans, 100, 137; basketball
  for, 12–34; community and, 92, 107;
  firsts for, 200, 207, 225; general
  managers, 200, 201; Olympic athletes,
  161–162; physical education for,
  10–11; pioneers as, xii, 135–166;
  players as, 2, 157–159; professional
  basketball for, 1–34; recognition for,
  38–39; recruitment of, 50, 142–143,
  216; rising stars, 169–201; social scene
  for, 17–19; in sports, 11–12; starting
  five with, 169–170; YMCA and, 13
Ahearn, Jake, 53, 60
Alcindor, Lew. *See* Abdul-Jabbar, Kareem
Allen, Phog, 178
All-Mid-Valley Conference (MVC), 183
Amateur Athletic Union (AAU), 155;
  McLendon and, 198; teams of, 161

American Basketball Association (ABA),
  190–191
American Basketball League (ABL), 152;
  founding of, 20; integration of, 156;
  McLendon and, 197, 199
American Revolution, 4, 5
Amsterdam News, 50
Anderson, Harold, 100
the Anderson Chiefs, 82
Archibald, Gerald, 28
Army, 87, 104, 218; teams and, 59, 81
arrests, 76
Aschburner, Steve, 219–221
Ashe, Arthur, 20
Attles, Al, 195–196
Auerbach, Red, 110, 200; on Barksdale,
  164–165; on Clifton, 145–146;
  Halberstam on, 170; on integration,
  145–146; on owners, 157; on Russell,
  172–173, 174; starting five and,
  169–170

BAA. *See* Basketball Association of Amer-
  ica
Baird, Frank, 27
Barak, Steve, 76
Barksdale, Don, 155, 157, 160; Auerbach
  on, 164–165; Robinson, J., and,
  163–164; story of, 159–165
Barnett, Shannie, 97

baseball, xiii, 136; Davis and, 75; Hudson, K., and, 200; integration and, 116; Jordan, M., and, 207; nickname for, 101

basketball, 14, 185, 200; African Americans and, 12–34; brand of, 170–171, 186, 211; early black professional, 1–34; Gates and, 120–122; Henderson and, 10, 12–13; Lew, H., in, 5; military and, 87; Olympics and, 207; status of, 101; World War II and, xiii, 36

Basketball Association of America (BAA), 128; NBL merger with, 133, 141

Baylor, Elgin, 151, 188; influence of, 186, 214; injuries and, 188; the Minneapolis Lakers with, 187–188; Russell and, 187; story of, 186–190

Bayne, Bijan C., 187, 189

Bee, Clair, 49–50; Cooper, C., and, 147

beer, 163

Bell, Clarence ("Puggy"), 25, 40, 45; career of, 42–43; on racism, 25

Benjamin Franklin High School, 120, 122

Bennett, Carl, 142; on integration, 142–143, 144

BET. *See* Black Entertainment Network

Bickerstaff, Bernie, 197

Bidwell, Bill, 107

Bird, Larry, xi; on Jordan, M., 204; rivalry with Johnson, E., 209, 211–214

Bjarkman, Peter C., 49

Black, Timuel D., Jr., 46, 48, 92; Strong on, 92–93

Black Athletes Hall of Fame, 12

Black Entertainment Network (BET), 225

Bleach, Larry, 40

Blinebury, Fran, 223

the Boston Celtics, 144–145; championships for, 169, 213; Cooper, C., with, 149–150; Russell on, 173

the *Boston Globe* newspaper, xi; Himmelman for, 8; Ryan for, 210

Boswell, Wyatt ("Sonny"), 46; career of, 61; photograph of, 62; records by, 60; shots by, 112

The Boys and Girls Club, 218

Brookins, Tommy, 31

Brown, Roscoe, 71

Brown, Walter, 144; Auerbach on, 145–146; Cooper, C., and, 150

Bryant, Joe, 221

Bryant, Kobe, 219–223

the Buffalo Bisons, 96

Bush, Jerry, 60

The Call newspaper, 74

the Capital club team, 71

career, 150, 189; of Bell, 42–43; books about, 214; of Boswell, 61; contemporaries during, 8; of Cooper, T., 68–71; of Isaacs, 71–74; of Johnson, E., 208–214; of O'Neal, 217–219; of Robertson, 186; of Stokes, 165–166; of Thomas, I., 214–217

Carpenter, Shorty, 162

Central Intercollegiate Athletic Association (CIAA), 136, 198

Central State University, 200

Chamberlain, Wilt, xii; Russell rivalry with, 174–177; scoring and, 178; story of, 177–179

championships, 173; the Boston Celtics, 169, 213; coaches and, 174; match-ups and, 196; NCAA, 172. *See also specific championships*

the Charlotte Bobcats, 225

the Charlotte Hornets, 207

Chicago, Illinois, 40, 95; Cicero Stadium in, 103, 112

the Chicago American Gears, 79; Mikan with, 127

the Chicago Bruins, 49; Halas and, 107

the Chicago Bulls: playoffs for, 203–204; titles for, 205, 207

the *Chicago Daily News*, 85

the *Chicago Defender*, 41–42; on Boswell, 46; on the Dayton Rens, 132; game coverage by, 76; NBL and, 103, 112–113; on players, 58, 59

the Chicago Harmons, 41

the *Chicago Herald American*, 37; Fischer for, 41; game recounts in, 65, 75; Wilson, H., in, 78

the Chicago Studebakers, 61, 65, 101; Price, B., and, 107; story of, 107–109

Chuckovits, Chuck, 49, 96; *Oshkosh Northwestern* on, 97–98; transition of, 106

CIAA. *See* Central Intercollegiate Athletic Association

Cicero Stadium, 103, 112

the Cincinnati Royals, 185; Embry with, 201

civil rights, 46, 49, 170; Henderson and, 12

Clayton, Zack, 17, 19, 76

the Cleveland Allmen Transfers, 82

the Cleveland Slaughter Brothers, 113

Clifton, Nat ("Sweetwater"), 143; Auerbach on, 145–146; NBA and, 152–154

clubs, 15

coaches, xii, 199; Anderson as, 100; championship for, 174; Cooper, T., 66–68; Illidge, 88; integration and, 79; Lloyd, 139; nonplayers as, 68; players as, 193–194, 195; Robinson, E., 199; Russell as, 174; on Thomas, I., 214; titles and, 197

Cochrane, Edward, 37

Cohen, Haskell, 142

colleges, 24; Chamberlain and, 178; opportunities and, 122; opt out of, 223

Collins, Doug, 210

Colored World Basketball Championship, 13

community, 92, 107; segregation and, 136, 183

competitiveness, 221

contracts, 5, 29, 81, 218; inclusions and, 163

Cooper, Charles, 144–145, 148; Brown, W., and, 150; story of, 147–152

Cooper, Michael, 193, 211

Cooper, Tarzan, 21, 24, 40, 70; career of, 68–71; as coach, 66–68; return of, 53

Cousy, Bob, 164

Crowe, George, 84; recollections of, 89

Crowe, Ray, 183

Cunningham, Fred, 7

Dancker, Ed, 109

D'Antoni, Mike, 217

Darling, Lonnie, 104, 105

Davies, Chuck, 147

Davis, Piper, 75

the Dayton Mets, 87

the Dayton Rens, 52; entrance of, 130; NBL and, 129, 130–133

the Dayton Sucher Wonders, 53

defense, 84, 205; Attles and, 195; Gates and, 127; Lew, H., and, 6–7; players and, 6

Dehnert, Dutch, 58

DeJulio, Hal, 171–172

desegregation, 11

the Detroit Eagles, 53; the Harlem Globetrotters and, 57–59

the Detroit Pistons, 139; playoffs for, 203–204; Thomas, I., with, 216–217

the Detroit Suffrins, 75

the Detroit Vagabond Kings, 129–130

DeWitt Clinton High School, 54

DeZonie, Hank, 74, 80; NBA and, 154–155

discrimination, 7, 8, 33; Gates on, 122; King, D., and, 52; racism and, 140–141

Dolby, Larry, 50

Douglas, Bob, 13–17, 21; on barnstorming, 24; on chances, 80; Hall of Fame, 30; interview with Smith, Wendell, 81; Isaacs and, 72; league attempts by, 132; nomination for, 29; recollections of, 43; regrets of, 83; respect and, 28; on technique, 27; Yancey on, 29

the drop step, 217

Drucker, Norm, 153–154

Duffey, Isaac ("Ike"), 82

Duffey, Mike, 130

the dunk, 190, 191–193

Duquesne University, 147

the DuSable Museum, 5

Eastern Board of Officials (EBO), 11

the Eastern League, 156

EBO. *See* Eastern Board of Officials

Ebony magazine, 162–163

education, 200

Ehlo, Craig, 203

Ellington, Duke, 4

Embry, Wayne, 200–201; the Cincinnati Royals with, 201

encephalopathy, 166
Enright, James, 67–68
Equal Rights Convention, 4
Erving, Julius ("Dr. J."), 190–193
Evans, Dick, 111, 113

fans, 41, 89, 104
Farrow, Bill, 127–128
fights, 150
Finn, Gerry, 2
Fischer, Leo, 37, 61; on games, 41
floods, 84
football, 101; integration of, 116–117. *See also* National Football League
Forbes, Frank, 16
For the Love of the Game: My Story (Jordan, M.), 207
Fort Meigs Hotel, 100
Fort Wayne News-Sentinel, 98
Fort Wayne Zollner Pistons, 38, 75; Toledo Jim Whites Chevrolets and, 98–99
fouls, 54
Frankel, Nat, 78
free agency, 218
Freedman, Lew, 170; on Chamberlain/Russell rivalry, 174–175
Freedom to Play exhibit, xii
Funke, Michael, 107–108; on incidents, 112

games, 16–19; advertising for, 27, 66; cancellation of, 50; the *Chicago Defender* on, 76; excitement and, 171; Fischer on, 41; history and, 39; planning for, 89; postponement of, 98, 99; recount of, 65, 75; Saitch on, 20; World Professional Basketball Tournament, 35
Garnett, Kevin, 225–227
Gates, Pop, 21, 27, 121, 131; on bus culture, 24; on conditions, 22, 23; on NBL, 132–133; pay for, 21; on racism, 24; recollections of, 78; on the Renaissance Ballroom, 17; on the Rens, 30; on Sidat-Singh, W., 56; story of, 119–127; on the Washington Bears, 66–67
general managers, 200, 201

Gerber, Bob, 96, 104
Giles Post American Legion squad, 30–31
Gladden, Jimmy, 50
Glamack, George, 78
Gola, Tom, 177
Goldberg, Sid, 95–107; on racism, 105
Gordon, Morris, 48
Gottlieb, Eddie, 29
the Great Depression, 36, 84, 100
greatness, 207
Green, Ben, 39–40
the Grumman Flyers, 59–60; Harlem Globetrotters and, 64

Halas, George, 39; the Chicago Bruins and, 107
Halberstam, David, 170
handshakes, 29
Hanin, Harry, 37
the Harlem Globetrotters, xi, 146; Cooper, C., on, 149; Detroit Eagles and, 57–59; the Grumman Flyers and, 64; NBA and, 33; New York Renaissance and, 35–36, 39, 41–42; origins of, 30–33; popularity of, 141–143; Saperstein on, 75; seeding of, 43
the Harlem Renaissance, 120
Harp, Dick, 178; on Robertson, 185
Harrison, Les, 117–119, 118; on Saperstein, 166
Hartman, Sid, 144
Harvard University, 9, 14
Hauser, Joe, 105
Haynes, Marques, xi–xii, 90; dribble of, 91; on Gates, 124; opportunity for, 158–159; story of, 91–94
Hearn, Chick, 189; *Rock the Baby* term by, 193
Heathcote, Jud, 209
the Hellcats, 77–79
Helms Foundation All-America Honors, 159; Baylor and, 187
Henderson, Edwin Bancroft, 9–14
Himmelman, Bill: on integration, 102; on Lew, H., 5–9
Hintz, Pat, 96
history, xiv, 213; the Dayton Rens in, 52; games and, 39; integration and, 48;

King, D., and, 79; Lew family in, 2–5; NBL and, 129; Nelson on, 112–113; wins and, 43

Holman, Nat, 29, 39

Holzman, Red, 123

hotels, 22, 105, 125, 151, 161

Hough, Harry, 5, 7

Houston Rockets, 213

Howard University, 11, 138

Hudson, Dick, 30

Hudson, Ken, 200

Hudson, Roosie, 63–64, 111

Hunter, Harold, 138, 139

Illidge, Eric, 21, 25; challenge from, 35–36; as coach, 88; on Gates, 124; interview with Smith, Wendell, 88

incidents, 104; Cooper, C., on, 150–151; Funke on, 112; racism and, 147–149, 153–154

Indiana, 26; treatment in, 140–141

the Indianapolis Stars, 80

injuries, 151; Abdul-Jabbar and, 209; Baylor and, 188; Stokes and, 166

integration, xiii, 60, 99; ABL and, 156; Auerbach on, 145–146; baseball and, 116; Bennett on, 142–143, 144; coaches and, 79; of football, 116–117; history and, 48; King, W., and, 128; leagues and, 156–157; Lew, H., and, 2–3, 8–9; narrative of, xiv; NBL and, 52, 65, 102–103, 108; owners and, 143–147; teams and, 46, 77, 101, 108, 111, 126, 161; tournaments and, 39, 74

Inter-Scholastic Athletic Association (ISAA), 11

Irish, Ned, 143–144

ISAA. *See* Inter-Scholastic Athletic Association

Isaacs, Johnny, 20, 40, 43; career of, 71–74; on racism, 25; recollections of, 25–26, 42; on Sidat-Singh, W., 54, 56

Jackson, Bruce, 147

Jackson, Inman, 45

Jackson, Phil, 205

James, LeBron, 224–225, 226

Jenkins, Fats, 18, 21, 23

Jenkins, Sherman L., 58

Jewish Americans, 117

Jim Crow, 23, 50

Johnson, Ervin ("Magic"): career of, 208–214; on Dr. J., 190, 193; on Jordan, M., 204, 205; the Los Angeles Lakers with, 209–210; rivalry with Bird, 209, 211–214

Johnson, Robert, 225

Jones, Bill, 48–49; performance by, 99; scoring and, 57; story of, 100–101

Jones, Casey, 97

Jones, K. C., 182, 196–197

Jordan, Johnny, 111

Jordan, Michael: Jackson, P., on, 205; shadow of, 203–227; titles and, 205–207

Josephs, Arthur, 122

Journal Gazette, 111

Kansas, 197

the Kansas City Monarchs, 114

Kase, Max, 80

the Kenosha Royals, 43, 53

Kerner, Ben, 154

Kerr, Steve, 207

King, William ("Dolly"), 49–53; inspiration of, 147; the Rochester Royals with, 127

King, Willie, 119, 127; integration and, 128

Knight, Bob, 216

Kundla, John, 159, 173

Lacy, Sam, 66

Langston University, 91

Lapchick, Joe, 71

leagues, 155–157. *See also specific leagues*

legacy, 190

Lehman, Jack, 190

Levane, Fuzzy, 141

Lew, Barzillia, 4, 5

Lew, Harry ("Bucky"), 1–9

Lew, Margaret, 3

Lew, Phyllis, 8

Lew, Primus, 3

Lew family, 3–5

Lichtman, A. E., 66

Lind, Al ("Chake"), 120

LIU. *See* Long Island University

Lloyd, Earl, 135–141; on Baylor, 186; distinctions for, 193
the *Long Island Daily Press*, 77
Long Island University (LIU), 49–52
the Los Angeles Lakers, 180; Johnson, E., with, 209–210; origin of, 188; playoffs for, 203–204; titles for, 211
the Los Angeles Rams, 116
losses, 101, 103, 173
Louisiana State University, 218
Lowell Courier-Citizen, 2, 5
the Lowell Five, 8
Lower Merion High School, 223

Madison Square Garden, 143; the Harlem Globetrotters in, 146
Magic Johnson Enterprises, 214
Malaska, Pat, 28
Marin Junior College, 159
marketing, 208
Mason-Dixon line, 149
Massachusetts, 1; slaves in, 3
Mays, Willie, 75
McDermott, Bobby, 99; Gates and, 123–124
McKinney, Bones, 138
McLendon, John, xii, 138; ABL and, 197, 199
McMahon, Jack, 182
media, 212
Meehan, John ("Chick"), 127
Meschery, Tom, 194
Messenger, Nat, 76
Metropolitan Basketball Association, 16
Meyer, Ray, 88
the Miami Heat, 218
Miami University, 201
Michigan City North Indiana Steelers, 60
Michigan State University, 208
Mikan, George, 84, 88–94; the Chicago American Gears with, 127
military, 108, 128; basketball and, 87; draft into, 138; players and, 59, 81; Price, A., in, 60
Miller, Eddie, 164
the Milwaukee Bucks, 180
the Minneapolis Lakers, 84; Baylor with, 187–188; roster of, 90. *See also* the Los Angeles Lakers

Minneapolis Rock Spring Sparklers, 65
Minor, Davage, 157
Mississippi River, 84
Monde, Leon, 16
the Montreal Royals, 116
Morgan, William, xi
Morse, Walter, 1
Most, Johnny, 164
music, 33
MVC. *See* All-Mid-Valley Conference

NAIA. *See* National Association of Inter-collegiate Athletics
Naismith, John, xii; McLendon and, 197–198
Naismith Memorial Basketball Hall of Fame, xi; Cooper, C., induction into, 152; Douglas induction to, 30; Gates induction to, 125; Wilkens induction into, 194
Nathaniel, Clifton ("Sweetwater"), 84–89
National Association of Intercollegiate Athletics (NAIA), 198
National Basketball Association (NBA), 33; ABA and, 191; African American stars in, 169–201; All-Star Game of, 165; DeZonie and, 154–155; franchises in, 38; integration of, 102–103; merger to form, 133, 141; pioneers of, 135–166; playoff finals of, 203–204; on Thomas, I., 214
National Basketball League (NBL), 37, 95–133; BAA merger with, 133, 141; history and, 129; integration of, 52, 65, 102–103, 108; seasons of, 128, 133
National Collegiate Athletic Association (NCAA), 36, 172
National Football League (NFL), 20, 116–117
National Invitation Tournament (NIT), 165, 194
National Professional Basketball League (NPBL), 155
Naulls, Willie, 169
NBA. *See* National Basketball Association
NBL. *See* National Basketball League
NCAA. *See* National Collegiate Athletic Association

NEBL. *See* New England Basketball League

Neft, David, 108–109

Nelson, Murry, 103, 130; on history, 112–113; theories by, 117

New England Basketball League (NEBL), 5–9

News Sentinel, 111

New York, 179; Brooklyn in, 194, 204; Long Island in, 190

New York Journal American, 80

the New York Nets, 191

the New York Renaissance, 13, 20–34; Harlem Globetrotters and, 35–36, 39, 41–42; losses to, 101; the Oshkosh All-Stars versus, 61–63; photograph of, 45; wins by, 38

NFL. *See* National Football League

Nike, 208

NIT. *See* National Invitation Tournament

Nixon, Norm, 180

North Carolina A & T University, 195

North Side High School Gym, 98

Novak, Mike, 112

NPBL. *See* National Professional Basketball League

the Oakland Bittners, 155; Barksdale with, 161

OAL. *See* Olympian Athletic League

O'Brien, John J., Jr., 19

Official National Basketball League Pro Magazine, 129

Ohio, 130, 224

Olympian Athletic League (OAL), 13

Olympics, 183; basketball and, 207; in Melbourne, 172; U.S. trials for, 161–162

O'Neal, Shaquille ("Shaq"), 217–219

opportunities, 227; colleges and, 122; Haynes and, 158–159

Oram, Eddie, 48

O'Ree, Willie, 102

the Original Celtics, 20

the Orlando Magic, 218

the Oshkosh All-Stars, 38, 42; the Rens *versus*, 61–63, 104

Oshkosh Northwestern, 97–98

Overbrook High School, 177

Owens, R. C., 187

owners, 123, 198; concerns of, 142, 157; Harrison as, 117–119; integration and, 143–147; Johnson, E., as, 214; Jordan, M., as, 207; vote by, 144

parks and recreation systems, 152

passing, 189–190; Johnson, E., and, 211

payments, 21, 25, 36

Pennsylvania, 165; Philadelphia in, 177; Warren in, 28

Peyton, Tony, 63; recollections of, 111, 112; on treatment, 110

Philadelphia 76ers, 191

photographs, 67, 73, 93, 108, 188, 220; Barksdale in, 160; Bell in, 44; Boswell in, 62; Clifton in, 86; Cooper, C., in, 148; Cooper, T., in, 70; Douglas in, 15; of Erving, 192; Gates in, 121, 131; Harrison in, 118; Henderson in, 10; Hudson, R., in, 64; Jenkins. F., in, 18; Johnson, E., in, 212; Jordan, M., in, 206; King, D., in, 51; Lew, H., in, 3; Lloyd in, 137; New York Renaissance in, 45; Price, B., in, 32; Robertson in, 184; Saperstein in, 31; Sidat-Singh, W., in, 55; Smith, Willie in, 115; Strong in, 47; teams in, 126, 131, 140; Thomas, I., in, 215; 12th Street Basketball Team, 13

physical education, 9–11; African Americans and, 10–11; student of, 198

pioneers, xii; NBA and, 135–166

Pippen, Scottie, 205; on James, 224

the *Pittsburgh Courier*, 36, 43; on Ricks, 49

players, 2, 16, 171; African Americans, 2, 157–159; aspirations of, 21; the *Chicago Defender* on, 58, 59; Clayton as, 19; coaches as, 193–194, 195; defense for, 6; dominance of, 175, 209, 220; early years for, 38; employees as, 107–109; for Giles Post, 31; influence of, 186, 214; Lloyd, 135–141; military and, 59, 81; in NEBL, 7; pairs of, 219; popularity of, 109; positions for, 88, 210; recognition for, 38–39; recruitment of, 50, 142–143, 216; Robertson, 181–182; roster of, 90;

style and, 153, 185, 191; talent of, 60–61; teams and, 156, 158; tryouts for, 21

Podoloff, Maurice, 145–146; Cooper, C., on, 151

Pollard, Jim, 88–89

popularity, 109, 113; the Harlem Globetrotters, 141–143; shoes and, 208

poverty, 122, 216

Pressley, Babe, 79

Price, Al, 60, 97

Price, Bernie, 32, 33–34, 48; Chicago Studebakers and, 107; recollections of, 110; scoring by, 103

promotion, 85

Public School Athletic League (PSAL), 11

racism, 72; Bell on, 25; discrimination and, 140–141; Gates on, 24; Goldberg on, 105; incidents and, 147–149, 153–154; poverty and, 122; schools and, 184. *See also* Jim Crow

Rayl, Susan, 81

rebounds, 6, 174

records, 180; Boswell and, 60; Chamberlain and, 179; tournaments and, 83

referees, 106; calls by, 110; Hudson, K., as, 200

Reinsdorf, Jerry, 208

the Renaissance Ballroom, 16–17

Renick, Cab, 162

the Rens. *See* New York Renaissance

respect, 113; Chamberlain on, 177; for Gates, 124; opponents and, 213–214; wins and, 123

restaurants, 105

Reynolds, Bill, 102–103

Rice, Grantland, 54–56

Rickey, Branch, 114–117

Ricks, Pappy, 49

Riley, Pat, 210, 213

Riska, Eddie, 64

rivalry, 13, 39–40; Bird/Johnson, E., and, 209, 211–214; Russell/Chamberlain, 174–177

Roach, William, 16

Robert G. Cole High School, 218

Robertson, Oscar, 180, 201; McMahon on, 182; player, 181–182; story of, 183–186

Robinson, Ermer, 93, 94; coach, 199

Robinson, Jackie, xiii, 102; Barksdale on, 163–164; comparisons to, 139, 141, 151–152; rise of, 114–117

the Rochester Royals, 52, 82; King, D., with, 127; players on, 158; Stokes on, 166

Rosenblum, Max, 52, 79

Roth, Carl, 105

Rupp, Adolph, 161–162

Russell, Bill, 66; Auerbach on, 172–173, 174; Barksdale on, 165; Baylor and, 187; Chamberlain rivalry with, 174–177; coach, 174; Hudson, K., and, 200; stature of, 151; story of, 171–177

Ryan, Bob, 210

Sadowski, Ed, 53

Saitch, Eyre ("Bruiser"), 16, 17; on games, 20

the San Francisco Warriors, 195

Saperstein, Abe, 31–33; business for, 58, 142–143; challenge to, 36; on Globetrotters, 75; Harrison on, 166; Levane on, 141; monopoly of, 145; Podoloff and, 146; scoring and, 33; treatment by, 149

Sarachek, Red, 52, 72; recollections of, 154

the Savoy Ballroom, 31

the Savoy Big Five, 30

Schayes, Dolph, 138

Schleppi, John, 36–37

scholarships, 91, 200; Baylor and, 187; Jordan, M., and, 204; UCLA on, 159

Schroeder, John, 54

scoring, 6, 45, 57; by Ahearn, 60; Barksdale on, 163; Chamberlain and, 178; Chuckovits and, 96, 104; Jordan, M., and, 204; by Price, B., 103; Saperstein and, 33

the Seattle Supersonics, 194

segregation, 9; community and, 136, 183; conditions and, 22–25; DeZonie on, 155; squads and, 56

Sharman, Bill, 196

the *Sheboygan Press*, 40, 106, 109
shoes, 208
Sidat-Singh, Samuel, 54
Sidat-Singh, Wilmeth, 53–56
signature moves, 191–193, 217
Simmons, Roy, 54
skyhook, 180, 181
slaves, 3
Slocum, Harold, 16
Smallwood, John, 171
Smith, Dean, 204
Smith, Wendell, 36; on the Dayton Rens, 132; Douglas interview with, 81; Illidge interview with, 88
Smith, Willie, 103, 113–114, 115
society, 170
South Philadelphia Hebrew Association (SPHAS), xiii, 29, 52
Space Jam movie, 208
the Spartan Field Club, 14–15; Douglas and, 16
SPHAS. *See* South Philadelphia Hebrew Association
sports, 107, 146; African Americans in, 11–12; heritage of, 125; integration of, 102; marketing and, 208
Sports Arena (Rochester, New York), 135
Stagg, Amos Alonzo, 85
starting five, 169–170
statistics, 179, 184
Steinbrenner, George, 198
stickball, 120
Stokes, Maurice, 167; career of, 165–166; injury and, 166; the Rochester Royals with, 166
Strong, Ted, Jr., 46–47; biography of, 58; Black on, 92–93; performance by, 65
Sukeforth, Clyde, 114
Sullivan, George, 240n28
the Syracuse Nationals, 138, 140
Syracuse University, 54–56

teams, 5, 42, 95, 210, 216; AAU and, 161; African Americans and, 12–34, 38; Army and, 59, 81; belief in, 89; Boswell on, 61; Cooper, C., on, 150; difference in, 176; emergence of, 13; as independent, 56, 100; integration and, 46, 77, 101, 108, 111, 126, 161; Isaacs

and, 72; the Lowell Five, 8; military and, 59; NBL and, 97, 118; New England Basketball League, 7; New York Renaissance as, 21, 30; players and, 156, 158; popularity of, 113; story of, 107–108; tournaments and, 35; trades between, 164, 194, 201; travel for, 30, 58. *See also specific teams*
technique, 205; Douglas, B., on, 27
Tenny, Ben, 111
terminology, 193
Texas Western University, 110
They Cleared the Lane: The NBA's Black Pioneers (Thomas, R.), 156–157
Thiel, Art, 208
Thomas, Isiah, 203; career of, 214–217; the Detroit Pistons with, 216–217
Thomas, Ron, 141, 156–157
titles, 104, 173; the Chicago Bulls and, 205, 207; coaches and, 197; Jordan, M., and, 205–207; the Los Angeles Lakers and, 211
Toledo Blade, 106–107
the Toledo Jim White Chevrolets, 95–107
Toledo University, 100
tournaments, 35–94; integration and, 74; records and, 83; Rosenblum and, 52, 79; Stagg and, 85. *See also specific tournaments*
Townsend, Johnny, 96
track and field, 11, 177
the Tri-Cities Blackhawks, 84, 125–127
Turner, Joe, 66
Tuskegee Airmen program, 56
12th Street Basketball Team, 13
Twyman, Jack, 166

UAW. *See* United Auto Workers Union
UCLA. *See* University of California, Los Angeles
Underground Railroad, 4
United Auto Workers Union (UAW), 108
United States Basketball Writers Association (USBWA), 183
University of California, Los Angeles (UCLA), 159; Abdul-Jabbar at, 180
University of Cincinnati, 149, 183–184
University of Kansas, 178
University of Kentucky, 110, 162

University of Massachusetts, 190
University of Miami, 149
University of North Carolina, 204
University of San Francisco, 171–172
University of Seattle, 187
University of Southern California (USC), 159
University of Tennessee, 147
urbanization, xiv
USBWA. *See* United States Basketball Writers Association
USC. *See* University of Southern California

venues, 38; challenges with, 98, 129, 130; Madison Square Garden, 143
the Virginia Squires, 190–191
Vitti, Gary, 221
volleyball, xi

Wade, Dwayne, 218
Walker, Chet, 182
Walton, Bill, 193
Warhol, Willie, 65
Washington, D.C., 186
Washington, Kenny, 102
the Washington Bruins, 66
the Washington Bullets, 196
the Washington Wizards, 207
Webb, William. *See* Sidat-Singh, Wilmeth
Wendall Phillips High School, 30
West, Jerry, 188

Westchester High School, 147
West Virginia State University, 136
Whitaker, Lang, 223
Wilkens, Lenny, 193–195
Williams, Hank, 96
Wilson, Bob, 157
Wilson, Harry, 37; the *Chicago Herald American* and, 78; on Oshkosh-Rens contest, 62–63
wins, 146; respect and, 123; Russell and, 173
Winter, Max, 94
Wolfe, Red, 53
Wood, Robert ("Sonny"), 75, 77
Wooden, John, 26, 114
Woodson, Mike, 216
World Professional Basketball Tournament, xiii, 35–94; first, 123; Jones, B., in, 57; titles and, 104
World War II, 59, 95; basketball and, xiii, 36; changes after, 114

Xavier University, 87

Yancey, Bill, 23; on Douglas, 29; as shooter, 26
YMCA, 120; African Americans and, 13; International Training School, 1

Zeigler, Vertes, 90
Zollner, Fred, 142

ABOUT THE AUTHOR

Douglas Stark is the museum director at the International Tennis Hall of Fame in Newport, Rhode Island. He is the author of three basketball books—*The SPHAS: The Life and Times of Basketball's Greatest Jewish Team, Wartime Basketball: The Emergence of a National Sport During World War II*, and *When Basketball Was Jewish: Voices of Those Who Played the Game*—and coauthor of the children's book *Shikey Gotthoffer*. He and his family live in Rhode Island.